THE UPPER ROOM
Disciplines
2011

UPPER
ROOM BOOKS®
NASHVILLE

AN OUTLINE FOR SMALL-GROUP USE OF DISCIPLINES

Here is a simple plan for a one-hour, weekly group meeting based on reading Disciplines. One person may act as convener every week, or the role can rotate among group members. You may want to light a white Christ candle each week to signal the beginning of your time together.

OPENING

Convener: Let us come into the presence of God.

Others: Lord Jesus Christ, thank you for being with us. Let us hear your word to us as we speak to one another.

SCRIPTURE

Convener reads the scripture suggested for that day in Disciplines. After a one- or two-minute silence, convener asks: What did you hear God saying to you in this passage? What response does this call for? (Group members respond in turn or as led.)

REFLECTION

• What scripture passage(s) and meditation(s) from this week was (were) particularly meaningful for you? Why? (Group members respond in turn or as led.)

• What actions were you nudged to take in response to the week's meditations? (Group members respond in turn or as led.)

• Where were you challenged in your discipleship this week? How did you respond to the challenge? (Group members respond in turn or as led.)

PRAYING TOGETHER

Convener says: Based on today's discussion, what people and situations do you want us to pray for now and in the coming week? Convener or other volunteer then prays about the concerns named.

DEPARTING

Convener says: Let us go in peace to serve God and our neighbors in all that we do.

Adapted from *The Upper Room* daily devotional guide, January–February 2001. © 2000 The Upper Room. Used by permission.

CONTENTS

FOREWORD

On my bookshelf at work sits a volume published in 1959 titled *The Upper Room Companion*; the next volume in the series published in 1960 bears the title *The Upper Room Disciplines*. So, for over half a century this little book has provided spiritual nourishment for many across the globe and has expanded far beyond its original intent as stated by the editor Gerald O. McCulloh:

> *The Upper Room Companion* is a new venture in the publishing of devotional materials. It is designed especially for ministers, theological students, chaplains, and all those whose vocation lies particularly within the program and structure of the Church.

Thus, *The Upper Room Disciplines* began as an opportunity to look more deeply at scripture by offering a week of meditations by a single author on a particular theme. The book's larger size afforded more development space than that of *The Upper Room* daily devotional guide.

By 1976, the staff of *The Upper Room Disciplines* began to assign scripture passages from the common lectionary to guide writers' thoughts and weekly theme development. The use of the lectionary allows for a common pattern of study and proclamation of biblical texts across churches and denominations. Individuals and groups may read, study, and pray the Bible in tune with the church's life of prayer and preaching. The flow of the church year provides a rhythm with a cadence all its own. A friend of mine wrote the following:

> We see patterns.
> We sense rhythms.
> We respond instinctively
> to repetition, to likeness,
> to sequence.
>
> Patterns are the result
> of the cognitive equipment
> we use to know our world.

After two years away from this task, I once again resume editorial responsibility for *The Upper Room Disciplines*. Once again I find myself immersed in scripture as we follow the familiar Jesus story and discover *our* place in the narrative of God's salvation history. I take comfort in the familiarity of the annual cycle of scripture—the pattern of holy seasons and ordinary time together. Yet to bear witness to God's work in the world, the cycle will need to move from page to life, from head to heart. That is my prayer for us all.

— Rita B. Collett
Managing Editor • Upper Room Books

Epiphany's Light

JANUARY 1–2, 2011 • ANNA LEE

SATURDAY, JANUARY 1 ~ *Read Revelation 21:1-6*

The beginning of a new year fills me with hope, excitement, and anticipation. However, I know that many of my brothers and sisters around the world face the new year as their first without a loved one or a job or a home. Despite the joy of a new day and a new year, pain still marks our world. Yet I call to mind the fact that the world in which we live is not creation's final state.

Today's passage confirms God's promise of the renewed creation to come: God dwells with the people and lovingly wipes away every tear. Death, pain, and mourning will be no more. God's promise of a renewed creation enables us to look with hope toward a sometimes uncertain future.

However, God does not abandon us while we wait. We stand on the cusp of a new year with the renewed assurance of God's presence, which we celebrated in the season of Advent. We do not face a new year or a new day alone; through the miracle of the Incarnation, we affirm that God is with us, even now.

Through the Holy Spirit, God fills our hearts and lives each day; and, as followers of God, we also manifest God's presence on the earth. God leads us to act with love and compassion toward others, making God's loving touch known to all around us during this and every year as we enact the reign of God on earth today.

Loving, compassionate God, we rejoice in the already and the not yet of your presence. We thank you for your abiding presence with us now in the Holy Spirit and in the witness of others, and we await with great anticipation the day in which creation is fully renewed. Amen.

Recent graduate of Vanderbilt Divinity School; member of the Holston Conference of the United Methodist Church

SUNDAY, JANUARY 2 ～ *Read Matthew 25:31-46*

The righteous and the accursed seem equally surprised by Jesus' revelation; both groups act out of a lack of self-consciousness. Seemingly all are part of the throng. Yet only the righteous willingly embrace those on the margins of society, those in need, those who are outcast.

"We don't know anyone in prison, and we're not allowed to just walk in the jail to visit. So, what can we do?" During a Wednesday night Bible study series, the youth in my church studied the various portions of Matthew 25 and sought ways to live out Jesus' call. A few weeks before Christmas, the chaplain of the local jail came to speak to the youth, bringing along an inmate who told his story. They addressed the needs of those in jail, including the desire to remain in contact with their families.

After the program, a group of youth acted to help those in the jail. They organized a Christmas card and stamp drive in our congregation. They collected the cards and delivered them to the jail where the inmates selected cards and wrote messages to their families. The youth then picked up the cards, stamped them, and mailed over eight hundred Christmas cards to the inmates' families.

The young people envisioned a creative way to use their gifts to minister to the "least of these" in their community. As we remember today the gifts of the Magi to the young Jesus, God calls us to consider our gifts. As we begin a new year, how might we share the gift of God's presence and love with the "least of these"? May we find ourselves "surprised" by a verdict of grace when we engage in the essence of discipleship.

God, on this Epiphany Sunday we thank you for the gift of your presence. May we unself-consciously serve those on the margins, acknowledging that service as appropriate discipleship. Amen.

Channels of Peace

JANUARY 3–9, 2011 • PAT LUNA

MONDAY, JANUARY 3 ~ *Read Psalm 29*

The closing petition of Psalm 29 surprises me. The psalmist does not call for God to quiet the storms or quench the fires. The psalmist asks that God give the people strength and peace.

Life abounds with disasters, both natural and humanmade. As I write, the United States is at war on foreign soil. At home, we battle an economic slump that has stripped jobs and homes from millions of people—with no end in sight. News anchors direct our attention to new storms brewing in the Atlantic. Tornadoes swirl, and earthquakes shake. Wildfires destroy homes. *Where is the peace of God in all this?* I wonder.

And then the beautiful words of a familiar prayer pour into my heart: "Lord, make me a channel of your peace." God's peace flows like water and requires channels—lots and lots of channels—to reach all those who suffer throughout the world.

I thought about the creek that runs behind my house and empties into the Intracoastal Waterway. The natural result of weather and the winds and rains that pummel the ground is that sludge accumulates and threatens to block the flow of the water through the channel, rendering it useless. The Army Corps of Engineers has to dredge the channel constantly to remove the sludge and to restore deep water and safe travel.

Our everyday life circumstances and human interactions cause a sludge build up in our hearts. We must develop ways to remove the sludge if we are to be effective channels of God's peace in the world.

Gracious God, reach deep into my heart and dredge out all the muck that blocks the flow of your Spirit within me. Amen.

Retreat leader, The Upper Room Academy for Spiritual Formation; president, capital campaign consulting firm; Santa Rosa Beach, Florida

TUESDAY, JANUARY 4 ~ *Read Matthew 3:13-15*

Some of us would consider John a fanatic as he wanders the desert, seemingly caring little for what he eats or wears. Yet his total commitment to God yields amazing results. John sees the sludge in the hearts of those around him, and he advocates repentance as the remedy for sin, repentance to help remove sludge from the channels of the human heart.

John also sees a different Jesus than the one the crowd sees. John beholds the Holy One who has no need of repentance. So when Jesus requests baptism at the hands of John, John balks. "I need to be baptized by you, and do you come to me?"

I understand John's reluctance to immerse Jesus' sacred head in the same muddy water with which he has anxiously baptized the unruly mob of sinners. We can easily find ourselves caught up in righteous anger at the injustice that surrounds us. Our own judgment blocks the way of the peace that God would like to offer the world through us.

Jesus presents himself for baptism in order to "fulfill all righteousness," to do all that God requires. Matthew sets the stage for Jesus' obedient faithfulness, the Son of God who models by word and deed the Father's will.

Jesus offers himself in humility to John, thereby calming John's fury and signifying a loving confirmation of all those penitent souls who stand dripping on the shore, as well as those who remain timid and fearful of the baptismal waters. Jesus elevates a ritual of cleansing to a sacrament of blessing. Jesus offers himself to John and, suddenly, those baptized are not only forgiven of sin but stand in good company as God's own beloved children.

Jesus, in his mercy, understands what John does not. Self-centered human beings are not transformed into humble servants in a moment. There is a process, and it begins here.

God, let my words and actions today bless your people. Amen.

As Jesus rises from the waters of baptism, the heavens open, and, unlike the Gospels of Mark and Luke, seemingly all present hear God's affirmation of Jesus as beloved Son. It is not Jesus who must learn his identity but those gathered—and not simply Jesus' identity but their own.

My friend preached on this passage to a group of incarcerated teenagers. First, he gave an account of his own failures so that the young men understood his own undeserving human nature. Year after year, my friend had disappointed his teachers and parents, let his friends down. And the world made sure he knew that he had failed. Its discouraging words robbed him of his heart's desire and imprisoned him with the rules of others.

My friend read to that group of boys the account of Jesus' baptism, explaining that before Jesus ever did anything great for God, God spoke words of encouragement to this effect: "You are my Beloved, and with you I am well pleased."

My friend realized that God's words were intended not just for Jesus but also for him, and he described his feelings when he first understood that *he* was God's Beloved. In spite of all he had done or not done, God was well pleased with him. Then my friend walked through the crowd of boys, proclaiming each of them God's beloved son. One by one, he called down God's loving favor on their tear-streaked faces.

Those on the banks of the Jordan that day, those incarcerated young men, and we who read Matthew's account today struggle to grasp with our hearts the deep truth that our minds might never comprehend: the God of heaven and earth, the Creator of the sky and the stars, loves us more that we will ever fathom. This loving is not our doing but God's. We can only accept it and serve as channels of God's love and peace to one another.

Gracious God, help me to know I am your beloved. Amen.

THURSDAY, JANUARY 6 ~ *Read Psalm 29*

EPIPHANY

Peace is not the absence of conflict but the presence of God's love. The psalmist describes God's power from the perspective of confidence in God that inspires awe and wonder. When we feel confident in our faith, made bold through knowledge of our belovedness in God's eyes—not because of who we are but because of who God is—our perspective begins to change. Our vision, less obscured by fear, can focus more attentively on God's expansive power.

Psalm 29 describes a God of power and might who holds sway over all the natural world. The "voice of the LORD" seems to come as a thunderclap and God's presence as a raging storm! My experience with the creek behind my house tells me that sludge constantly accumulates. Yet this God who can break the cedars and shake the wilderness can dredge and open the channels of our hearts, releasing the fear and frustration that often block a sense of God's peace.

We are the beloved children of the Creator, who is pleased with us and whose deepest desire is intimate union with us. "The LORD is my light and my salvation; whom shall I fear?" (Ps. 27:1); God's "perfect love casts out fear" (1 John 4:18). When we allow God to clear the channels, the peace of God that "surpasses all understanding will guard our hearts" (Phil. 4:7).

Jesus understood that John's one-time repentance was insufficient; sanctification requires a process of continued dredging and cleansing. "The voice of the LORD is over the waters"; God's reign in our lives brings strength and peace.

God of peace, may I live in an ongoing process of sanctification. Dredge me; cleanse me. Amen.

FRIDAY, JANUARY 7 ~ *Read Isaiah 42:1-9*

Isaiah's proclamation that God will bring justice to the earth is not nearly as surprising as the description of the manner in which that justice will come. Without raising a voice, without breaking a bent reed, without extinguishing a dim candle, justice will come to the people. How is that possible?

Isaiah speaks to those in exile, identifying the servant as the instrument of God's justice. At any given time, the reader must determine who the unnamed servant is. Whom do you see bringing justice to the nations; whom do you witness working tirelessly for justice "in the earth"?

And yet, this week we hear the words: "This is my Son, the Beloved, with whom I am well pleased" (Matt. 3:17). We hear the echoes of Isaiah in the words spoken at Jesus' baptism. The writer of Matthew understands Jesus to be "my chosen, in whom my soul delights." It is Jesus who realizes that "former things have come to pass." And it is he who holds the vision of the new things God has planned.

Jesus does not need to be baptized, but the people need a living example. Jesus submits to baptism to demonstrate what is good and necessary. In this moment of consent, Jesus puts on the mantle of servanthood. Isaiah offers lovely metaphors for the tender mercy and healing touch that Jesus will offer the world. The broken and the lost, the lepers and prostitutes—the bruised reeds, the dimly burning wicks—will find no harshness in Jesus' forgiving words and the "new things" of God. Jesus' life and ours resides in God's keeping: a "covenant to the people, a light to the nations"—channels of peace to all.

Gentle Jesus, guide me by your Spirit so that my words and actions may create soft places where weary people may find rest and comfort. Amen.

One of the things I love most about the creek that runs behind my house is how quiet it is. There is little boat traffic, the water generally still. That very stillness can be problematic, however. Without a constant flow of water out to the Intracoastal Waterway, the sludge tends to build up in the bottom of the creek bed. I worry that I will wind up with an isolated pond, rather than a navigable waterway.

But then the rains come, and the natural flow of the current out into the larger channel removes the sludge. The water moves impartially; it just needs a channel. One channel is as acceptable as another. "God shows no partiality."

Peter is addressing the household of Cornelius, a centurion. God's Spirit has directed them to each other. Both have reason for wariness, but receptivity creates a channel for the Spirit's work. In verse 44 we will learn that the Spirit comes to the entire family of Cornelius.

God's Spirit and peace, like rainwater, pours into us, moves through us, and dredges the channel as it goes. The more we open our hearts and allow that peace to flow out of us to others, the broader the channel of peace becomes. Unlike the natural landscape, we have a choice. We can refuse to let God's peace move through us into the world. We can allow fear, anger, or resentment to block the flow. God desires our cooperation and receptivity; but God does not need us, anymore than the rains need a particular creek to arrive at the ocean. As Peter reminds us: "Anyone who fears [God] and does what is right is acceptable to him. " God shows no partiality—God will use any ready heart as a conduit for God's peace. The act of loving others becomes the means of our own sanctification.

Dear One, let me remember that all those who serve as channels of peace in the world are your beloved children. Amen.

SUNDAY, JANUARY 9 ~ *Read Acts 10:39-43*

BAPTISM OF THE LORD

A *willing heart and a receptivity to God's Spirit* are words that bring to my mind a woman named Mary, a resident of a correctional facility in Alabama. I met Mary as a volunteer with Kairos Prison Ministry. Mary had every reason to be depressed: incarcerated miles from family and her many health problems. As her sixtieth birthday approached, she learned she was losing her sight. I listened to Mary, month after month, knowing that I was helpless to ease her pain and depression.

Then one month the volunteers arrived at the prison and Mary greeted us with a broad smile. Her eyes danced. I could hardly wait to hear what had happened in her life. Clearly something wonderful. Had she been healed? "No, nothing like that," Mary said. Then she explained that a few weeks before, an elderly woman had been moved into the bed next to hers. The woman could barely walk and would often soil herself at night. She couldn't wash her clothes or change her bed. "I heard God tell me to do her laundry," Mary said. That was all.

These verses address the theme of Spirit-filled witnesses: Peter speaks on behalf of the disciples who lived and worked with Jesus, but he moves on to mention "those chosen by God as witnesses"—as channels, we might add.

In her prison setting, Mary perceived and seized her opportunity to witness. God's channel of grace in Mary was purged of the sludge of troubles, and Mary became a conduit for God's grace. We are all chosen by God to bear witness. May we, like Mary, sense the heavens part and feel God's peace descend upon us like a dove. Then we will hear the words of affirmation: "This is my Beloved, with whom I am well pleased."

Merciful God, open my eyes to see you at work in the world around me today, and make me a channel of your peace. Amen.

Calling and Ministry

JANUARY 10–16, 2011 • RON HILLIARD

MONDAY, JANUARY 10 ~ *Read Isaiah 49:1-3*

God is the one who first moves toward us and pursues us. Today's text invites us to recall God's initiative with God's servant. In verse 1 we read, "The LORD called me before I was born." God took the initiative to choose and appoint Israel as servant. Isaiah's writing about a call that occurs before birth reminds us that God's initiative typically has nothing to do with us and everything to do with God. Even before we can respond, God is at work in our lives.

I discovered this truth a few years ago when as an adoptee I decided to search for my birth mother. Throughout the search I had a sense of God's leading. When I finally met some members of my birth family, I was able to add the story of my relinquishment to the story of my adoption. During this time, I realized in a deeper way God's involvement throughout the whole process. Even before my birth I could now perceive God's working to bring me into relationship. In my coming to faith, I now acknowledge God as the one who took the initiative, working through circumstances and people to open my eyes to my need for a Savior. Before I had a clue about who God was, God pursued me, found me, and called me by name.

What is true in God's call to Israel is also true in God's call to each one of us. Divine initiative pursues us and works through people, circumstances, and events to bring us to God.

God, thank you for the specific ways you have worked in my life to open my eyes to you. Continue to open my ears so that I might hear you call me by name in this new year. Amen.

Associate pastor, First Presbyterian Church; North Palm Beach, Florida

God's call goes beyond mere invitation to fellowship. God calls us to join the work of the kingdom in order to make a difference in a hurting world. In today's reading, God calls the servant and issues a far-flung mission: bring the exiles home. But the mission entails more than saving Israel; the servant is to be a "light to the nations, that my salvation may reach to the end of the earth." Not just the Jews—but everyone on the planet! And how does the servant have the audacity to undertake such a task?

The key may lie in the first verses of this passage. Notice the shift from verse 4 to 5. In verse 4 the servant acknowledges that he has spent his strength and labored in vain. In verse 5, with his enlightened perspective of God's support, the One who has named and called the servant, God now becomes the servant's source of strength. His strength is in the Lord, who is faithful.

Throughout the millennia, God calls the chosen ones to be light to the nations, but we tend to forget the mission of taking the message of God's salvation to the end of the earth. "It is too light a thing that you should be my servant to . . . " What have you undertaken as a servant of God that may be "too light"? What task might require some heavy lifting? As disciples God calls us to worldwide mission. We, like the servant, may need to assess the source of our strength. Upon whose strength do we base our action?

Today we see the worldwide aspect of God's mission coming to fruition. The church in many parts of the world is exploding with growth. May we be faithful to our calling!

God, give me a heart for the people whom you love; make me your light to the world. Amen.

John the Baptist bears witness to Jesus. In a court of law a witness can testify only to what he or she has seen or heard. Secondhand stories and hearsay are not allowed. John provides testimony about who Jesus is and what Jesus has come to do; he speaks of what he *personally* has seen and heard. John moves from "I myself did not know him" to bearing witness.

The Fourth Evangelist allows John to speak for himself. It is as if the cross-examiner asks, "Now, Mr. Baptist, tell us your accounting of the facts on this particular day." And John steps up to speak. First, John testifies about the Spirit's descent upon Jesus—a divine revelation. John sets the record straight for all who were with him and all who will read this scripture about who Jesus is: the Son of God. John uses his witness to address others. Twice he sees Jesus and identifies him as "the Lamb of God." When referring to Jesus as the Lamb of God, John testifies to what Jesus will do. He lets others know about the work Jesus has come to accomplish. As the Lamb of God, Jesus is the sacrifice that will take away the sin of the world.

So John steps from the witness stand having identified Jesus as (1) Lamb of God who takes away the world's sin, (2) the preexistent one, and (3) the Son of God. The Fourth Evangelist stresses witnessing as the beginning of faith.

As modern-day witnesses we are to follow John's example and tell others what we have personally seen and heard concerning Christ. We relate our experiences, stories, and encounters with Jesus not to point to ourselves but to point others toward Jesus.

God, be at work in my life so that I have personal experiences with you to share with others. Help me recognize opportunities to testify, and give me the courage to do so. Amen.

THURSDAY, JANUARY 13 ~ *Read John 1:35-42*

The focus shifts from John's testimony to the believing engendered in others by his testimony. Andrew hears the testimony of John the Baptist and begins to follow Jesus. Andrew accepts Jesus' invitation to "come and see" and spends a day with Jesus. He discovers through John's testimony and his personal experience that Jesus is the promised Messiah. The first thing Andrew does when he realizes Jesus' identity is to go and find his brother, Simon. Andrew is so excited about meeting Jesus that he cannot wait to introduce his brother to him.

Andrew finds Simon and relays his startling news. Notice that Andrew witnesses to his brother by telling him what he has learned: a verbal aspect of witnessing. Then Andrew takes action by *bringing* Simon to Jesus. God uses Andrew as part of the process of Simon's meeting Jesus. God works through people and depends upon them to introduce others to Jesus.

Andrew's story remains unfinished until his witness brings others to Jesus. I am aware of a long list of people whom God has used to impact my spiritual life: my mother, grandmother, youth leaders, pastors, and friends. God has used them all to help bring me to Jesus. Their witness inspired my belief. Some brought me to Jesus by example. Others influenced my faith by simply spending time with me. Still others influenced my walk with Christ by teaching God's word and by telling me about God's work in their lives. How do you influence others to be followers of Jesus through your words and actions?

Jesus, continue to work in my life and give me both awareness and openness to be used by you to influence others for your kingdom. Amen.

FRIDAY, JANUARY 14 ~ *Read Isaiah 49:1-7*

When God calls and sends us on a mission, we must depend upon God. This is a lot easier said than done. We are often subtly taught that hard work, good preparation, right decisions, and correct analysis guarantee success. The corporate-leadership culture can subtly make its way into the life of faith and encourage us to believe that success depends more on us than upon God.

The servant, in today's scripture reading, has learned an important truth about trusting God. He says that his own strength in accomplishing his mission was not enough; God has been his strength. We too will discover God's strength only after we acknowledge that our own strength is not enough.

I have been a servant of God for over thirty years, yet I still give in to the temptation to rely upon my own strength. I make decisions before taking the time to listen to God. I work far more hours than I should because I believe that success depends upon me. I easily jump to action and later ask God to bless what I have done.

While I recognize this all-sufficient attitude about myself, I am also learning to trust God and to rely upon divine strength through the practice of several spiritual disciplines. In prayer I make my requests to God and wait for answers. In solitude I stay focused on God, attending to divine presence. In worship I regularly focus on God through praise, confession, and hearing the word. These spiritual practices keep me connected to the Holy as I continue to learn to rely upon God.

God, help me to stay focused on you so that you may become my strength. Amen.

SATURDAY, JANUARY 15 ~ *Read Psalm 40:1-11*

Avisiting seminary professor was teaching at our church, and he talked about how God shows up and shows off. He was reminding us of God's faithful presence and willingness to act on our behalf. Psalm 40 does the same in recounting God's saving activity in the life of the author. God hears the psalmist's prayer, intervenes in order to save, and transforms his life. Not only does the author of Psalm 40 recount God's faithfulness in his life, he also gives an example of appropriate response to God's action on our behalf. He becomes a witness to what God has done. He proclaims God's righteousness in the great assembly and speaks of God's faithfulness and salvation. He makes sure that others know what God has done.

Not only does the psalmist model the importance of sharing *when* God saves, but he also tells us *where* we are to do this: within the community of faith. A growing practice in my church at the contemporary worship service is to ask people to say aloud their "God sightings" from the past week. People will stand and tell how God "showed up" in their lives. The sharing often includes stories of God's faithfulness, awareness of God's presence in other people or in nature, answers to prayers, and so on. This time of sharing is a highlight of the worship service as people give witness to God's faithfulness. The blessings that come from this witness are profound. Not only is the whole community reminded of God's faithfulness, but those struggling in difficult situations are encouraged to remain steadfast while waiting for the Lord to turn and respond to their prayers.

Lord, thank you for your faithfulness to me. Teach me to wait with hope in your answers to prayer and to witness faithfully to your care and salvation. Amen.

SUNDAY, JANUARY 16 ~ *Read 1 Corinthians 1:1-9*

The most prominent word in today's passage is the word *called*. Paul uses this word four times in the introduction to his letter. I believe that Paul is pointing out from the start of his letter that all Christians are called by God! He begins by mentioning in verse 1 that God *called* him to be an apostle. Then in verse 2 Paul tells the church that those who call on the name of the Lord are called to be holy.

God does not call only those we consider professional church leaders; God calls all the "saints"—and they are then set apart for God's use. Each person is empowered for ministry.

Paul then goes on to mention how God assists us in our ministries. First, God provides spiritual gifts. We lack nothing, he says, in order to do the work of ministry. Second, God's strength is available to us so that we can faithfully serve. And last, God calls us into a fellowship of believers. We are not alone in ministry. Rather we are part of a great community of believers who are all called to ministry. That is the church!

The support, encouragement, prayers, and gifts of all the saints are available to each of us as we serve together. Paul insists on the equality of the laity with the ordained. The gospel's radical claims enter the life of every believer, and all are part of a community that requires full participation. Often the church's lack of power and failure to make a difference for God's reign result from division, broken relationships, and lack of unity. Our power to make a difference is multiplied as we serve together rather than separately. In a world of brokenness and fractured relationships, the church's power resides in its modeling of community.

God, help me to hear your call and to know that I am set apart to serve you. Amen.

Carrying God's Light

JANUARY 17–23, 2011 • CATHIE MCFADDEN

MONDAY, JANUARY 17 ~ *Read Isaiah 9:1-4*

A church faced a decision: to stay or to go. After months of meetings, weeks of worry, days in discussion, and hours in prayer, the vote was taken. The church would relocate.

These people had been the church for generations in this one place. The ministry had steadily grown, so much so that there was little room for all the new families coming each week. As the new building took shape, the church prepared for the move. This faith community needed to take with it all that had made it a church. They would not be starting over. The mission had not changed. Only the place.

The final worship service in the old church sanctuary stressed God's call to a new day. At the close of the service, a lantern was brought forward, and the candle from the altar was placed within it. People took turns carrying God's light at the front of the procession as they walked the one and one-half miles to the new church. Waiting at the new property were the "elders" of the church who graciously accepted the lantern light for the new altar.

God calls us out of darkness into the light. God also calls us to change. We give up the familiar, the old, and become new persons transformed by God's abiding love and perpetual presence. Will you carry God's light this week into a world of darkness?

*New every morning is your love, great God of light, and all day long you are working for good in the world. Stir up in us desire to serve you, to live peacefully with our neighbors and all your creation, and to devote each day to your Son, our Savior Jesus Christ. Amen. (*Upper Room Worshipbook*)*

Certified lay speaker; Hendersonville, North Carolina

TUESDAY, JANUARY 18 ～ *Read Psalm 27:1, 4-6*

Sometime between the ages of two and three, my grandson, Maxwell, was diagnosed with Sensory Integration Disorder. Things that most children would find fascinating like butterflies, bugs, wind, loud noises, car washes, scared Max. He refused to go into the backyard. He could not process sudden unexpected movements. His world became a frightening place.

Maxwell's therapy consisted of movement and accomplishing small tasks at the same time. He might swing in a hammock while putting together a puzzle. His mommy would scrub his whole body with a brush for tactile stimulation. He would wear headphones to reduce loud noise in crowds or movies. *My* therapy involved holding Max, speaking softly, reading favorite books, reinforcing love with words of acceptance, and telling him of the joy I experienced being with him.

J. Philip Newell, Celtic priest, author, and former Warden of Iona, told a group gathered for an Advent retreat that when one person suffers, we all suffer. My thoughts and tears were for Maxwell. I needed to be love and healing for him, and I had only one source from which to draw that love. As I had been loved, so shall I love.

In *The Wesley Study Bible*, the commentary identifies Psalm 27:1-14 as a hopeful prayer in the midst of suffering, a song of confidence, a confession of trust. In a hurting world, our confidence comes from the knowledge that we can call on God "in the house of the LORD" and live in the house of the Lord all the days of our lives without fear.

"The LORD is my light and my salvation; whom shall I fear?" We are called into the pain and fears of those we love, strengthened by the light of the Lord. Let there be healing.

Who might be calling to you out of their pain and sorrow? Will you carry the lantern this week?

Where do we find ourselves crying aloud, crying for graciousness, desiring to be answered? A retreat leader once called this state of being one of dis-ease: dis-ease in church, dis-ease in families, dis-ease in society, dis-ease in the workplace.

Churches become places of dis-ease when personal agendas, functional processes, and infighting overshadow the discernment of God's will within the faith community. Church becomes what the leaders want, not what God desires for God's people.

Families become distracted in the rearing of children by the dis-ease of a culture of drugs, sex, and violence. Stretched to the limit by financial burdens, low wages, single parenting, homelessness, and the inability to climb out of soaring debt, families disintegrate.

God's word calls us to love our enemies, yet wars rage. Some Christians cling to the "one true faith." Skin color determines value in the minds of some, rather than God's love for all people. We are dis-eased by the stranger and by the traditions unlike our own.

Ruthlessness and greed have driven leaders in the workplace to cause the downfall of corporations, innocent workers, and clients. Survival from this dis-ease cannot be guaranteed.

The psalmist (or you or I) cries out for reassurance that God will always be gracious, that God will always show God's face, will never hide or turn away as he strives to overcome the dis-ease that surrounds him. What answer do you seek?

What is the dis-ease in your life today? Cry louder! Look for answers from the God of our salvation! Expect graciousness!

THURSDAY, JANUARY 20 ~ *Read 1 Corinthians 1:10-18*

Imagine being in Paul's inner circle. You've been called to a meeting where Chloe's people, who have returned from Corinth, will discuss the state of the church there. They have disturbing news. Factions have divided the people. Some pledge allegiance to Paul, others to Apollos, still others to Peter and, yes, some to Christ, the Messiah. This infighting has sidetracked the church. Proclaiming the gospel has taken a backseat to discussion over who was in charge, who had authority.

Eugene H. Peterson in *The Message* states Paul's word as these: "You *must* get along with each other. You must learn to be considerate of one another, cultivating a life in common." Paul restates the mission as proclaiming the gospel with the cross as the living center of the ministry.

Some things never change! Being the church can be difficult. At times God's light seems extinguished. Like the church at Corinth, we may argue over "priorities" of no eternal value. We bring agendas that have little to do with discerning God's will (light) for our church. Laity assumes power without purpose. Sometimes clergy do the same.

The church is not about choosing sides, personal agendas, self-interest, hubris, or power. The church is about Christ crucified, the message of love to a hurting world. We are the light bearers for the Christ who sacrificed all. Church is about transformational change in our hearts and dedication to the work God calls us to in community.

Years ago, I was first introduced to doing worshipful work, discerning God's will, following the Christ as the only leader of the church today, and acknowledging the Holy Spirit's presence. So let it be!

Holy Three-in-One, transform our lives this very day. Amen.

FRIDAY, JANUARY 21 ~ *Read Matthew 4:12-17*

Let us return to the church that relocated. The church had hired a consultant to lead the church through the process of discernment. The question the consultant raised that caught the church completely off guard was this: "Do you have the right leader?"

Today's text focuses on a change in leadership. John, who had been the light bearer, has been arrested. Now Isaiah's spoken word is to be fulfilled. Jesus brings the light to Galilee, to Capernaum by the sea. "He picked up where John left off: 'Change your life. God's kingdom is here'" (THE MESSAGE).

The consultant's question has haunted me for years. Looking back on our country's political leaders, we note years of enlightenment and progress but also years of darkness.

In his book *Where Have All the Leaders Gone?*, Lee Iacocca lists the qualities of good leadership: curiosity, creativity, communication, character, courage, conviction, charisma, competence, and common sense.

Charisma comes from the Greek *kharisma*, meaning "gift of" or "favored by God or the divine." Iacocca uses an old word, one we as the church recognize not only in John and Christ Jesus but in ourselves. Two charismatic leaders, each with a gift from God: John and Jesus. One prepared the world for the coming of the other. Christ, the kingdom Light returns to Galilee, fulfilling the centuries-old prophetic promise. Jesus' time of leadership is at hand. Are you following the right leader? How might the charismatic Christ change your life?

Gracious God, mold me and equip me to be Christlike today. May I be about your work. Amen.

SATURDAY, JANUARY 22 ~ *Read Matthew 4:18-22*

In the practice of *lectio divina* (holy reading), one question among many might be, Where are you in this passage? In today's scripture, we find fishermen working by the Sea of Galilee. This common, everyday occupation involved mending nets, repairing boats, preparing to fish. Put yourself into the story. What do you hear, see, feel, or smell? Which person might you be?

Simon and Andrew are the fishermen along with Zebedee and his sons, James and John. Jesus approaches. Jesus speaks a few words and says something significant enough to change the lives of these men, significant enough for them to give up their jobs and take on the task of "fishing for people." Think about it. Does this look like any evangelism team you have ever met?

If you had been there, would you have answered the call? Would you have gone with the others, or would you have stood by in stony silence, watching as the four leave with Jesus? Would you have seized the opportunity to grab the left-behind nets and boats for your own enterprise? Where are you in this story?

I have never been to the Sea of Galilee. I have, however, been called. As a young girl, I, along with several other confirmands, made a decision to follow Christ. There were no boats or nets, and I didn't make the decision to leave my family. What I still remember after all these years were the words I heard that day. "I have chosen you. Come! Follow me." Dramatic and life changing? Yes. Simon, Andrew, James, John, you, and me. We can all be a part of the story.

Lectio Divina
Reread the Matthew 4:18-22 text.
Listen for a word.
How does this word fit into your life?
What is this word calling you to be?
How do you answer?

SUNDAY, JANUARY 23 ~ *Read Matthew 4:23*

Carrying God's light had its beginning (or was it the ending?) in this verse. Jesus becomes the light bearer, evidencing his *charisma*, God-through-him, in his preaching and healing—kingdom work!

Maureen Dallison Kemeza, an Episcopal priest, quoted a line from poet Seamus Heaney in the *Christian Century*, April 24, 2009: "Jesus was emptied into us to keep."

Looking back, I can see Jesus being emptied in a church's decision to expand its ministry, welcome newcomers, and grow into a large community of faith doing kingdom work.

Jesus is emptied into this grandmother's nurturing love for a grandchild. May we be vessels full of the healing love of Christ.

Jesus is emptied into a place of dis-ease, shedding light that changes people—whether in recognizing things of eternal value, giving up power or corruption in selflessness, or radically changing their life's direction and work.

Jesus is emptied into the church to heal divisions. The church becomes one in the spirit of all that is good and promotes the good news of God's love. Let the church be about worshipful work.

Jesus is emptied into those who will lead the church. Leaders must help us discern our own gifts, listening when congregants hear the call to serve and encouraging us to be the church.

A pastor asked this question from the pulpit: "When did you know when love became apparent?" Love came to me when I was eleven years old. How about you? When was love emptied into you?

Annie Dillard says this: "I cannot cause the light. The most I can do is put myself in the path of its beam." Receive the lantern. Light the path. Someone lives in darkness along the way.

Receive this day the love of God the Father, Christ the Son, and the ever present Holy Spirit.

What God Requires

JANUARY 24–30, 2011 • DOREEN KOSTYNUIK

MONDAY, JANUARY 24 ~ *Read Micah 6:1-5*

Micah, one of the lesser prophets, carries the passionate voice of God condemning the ruling class and the elite for ruthlessly taking over the land of peasants, oppressing the poor, and failing to serve the cause of justice. Micah cries out God's anguish about the abuse of power and the lack of justice.

I find it tempting to critique our own temple politics, our own political systems, without bringing the controversy of God closer to my own examination of conscience and of my own collusion with systems of injustice. But we too are meant to carry God's anguish for justice, to become a presence of hope.

Anguish is carried by a heart full of love, loss, and grief. The emotion of anguish, if not embraced and dealt with, can lead to a broken heart—or to anger, blame, and other forms of projection that lead to hatred and violence. We stand before the grieving God who is always moving toward relationship and is rendered invisible, not seen or known as present. God the creator of life and love, of freedom and relationship anguishes because those created out of God's very nature choose slavery over freedom, greed over justice, violence over reconciliation.

God calls us to reflection, to attentiveness, back into a relationship that we have left. We are meant to be attentive to the poor, to the marginalized, to the suffering born out of violence. When I am in anguish, I call a friend or my spiritual director. Here, God calls to the whole of creation to hear the anguish, the controversy of God's own heart.

Today may I be conscious of the anguish around me and be a presence of compassion, of listening and mercy.

Writer, spiritual director, therapist; New Westminster, British Columbia

Micah's passionate God voice continues. "With what shall I come before the LORD?" When falling into the reality of Great Love, what is required? What response allows it to reach our heart and root there, transform us so that we become more fully what we have received? I recall a recent experience with my brother who came to help me repair a broken windowpane. Looking at him I remembered how we both came out of a fractured family where love was measured in spoonfuls and by performance; we never quite felt that we were good enough. Our parents came out of the same reality. Who can give what hasn't been known or received?

As I looked at this man, much younger than I, I marveled at his great gentleness and tenderness as he worked with this glass and directed me as I helped. I knew that from his marriage of twenty years he had learned about loving and being loved. He had learned to be vulnerable, open, and transformable. He had learned to rest in the love given deeply enough that he could believe it, receive it, and respond in kind.

As we lean into this passage from Micah, we are invited to do the same: to receive deeply the love God has given and from there learn what is essential to life, what this Great Love requires: to do justice, to love kindness, and to walk humbly with our God. What is required is that we receive the great gift of love from which we are created. Made in the image of God, we are meant to find and know that image in ourselves so that we can exercise it fully and live the likeness.

Gracious God, help me to be simple enough, available enough, open enough to be fully present to the love you have written into me that I may indeed do justice, love kindness, and walk humbly with you this day, bringing your presence into all that lies before me. Amen.

Always when we pray the psalms, we find ourselves in the presence of our common humanity. The psalms do not carry God's voice addressing us; rather, they record our voice addressing God. The psalms give us voice for those times when we feel settled, for times of unsettledness and disorientation, and for times when we once again find our place in life and in God.

Psalm 15 addresses our reorientation to live in relationship with God and, out of that, in relationship with one another. The psalmist asks, and we ask: what kind of person abides in God's tent? What mindful, responsive stance is necessary? The psalmist, listening deeply to the interior voice of wisdom, then gives us the direction. The psalmist describes a holy person, one whom we can model.

In our moments of quiet, when we ask the same kinds of questions, seek to find the learning, the direction that leads to right relationship with God and with one another, our own inner wisdom draws us into clarity of spirit, and we are empowered to move out of those situations of challenge, those moments of darkness and aloneness. To place ourselves before God with such questions requires great humility. We see ourselves as we are, no more and no less; we see reality as it is, no more and no less, and seek to place ourselves before God and one another with an openness to truth and justice in an attitude of love. That is the invitation of the psalmist so that we may abide in God's tent and dwell on God's holy hill.

> *Where do I need to speak truth from the heart, do what is right, be without blame, or be reconciled? On what holy hill will I dwell and with whom?*

THURSDAY, JANUARY 27 ~ *Read 1 Corinthians 1:18-31*

Paul writes from the perspective of the risen Christ, the one who has conquered death by death, and given new life through the power of love and truth, compassion and mercy, justice and right relationships. For Paul, the cross is the point of transformation, a point of passage that leads from conventional wisdom to the wisdom of the heart, to the alternative wisdom given us through the life of Jesus. One of my earliest disciplines involved "following" Jesus through the scriptures to observe his actions, to notice how he looked at and touched people.

Next I would let Jesus live that look, that touch, toward me. Then I practiced being the look and living that touch of life and love. I often found the practice challenging, but it taught me about the reality of the cross, the struggle of holding the tension long enough to see the light and discern a direction so I could respond rather than react.

I invite others to make the same journey. Recently one of my fellow pilgrims had a challenging experience with a small claims lawsuit. Holding the tension, remaining rooted in truth and integrity, grappling with the anger of injustice, and staying out of the desire for retaliation formed the heart of conversation again and again. The judge ruled that the case had no merit, and this person was awarded a small sum for his lost workdays. He decided to use these funds in a way that carried a consciousness for truth and justice, so he bought a beautiful watercolor that depicts hospitality and the graciousness of creation. The art daily reminds him to live as an agent of truth and nonviolence. My friend grappled with the cross and was empowered by the grace of resurrection to live out of an alternative wisdom.

At what moments in my life have I been challenged by the cross and chosen a path of alternative wisdom?

We now turn toward the challenge of the Beatitudes. The Western mind will not easily grasp them unless a person has dealt with loss or pain or known some form of tragedy that has led to a point of passage. Pain not dealt with well gets buried alive and then projected onto some other person, situation, or event, perpetuating and passing on that pain. The attitudes lived out are ones of blaming, bitterness, getting even, or self-pity.

The Beatitudes provide pathways for the transformation of mind and heart. In effect, they celebrate that transformation by saying, "Good for you! Congratulations! Blessed are you who are poor in spirit, who know mourning, who have learned mercy, who have purified your hearts!" They empower us to come at things from the underside of God, where an understanding of our own poverty and brokenness has been held and received.

In my Eastern Byzantine tradition we speak of people being beatified: where people have held the darkness, the pain, the struggle long enough to find their way into resurrection and life and, in their humanity and even before their death, are made holy. The Beatitudes carry the invitation to emulate the attitudes of God. The Hebrew word for this is *Kadosh*, that is, "be sacred being." Be sacred being, and live the hunger and thirst for justice and right relationship. Enter deeply into these Beatitudes of sacredness so that you may know God's reign by your involvement in challenging that which keeps people poor, women and children trafficked, and the marginalized absent from our tables of sacred gathering.

Today which beatitude speaks most of your passion? What in your life's experience emulates the presence and attitude of God?

I was waiting in a bus shelter when a man who looked much like a street person came to stand and wait with me. He held in his hand a basket of fresh strawberries from a market not a stone's throw away. He saw me look at the strawberries and at him and proceeded to offer me one. I looked at him and at the strawberries and refused. Somehow because of his unkemptness I decided he might have contaminated the berries. He might have touched one with his dirty hands or put them too close to his face and breathed on them.

Conventional wisdom had taught me that someone who looks like a street person is not worthy of trust or respect, let alone kindness or a sense of mutuality. That experience was some forty years ago, and this man still teaches me about my capacity for arrogance, self-righteousness, and judgmentalism. The Gospel of Matthew gives us the Beatitudes, the attitudes of Jesus, as an "examination of consciousness" (the term I employ in spiritual direction and therapy). Jesus addresses our hearts not with rules and regulations or with shoulds, oughts, and have-to's but with handrails for our salvation, our growing consciousness, our being transforming agents in the world. Jesus welcomed the poor, touched the untouchable, healed the sickness of self-centeredness, stood up those who were bowed down. He did this not by doctrine or lecturing; rather, he did all by his touch, his look, his word of truth and love. He displayed fearlessness before the judgment of Temple politics and the tiered reality of the class system. He did all of this by his life, through his prayer and reflection, and, having received love, experienced God as love.

Today as I pray the Beatitudes, how am I invited into a deeper awareness of Jesus' attitudes toward all persons? Which beatitude speaks to my heart, invites me to want and to do more kingdom living?

SUNDAY, JANUARY 30 ~ *Read Matthew 5:1-12*

The Beatitudes call us to know God and do justice; to be humble and live truth; to move from imperial power to God-power as Jesus did. It was not until the third century when Christianity became the religion of the empire that Christians could take up arms. Until this time, no Christian could be a soldier. This week's reflections invite us to put our life on the line for that which brings peace. We can do this only through total reliance on God, letting God be God, entering into the freedom of God, and being led from within by the Spirit and wisdom of God as Jesus was.

Such attentiveness demands contemplation, insists on prayer and reflection, calls for discernment to separate our own way, to follow a path laid out by the Risen One. So many of us have been taught to *be good* rather than live from our goodness; we have been taught to use scripture for judgment rather than entering it deeply to unveil the dream of God for a just world; a society based on equality, mutuality, and right relationships.

Jesus by his life signaled God's concern for the poor, the downtrodden, the broken, the lost—both within ourselves and around us. Jesus lived as the dream of God and died because of sin and all the ways that sin continues to feed our insecurities and uncertainties.

This week of reflection calls us to bend deeply into God and to enter the stillness that activates God's deep inner movement in us so that we can be God's action. "Blessed are you who walk in my ways, who are meek and humble of heart, who mourn, who hunger and thirst for justice, who are persecuted for righteousness, who are peacemakers: For you will be called children [people] of God."

In what ways has this week led me more deeply into contemplative prayer and action?

Having the Mind of Christ

JANUARY 31—FEBRUARY 6, 2011 • DAN JOHNSON

MONDAY, JANUARY 31 ~ *Read Isaiah 58:1-12*

Israel isn't alone in its propensity to say one thing and do another. We all have this tendency. And it takes a prophet to point it out with clarity and power, as we have in this chapter of Isaiah. God calls on the prophet to "shout out, do not hold back! Lift up your voice like a trumpet! Announce to my people their rebellion." They are religious in the sense that they observe certain religious rituals, like fasting, but this religion is an outward garment all for show. It doesn't come from the heart, from the inner soul, from a changed and transformed mind; therefore it doesn't translate into action that helps anyone. Then the prophet gets very specific in naming the actions God expects of God's people: to work to end injustice, to free the oppressed, to share bread with the hungry, to shelter the homeless, and to provide clothing for the naked.

This sounds a lot like Matthew 25's recording of the Judgment when people ask, "Lord, when did we see you hungry or thirsty or a stranger or needing clothes or sick or in prison?" In fact, this theme resonates throughout scripture because of its closeness to the heart of God. True religion actively cares, feeds, and clothes. It's a "helps others" kind of religion.

As I write this, members of my church are preparing to host four families who are temporarily homeless. With help from the Christian community, they will get back on their feet again. I imagine you are already putting hands and feet onto your Christian faith.

Dear God, may I see those in need and have the courage and will to do something about it. Amen.

Senior minister, Trinity United Methodist Church; Gainesville, Florida

TUESDAY, FEBRUARY 1 ~ *Read Isaiah 58:1-12*

What do you do when you're going through a desert time in your soul?" I asked my old preacher friend. "I go to the hospitals and nursing homes and visit folks," he replied. "I get outside of myself and do some good, and pretty soon I start to feel a lot better." He knew the reality that Isaiah describes. Something happens deep within persons when they live in sync with God's own heart, when they act on behalf of others as God would have them act.

Studies are clear and overwhelming: the happiest people are serving people. Is that a sudden revelation? Is it the latest fad? No, it goes back to the deepest parts of scripture. God created us in such a way that we are our best, healthiest, and most creative selves when we serve others and work for the causes that please God's heart.

Of course, this is most true when and if we act out of authentic love for others and not for ourselves. That's probably why the two greatest commandments come in the order they do: First, love God with all your heart, soul, mind and strength—get that right, let that reality grasp you, and change you; and *then* love your neighbor as yourself.

A team from my church recently returned from a trip to a remote region of El Salvador. They went to dig a well for people who had no clean drinking water, whose children often died of illnesses that come with contaminated water. When the clear fresh water came gushing forth, there was celebration and life! And I can tell you that the celebratory note for our team continues and will continue—just like the prophet said!

Dear God, may my heart feel as your heart does, and may my actions reflect a heart turned to you. Amen.

WEDNESDAY, FEBRUARY 2 ~ *Read Psalm 112*

This psalm relates the blessings that come to the faithful who keep God's commands. It is part of the theological tradition that grows out of Deuteronomy that says if you obey God's commands, you will receive blessings; if you disobey, you will receive curses. (See Deuteronomy 28.) This teaching contains a great truth. But I can't comment on the truth of this psalm without first offering an important caveat—from our Old Testament friend Job.

You remember Job: a righteous man who did all the things this psalm suggests. He was faithful, obedient, and true. Still disaster struck, and he lost everything. Bad things do happen to good and faithful people.

Nine years ago, our twenty-two-year-old daughter, Shevon, a religious and faithful-to-Jesus-type person—very careful not to sin or disobey God—was hit by a car that ran a traffic light. Shevon suffered several broken bones, was in a coma with a traumatic brain injury, and hovered between life and death for many days. Before she could speak, she looked up to the ceiling to ask with her eyes: *Why did God let this happen to me?* I could only answer with tears in my heart, "I don't know why this happened, but I know God loves you." Shevon has gained partial recovery, remaining mostly in a wheelchair; her memory and personality have come back. She and her husband have had two precious children, and we thank God every day. Her heart is "firm, secure in the LORD."

Dear God, we hold to the reality that you are a loving God, always working for your children's good—even when we don't understand. Amen.

THURSDAY, FEBRUARY 3 ～ *Read Psalm 112:5-10*

I move now to the reality that God has created us and our world in such a way that when we live as God intends, then life tends to go well for us. We experience an inner harmony and joy that comes from being "at home" in God and in God's world. When we take Christian discipleship seriously, we try to align our priorities with God's, along with our values and behavior. And that makes for a healthier and happier life than the alternative.

The psalmist spells it out in some detail. Look again at verse 5. Generous people *are* happier people, partly because we are made in God's image and God's nature is to be generous. When we are generous, we are in tune with God and how God created us. Moreover, honest actions free our consciences, and we live in a sense of trust.

In our daughter's situation, even in the midst of our heartbreaking disaster, we held on to our deep faith. We were even drawn closer to God. Shevon has since spoken in several churches; she titles her talk, "Faith Makes Things Possible, Not Easy."

Our family returned to the hymns of our faith, the scriptures and creeds. The knowledge that Jesus walked beside us gave a secure and rock-solid foundation that provided the basis of what the psalmist tells us.

When we look carefully, this psalm evidences a faith and trust in God regardless of outward circumstances. The "wealth" comes in the security, strength, and steadfastness that overcomes any adversity.

Dear God, you are our strength and our hope always. Amen.

Having the Mind of Christ

FRIDAY, FEBRUARY 4 ～ *Read 1 Corinthians 2:1-8*

The older I become, the more I affirm the truth of this passage. The wisdom inherent in scripture differs from the wisdom we find anywhere else. With a doctoral degree, I love gaining wisdom from wide-ranging arenas; but, at the end of the day, I am certain that the wisdom revealed in scripture surpasses all else.

As God said through Isaiah long ago:

My thoughts are not your thoughts, nor are your ways my ways. . . . As the heavens are higher than the earth, so are my ways higher than your ways and my thoughts than your thoughts (55:8, 9).

Christ is God's wisdom incarnate. Christ and his teachings reveal to us God's higher ways and express God's higher thoughts in words we can understand.

The Greeks prized wisdom above all else. Paul knows his audience. He also knows that wisdom, as an end in itself, leads to hubris and self-centeredness, characteristics prevalent in Corinth and in the Corinthian church. Paul's task then, as is our task now, is to bring the focus back to Jesus, to have the mind of Christ and see the world through his perspective.

Paul can share his erudition with the best of them, but he affirms that life at its essence is not about that. He knows what the Hebrew Bible attests: reverence for God is the beginning of wisdom. Only with the humble spirit of Jesus can the members of the Corinthian church turn from their divisions, immorality, and false wisdom to become a loving, serving church worthy of the name of Christ. So it was, so it always shall be for any person or any church.

Lord Jesus, may I walk humbly with you, eager to learn of you and your ways. Amen.

SATURDAY, FEBRUARY 5 ~ *Read 1 Corinthians 2:9-16*

Paul uses the word *Spirit* six times in the last six verses of chapter 2. Clearly, Paul believes that the Spirit of God reveals God's wisdom to us. Toward the end of his life, Jesus told his disciples that he would ask the Father to send another Advocate, the Spirit of truth; this Advocate "will teach you everything" (John 14:16, 26).

I believe four keys open us to receive the wisdom that the Spirit reveals:

1. *Humility.* Humility puts us in a posture of receptivity. We understand that while God gives us brains and intelligence, we become open to the deeper wisdom only when we open ourselves to God.

2. *Asking.* I often charge forth into my day without asking God to guide me. I am learning to pause and ask the Holy Spirit to guide me into all the truth I need for this day. I see a difference when I pause.

3. *Others.* A couple of years ago, I formed a weekly Bible study that became my "sermon research" group. The members focus on the scripture that I will be preaching on the next Sunday. I gain amazing insights from this group!

4. *The mind of Christ.* Paul closes this chapter on wisdom and the Spirit by affirming that "we have the mind of Christ." Living in the Spirit can be quite subjective; we can fool ourselves into thinking that our thoughts are really the Spirit's. We need the concrete specificity of "the mind of Christ" to keep us on track.

Dear God, may the mind of Jesus be in me, that I might think his thoughts and do his will. Amen.

I did my PhD work in Old Testament. So I am a strong proponent of the Old Testament, of the whole Bible. Too often I have witnessed a practical disregard of the Old Testament and a preferential exclusivity for the New Testament. The church has never condoned this belief and, more importantly, it flies in the face of Jesus' own teaching. He cannot state it more strongly than when he proclaims in his Sermon on the Mount: I didn't come to abolish the law or the prophets but to fulfill them!

Jesus comes to reveal or recover the deeper, intended meaning that has gotten lost in the encrustation of human tradition. In these verses, he sets forth two strong images of Christian community: salt and light. Both serve particular purposes with specific intentions. When salt no longer seasons food, it becomes useless, no longer serving its intended purpose. We who hear Jesus' words acknowledge the warning to take our call to discipleship seriously.

As for the light—either of city or home, with a lamp—the intended purpose is visibility. Placing a lamp under a basket thwarts its reason for being. And we affirm God's intended purpose for us as we witness to God's glory and bring light to the nations. We are the light of the world.

Throughout the Sermon on the Mount, Jesus says often, "You have heard it said . . . , but I say. . . . " In every instance, he does not negate the saying but presses on to its intended meaning. Jesus doesn't destroy the law but fulfills it. And he insists that we do as well. So we move forward to fulfill God's intended purpose for us: to be salt and light.

Gracious God, grant me insight into your word that I may walk in its light daily. Amen.

The Discipline of Choices

FEBRUARY 7–13, 2011 • BERT COBB

MONDAY, FEBRUARY 7 ~ *Read Deuteronomy 30:15-20*

Ultimately, our choices in life determine who we are and whose we are. Jesus was a practicing Jew, as were his disciples. Our ignorance of Torah blinds us to much of Christianity's foundation. Jews see Torah as the divine word of God delivered to the prophet on Mount Sinai. The non-Jew often fails to see the grace, love, and mercy contained in Torah.

These verses from Deuteronomy sum up a series of sermons delivered by Moses in which he explains his vision for the Israelites' future. Chapters 28 and 29 set the parameters for compliance and the outcomes for obedience or disobedience. These regulations touch every aspect of life. There is no fine print in the contract that Moses asks the people of Israel either to accept or reject. Acceptance of the commandments leads to blessing; rejection of the commandments leads to judgment.

True disciples are those who have consciously chosen to follow God and God's paradigm for their lives. Some of us kick against the briars and blame God for our ignorance when the choice is obvious: life and good versus death and evil. But ethics are what others see. Morals are what we do when no human eyes are watching. The basis of both is our decision as to who will be in charge of our life. As Moses warns the Israelites, not choosing *is* a choice.

Lord, grant me the discernment to choose wisely in keeping with your will. Amen.

Physician for thirty-one years, member of Christ the Redeemer Church; San Marcos, Texas

Psalm 119 celebrates Torah as a gift from God, as a faithful guide to right living. Torah might better be translated as "instruction" rather than law. These verses in Psalm 119 describe the wholeness of life that comes to those who attempt to follow God's leading. Those who want to affirm God's presence in their lives signal that choice by accepting God's "instruction."

Choices are easier when we can appreciate a present or future value for them. The psalmist calls for benediction upon those who have chosen to walk blamelessly in the law of the Lord and who honestly and wholeheartedly seek God. God's law benefits disciples in the present and in the future. Choosing to see God's guidance as beneficial versus punitive and limiting opens up the possibility of the joy of obedience. The psalm names as "happy" those who attempt to live in the light of Torah.

As children of God, we test the limits of God's love by trying to walk as close as possible to the edges of God's path of instruction. Two-year-olds test the limits of parental oversight. Eventually, they learn that the parents' guidance is for their well-being and blessing. God, the loving parent, gives guidance for our benefit and blessing. We grow up spiritually when we realize that God's parental advice and counsel has our best interests in mind. For present and future value, choose God, obey, and be happy.

Lord, make your ways my ways. Show me the path that leads to you. May I choose to be happy and blessed. Amen.

Personal responsibility provides the framework for God's instruction. From early childhood, the psalmist has known Torah and its precepts. The psalmist also understood the importance of diligence in following the revealed word of God it contained. Diligence is not a one-time event. Diligence implies a continual search and effort to understand and internalize the principles contained in Torah. Each of us will be responsible to God for our own words, thoughts, and deeds.

God desires that we voluntarily choose to follow divine precepts without shame, our eyes fixed on the joy of pursuing God's will. But we can choose to live a scattered or fragmented life by following our own precepts and will. We may follow the rules God set down for our happiness and blessing, or we may ignore God's instruction to our detriment.

The psalmist expresses his intention of keeping Torah, identifying God's instruction as the focus of his life, "having my eyes fixed on all your commandments." We, like the psalmist, acknowledge our desire to follow God's path of instruction even as we acknowledge our own human weakness in commitment to that path. Yet, we do not seek justice. We desire mercy.

Our God is the God of second chances, who grants grace and mercy when we stray from the path. God will never forsake us. Nothing we can do will make God love us less. God's love, mercy, and forgiveness exceed our wildest imagination. In response to this love, may we keep our eyes fixed on all God's commandments, reaping the joy that comes from such commitment, such obedience.

Lord, give me the joy of a relationship with you built upon honesty and personal accountability, that I might glorify you in my obedience to your righteous precepts. Amen.

*W*hat do I feed my baby is a question that arises in the mind of every first-time parent. No one would feed a newborn a steak or hotdog, yet we may attempt to cram the meat of doctrine and dogma down the throat of newborn Christians.

While Jesus and the twelve disciples witnessed primarily to people who had an understanding of God, Paul ministered to the Jews and the culturally polytheistic peoples. Paul, a teacher with a first-class education, understood the principle of starting from the basics to expand and explain Jesus' message. So he reminds the Corinthians that he fed them with milk until they were ready for solid food. Some in the community identify Paul as their savior because he first gave them the gospel. Naturally they want to cling to one who brought the good news of salvation.

Others claimed various other teachers as their spiritual leader. They so appreciated the light of the gospel and those who delivered it to them that confusion developed about the source of their salvation and healing. Paul clarifies the issue: he and others are mere mortals who are given the ministry of spreading the good news. They are servants of the Lord with an assigned task. Apart from God, they are powerless and unworthy of acclaim or special status.

Paul's opening salvo of spiritual baby food nourished the Corinthians until they could "eat" the spiritual food of adults. Identified as disciples of Jesus, they too will take up the call of ministry: to choose to follow Christ and faithfully deliver the good news to everyone in their world.

Lord, may I take in your spiritual milk until I am ready for solid food. Amen.

Because of Paul's notoriety in the early church, he could have chosen to receive special status and to draw disciples to himself. Instead, he chose to be honest with the Corinthians and give the full credit to God for the gospel and for the growth of the numbers of disciples. In an agrarian society, Paul once again draws upon a nurturing image that every listener would have understood when he uses the metaphor of planting seeds.

"I planted. Apollos watered." Quarrels about the merits of Paul and Apollos reflect the Corinthians' misunderstanding of the nature of Christian growth. Neither Paul's role, that of planting or initiating the church at Corinth, nor Apollos's role, that of watering or watching over the church, makes the church grow. The growth itself comes from God alone.

I have been a gardener for years. In faith I plant seeds, weed, and water my garden in the hope of a bountiful crop. In drought, I wait upon the Lord to water my crops and realize that my garden's success depends on the weather. I do my best to achieve success but realize that God is in charge of the seeds' sprouting, the growth of the new plants, and the miracle of the harvest.

Paul, fully aware of his part in this miraculous harvest of believers, plants the gospel in the hearts and minds of the church folks, but God helps it grow to maturity. The believer plants, and God gives the growth.

God is present with us as we plant, water, weed, and wait. The harvest occurs in God's time, so what we plant today may not produce fruit until long after the planting. Paul knew that his success ultimately lay in God's hands. We can choose to do our best and let God give the harvest. We can rejoice in God's faithfulness to fulfill our humble efforts to God's glory.

Lord, may I labor in faith, knowing that you give the growth. Amen.

Most of us have never killed anyone, but have we destroyed someone's ego or abused private knowledge to kill a reputation? Jesus, a rabbi familiar with Torah and the teaching of the Jewish leaders, compares current practice and standards advocated under Torah with his new covenant. Which is worse in God's sight: murdering the body or murdering the spirit or reputation? To understand the pain and suffering that hurtful words cause, visit a courtroom in any city when child custody or divorce cases are being heard. Unbridled tongues have "killed" more people than any sword or gun.

This passage is about personal responsibility and the choice to accept ourselves and others as equally sinful and in need of forgiveness. The early church and some modern fundamentalist groups had a period of confession and a time of forgiveness prior to partaking of the Communion sacraments. Before standing before the Creator, it is imperative that we make right our relationships with God's children by honestly seeking forgiveness for anything that might separate us from each other. For Jesus, any issue that disrupts relationship requires resolution. It does not matter who is right and who is wrong.

In Jesus' time, the religious authorities served as both judge and jury in civil and religious disputes. Settling petty disputes between parties before placing the facts of the dispute before those who had the power to imprison was both curative and preventive medicine. My relationship with God depends on my honest relationship with others and my desire for reconciliation.

Lord, make me an instrument of healing as I choose to appreciate and value others as I would like to be appreciated. Amen.

Jesus goes on to address adultery and divorce. Once more he emphasizes relationship. In biblical times, adultery was defined as extramarital sexual intercourse between a man and another man's wife. The concern about adultery grew out of the property laws of ancient Israel. The wife was viewed as the property of her husband; the extramarital relationship violated the rights of the husband. But Jesus' teaching affirms women as persons in their own right.

Adultery is a choice to share innermost thoughts and body with another human who has pledged an oath of allegiance in an equal relationship of intimacy. Adultery begins in the heart and mind and culminates in sexual intimacy. When the sexual urge overrides the mind's ability to exercise judgment and control, intimacy fails and chastity suffers. Jesus' warning about lust offers some protection for the disadvantaged woman, and his statements that follow emphasize the importance of a wholesome relationship.

In marriage, two parties pledge love and intimacy to each other. The oath, made before witnesses, enforces the gravity of the occasion on all involved. Jesus affirms the sanctity of marriage and encourages reconciliation. Once again, the matter of wholesome relationship comes to the fore.

We must keep our promises to each other just as we keep our commitment to God. Since we own nothing and owe everything to God, we can only pledge ourselves in payment of our oaths of indebtedness to God and to each other.

Lord, I desire to honor you with my life. Help me choose to keep my promises to you and to others. Amen.

Reaping to the Edges

FEBRUARY 14–20, 2011 • HELAENA W. PRITCHARD

MONDAY, FEBRUARY 14 ~ *Read Leviticus 19:9-10*

My husband and I work in developing countries. Every two or three years, crews of professional movers pack our household items to go by sea to our next country of assignment. Because shipping those items may take months, we get to send several hundred pounds of "critical" possessions by airfreight for use in the interim.

Our domestic staff (local residents who rely on the comparatively high salaries [$150–200 per month] and jobs that foreign diplomats, aid workers, and business people provide) help stack the boxes as they arrive. As the unpacking begins, I feel overwhelmed and ashamed by what I've acquired. I give much of it away—to the staff or to the elderly fellow who repairs shoes on the dirt street corner outside our house for pennies—whether out of a compulsion to help those in need of five pairs of khaki pants and seven bath towels or because I simply don't know where to put it all.

In Leviticus, God cautions us against hoarding and overconsumption. We are to leave some of what we possess for those who need it more than we do. We may do this by tithing to the church or to charities, giving time and resources, or not driving too hard a bargain with our neighbors or those we employ. Leviticus reminds us that we are not to "reap to the very edges of [our] field"—or our means.

God, remind us to give, knowing that someone is in need. Remind us of our affluence as we bask in the richness of your love. Amen.

U.S. Foreign Service officer; Nairobi, Kenya

TUESDAY, FEBRUARY 15 ~ *Read Leviticus 19:11-15*

These verses echo other words we know from Exodus and Deuteronomy. We read of not stealing, dealing falsely or lying to one another, and no swearing in God's name. These instructions foster good relationships among neighbors and serve to protect the weak. I witnessed systemic abuse of the weak when I lived in India, where the scale of poverty is shocking. I have felt compelled to deliver all my household possessions to the nearest slum and catch the next transatlantic flight back to my hometown, where poverty is less visible and thus easier to forget.

Ten-plus years ago, as a student in India, when I walked the streets, gangs of children would surround me, pulling at my clothing, asking for money. A devoted babysitter back home, I astounded myself by stomping and swatting these children away as though they were flies. Years later, when I returned to India as a professional, packs of unwashed children would surround my car at stoplights. An emaciated preteen might carry a limp, skinny infant. These children do not keep the money they earn begging. So do we leave it to the charities to assist them, or do we try to soothe in some small way the few we can?

"You shall not be partial to the poor or defer to the great," the God of Leviticus warns. Some of my colleagues began to hand out juice boxes, water, or snacks, often into the hands of the alpha child, who, desperate to survive in a cruel urban world, hoarded the bounty from his team. The limp baby remained with her empty bottle. And I, a comparatively wealthy foreigner, drove away feeling perplexed, saddened, and helpless in the face of the incomparable suffering of these children.

God, grant me the discernment to know when to favor the poor and when to defer to the great. Shine your light upon those who suffer. Clear my eyes of false judgment; may I seek your righteous justice. Amen.

The idea of God's Spirit dwelling within has never been more real to me than when I have been pregnant. As I incubate my second child, I feel a tangible blessing from God; I am mindful of the spirit within this child kicking in my womb, which is a vessel of God's creation.

Yet as I feel mindful of this holiness, one of my best friends is fighting a severe case of endometriosis, a condition that closes the window on her potential to have biological children. In our early twenties, she and I became fast friends, discovering that we shared our faith, common interests, and dreams of having children even as we pursued our careers overseas. On my first assignment in Asia, I met a humanitarian worker who became my steady and loving husband, while my friend was evacuated from her assignment in a neighboring country to have emergency surgery and recover alone.

My friend suffers terrible pain from cysts, multiple surgeries, and hormone therapies. Her dearest wish, like mine fulfilled, is to have children. She suffers through her condition and the side effects of her medications in the hopes of maintaining her ability to procreate until she meets her life partner.

My son recognizes her loving spirit and toddles to my friend with the same immediacy and delight he feels for my sisters or his grandmothers. Paul reminds us that we are God's temple and that God's Spirit dwells in us, no matter our physical conditions. My friend knows hope and love in the Spirit; the present and the future belong to her, for she belongs to Christ, who belongs to God.

God, you are within us even when we fail to perceive you. Make us mindful of your Spirit, and let us be vessels of your creation. Bring us new beginnings. May we carry you in our hearts just as you carry us through the blessings and trials of our lives. Amen.

Paul switches metaphors on us: We move from planting to building. In planting, God gives the growth; in building, humans become responsible for the finished product. We become responsible for what we build and how we build it.

I arrived at my job in Sri Lanka three months after the December 2004 tsunami, which killed thirty thousand people on the small island that had already lost twice that many through twenty-five years of civil war. As I drove south toward the beach during one of my first weekends in that country, I saw the crumbling concrete houses lining the railroad tracks and highway by the seaside. The roofs of these houses had been lifted off.

The people of the world responded with generous aid to rebuild the houses and lives of those who survived. But before long, rumors surfaced of the craftiness of human leaders: that the rebel group would only allow aid into the areas they controlled if they could oversee its distribution; that the majority politicians were favoring members of their own ethnic or religious communities; that building contractors were mixing too much sand into the concrete in order to maximize their profits.

Thus the politicization of that aid closely followed the goodwill between communities that the tragedy had first evoked. A year into my tour, I still saw villages of blue plastic tents lined along the coast, but the work had begun. The world can extend gratitude to those who chose to build a solid foundation and who knew that this world's wisdom is foolishness with God. They put aside politics to rebuild the foundations of human lives with care and faith.

Dear God, as we watch, report, and advise on the cycles of war, peace, unification, disaster, make us humble so that we may become wise in Christ. Guide us to alleviate the suffering of those near to us and far from us, to honor your Spirit through the care of your children. Amen.

FRIDAY, FEBRUARY 18 ~ *Read Matthew 5:38-48*

Acity's traffic, check-out lines, and public transportation often evidence the self-focused aspect of the metropolitan personality. A well-dressed university student or businesswoman may keep her seat when an elderly person boards the train, facing straight ahead as the man with the cane struggles to maintain his balance when the train lurches between frequent stops. A driver may be too impatient to turn left to wait for a pedestrian pushing a stroller to reach the other side of the crosswalk. I am guilty of pretending not to see the homeless veteran on the sidewalk between my train stop and office or the volunteer canvassing for a charity. In city life, many of us guard against being asked to give anything to strangers.

Currently I live and work in Washington, DC, my nation's capital, where many talented and ambitious persons have converged. One of my colleagues introduced me to the term *coopetition*, the art of competing with colleagues while demonstrating a positive "team spirit." Every one to three years, my colleagues and I are transferred. We compete for jobs across the globe and in Washington, some more highly prized than others for their interesting work or exotic locations. We rely on the confidential recommendations of our former supervisors, peers, and supervisees. It's important to know your friends from your "frenemies" when requesting recommendations.

Jesus reminds us that loving our friends is the easy thing to do. To love strangers and those with whom we are inclined to compete or dislike requires us to tune in to the Spirit of God within and open ourselves to those around us.

God in heaven, teacher Christ, Holy Spirit within us, help us to love our neighbors, be they strangers, friends, or enemies, so that we may spread your love and light in our world and thus be your worthy children. Amen.

Once again the psalmist turns our thoughts to the life-giving Torah, employing a string of synonyms: "statutes," "law," "commandments," "decrees," "ways," "promise" and "ordinances." And humankind's urgent prayer calls upon the grace of God: "Teach me . . . "; "Lead me . . . "; "Confirm . . . " to save us from life's pitfalls and struggles.

As a child in the "Bible Belt," I understood that there were three main "religions": Methodist, Baptist, and Presbyterian. (My Jewish uncle lived in faraway Boston and didn't seem too concerned with keeping kosher.) The theological differences involved the fact that Presbyterians liked to vote on committees and we Methodists couldn't chat too long after church if we were going to beat the Baptist lunch crowd to our favorite restaurant. I attended a Methodist university and actively participated on the interfaith council. Despite my exposure to world religions, I never had to stray far beyond the theology of my Christian comfort zone.

In recent years I have belonged to church communities overseas, in countries where Christians are the minority and the foreigners come from a greater variety of backgrounds. I have encountered more varieties of Christians in my adult life: austere Canadian Mennonites, Korean converts, Scottish Presbyterians, and Evangelical Anglicans from Australia. Yet, we all, like the psalmist, acknowledge God's instruction as a gracious gift that allows us to live peacefully with God and with one another. Torah brings life.

> *God, may we observe your laws with our whole hearts. Turn our eyes from vanities and petty differences; may we remember our unity in Christ and continue to long for your precepts. Amen.*

SUNDAY, FEBRUARY 20 ~ *Read Leviticus 19:16-18*

In Laos, the last overseas country in which my husband and I lived, Christian evangelism by foreigners was illegal. Some of my Christian neighbors, many of them missionaries, introduced me to theological concepts I had not considered: the quality of everything in the universe as either good or evil, rather than shades of gray; spiritual warfare as a reality. My new Christian neighbors introduced me to more literal biblical interpretations. I had always assumed that when Jesus cast out the demons he had cured the man of schizophrenia, or that childbirth was painful because of narrow pelvic bones rather than the sin of Adam and Eve.

Our Laotian pastor always reminded church members that we are one family in Christ despite our denominational personalities. Some of my new siblings wondered if my Church of England husband might not be saved because he didn't get emotional in church and avoided Wednesday evening Bible study (but not Sunday lunch) whenever possible. One new sister told me she prayed that my husband would be struck by the Spirit!

Members of the congregation spent many hours discussing God's presence in their lives. Sometimes they ventured into areas in which my husband and I could not agree in our hearts. Sometimes I became more open to new biblical interpretations. Mostly, I reverted to the guidance of my father, an Old Testament scholar, and my mother, a gentle lay minister. Praying together with them provided some of the most spiritually moving moments of my life.

"You shall love your neighbor as yourself: I am the LORD." Despite our theological differences, I found much comfort in those neighbors in Christ.

Creator God, we are all your children. Help us consider and learn from our differences. Guard our hearts from hatred of any who love you. Amen.

A Transforming Wait

FEBRUARY 21–27, 2011 • CHRISTINA M. SAENZ

MONDAY, FEBRUARY 21 ~ *Read Isaiah 49:8-14*

The psalmist records words that testify to God's faithfulness: *answered, helped, kept, given*. God is faithful to the end. We have heard this said many times, and we may even profess it and encourage others to acknowledge it. However, a disconnect occurs when we ourselves realize that we don't know the "end" of our problems, our anxieties, our confusions. If we did, we might consider God's faithfulness irrelevant. If Zion had known that God would show up and attain the victory, the nation might have ignored God's faithfulness and become self-indulgent in its accolades. God protects us from self-absorption. God knows the strength we possess, our tendency to rely on ourselves; and, most importantly, the moment in which we will learn to fully rely on the divine. God waits for us until we wait on the Lord.

Despite the psalmist's assertion of God's ongoing care for us, we often ignore the provision and assume control. We respond, like Zion, "I don't get it! God has left me, forsaken me, forgotten I even exist." The question is, has God forsaken us or have we forsaken our faithfulness to God? When a child attends a public school in my country, the law guarantees the provision of a meal. But the child must decide to eat it.

God offers comfort and has "compassion on his suffering ones." How have we experienced this comfort and compassion? As God's children, we can expect God's provision. How will we respond to this gracious offer?

Dear Lord, help me recognize your provision in my life. Please wait for me as I learn to wait on you. Amen.

Youth pastor, El Buen Pastor United Methodist Church; Edinburg, Texas

TUESDAY, FEBRUARY 22 ～ *Read Isaiah 49:15-16*

I will never forget you." Those are the words a parent longs to hear when children leave home to begin their life. They are the words that friends speak when they will be apart for a period of time, and the words significant others exchange when they are moving on. We want to be remembered, loved, never forgotten, always relevant. Human beings innately need to be loved and accepted. At day's end, we perhaps recall the people we encountered throughout the day. We hope that they are remembering us as we remember them. The thought of being forgotten or irrelevant pushes us into a state of insecurity and self-pity. Yet the more we seek our worth from those within reach, the less likely we are to look all around us, even to the depths of the earth and the endless heights where God resides.

Out of sight and out of mind may be our biggest fear, though we know that losing sight of something or someone is easy to do. Often we accept responsibility to "watch" over another. When that person is no longer in our care or our presence, we tend to move on to new experiences, new relationships.

God assures us that we are never out of sight or mind of the divine. Being in God's sight every second of the day may overwhelm us. Maybe we disregard that fact because we do not want to accept its reality. Yet God assures us, "I will not forget you." Others may pale in our memories over time; we may no longer be remembered in the minds of others. But God imbues our human lives with eternal significance through holy viewing and care. Like a parent who takes a child out to play, God is always observing, waiting, and encouraging. We are inscribed on "the palms of [God's] hands."

Dear Lord, may I not forget that I am always in your sight and that by you, I will never be forgotten or rejected. Amen.

For God alone the psalmist waits. For what are you waiting? A life change? A new job? A spouse? Money? Maybe you have been waiting so long that the act of waiting has become an inseparable part of your existence. The wait has been long and exhausting, leaving you void of hope.

Many of us waken daily to another day of mundane existence. Rather than search for an eternal cure for our longing, we seek a quick resolution. Our cultural conditioning provides instant gratification. Days go by; the horizon seems to drift off in the distance and the light at the end of the tunnel is eventually blocked by an obstruction.

This psalm asks us to reflect not only on what we are waiting for but also in whom we place our trust. The psalmist advises us to trust in God. However, rather than clinging to the "rock" as the psalmist suggests, we cling to pebbles. The psalmist mentions some of these illusory pebbles: wealth and power. We grab up these pebbles in desperation, in fatigue, and in impatience. They can scarcely satisfy the "wait," but we compromise an eternal answer for a temporal satisfaction. Carrying around multiple pebbles can result in unnecessary discomfort (annoyance, sweat, etc.). Instead, hold fast to the Rock that offers comfort, strength, courage, hope, and refuge. Escape from the mundane way of life to be held in God's embrace, from which flows eternal satisfaction. Do not sell yourself short during the "wait." Hold steady. Reject the temptation of immediate gratification. As my dad, Rev. Ruben Saenz (a fearless disciple of Christ), proclaimed, "Waiting allows for the acquisition of spiritual muscle." Victory comes only when we build our strength.

Dear Lord, rid me of my dependency on the pebbles of life. Help me develop the sustaining power of holding fast to you, my Rock. Amen.

Once again our scripture passage calls to mind a mother's love and support for a child. The parent serves as a calming influence. For those who waken to a mundane existence, the psalmist goes on to reflect briefly on a life in which some parts were unfulfilled. His eyes are not raised too high, and he leaves the great and marvelous alone. His heart is not lifted up. The psalmist comes humbly before God, aware of his personal limitations—no inflated ego here.

When we, like the psalmist, seek after God's heart rather than the gratification of our own heart, we decrease and God increases within us. As much as our heart illuminates our passion and desires, it can also lead us down a path of deception and pride. When our heart loses a battle of love or when a passion is dissolved, our defense mechanisms accelerate; slowly our heart is subject to dangerous pride and overconfidence. The place of God's residency becomes inhabited by self-centered kudos. Entitlement lurks just around the corner from self-centeredness, all too often propelling us into a state of self-advocacy, selfishness, and justification. Give an inch to pride, and expect it to take a million miles. Allowing pride and entitlement to dictate our actions and relationships blocks the unconditional love God offers to others through us.

God's power comes wrapped in paradox; simple, yet deep enough to sustain the width and depth of the universe. Our feeble attempt to understand God fully may elicit self-dependency rather than spiritual revelation. As we come to trust and rest in God's promise of perfect love, we will find our soul calmed and quieted.

Dear Lord, may I decrease so that you may increase in me. Amen.

Ihave always believed that my dad and my older brother (both pastors) hold God's secrets. Every time I hear them preach, they unlock for me the mysteries of God's timing and plans. I know they are merely vessels who allow God to flow through them, but the thought that someone could be God's secret keeper sounds brilliant to me. Paul identifies us as servants of God and stewards of God's mysteries. Both servants and stewards take responsibility: servants over various things; stewards over the tasks of a household. Nothing powerful, nothing exotic: simply the care of matters. God requires our service and will hold us accountable.

Our judgments on others and their judgments on us are not the ones that matter, for "it is the Lord who judges." Paul reminds us that one day our inner motives and purposes of the heart will be brought to light—a rather terrifying thought, isn't it?

One day I asked my dad, "the secret keeper," what his greatest fear in life was. He responded by saying that he feared not doing enough for God. While we may not attain perfection and may allow imperfect inner motives to guide us, we may put on an attitude of "enoughness" for God as part of our daily wardrobe. This attitude decreases our selfish motives and increases our selfless motives, knowing that none of us can stand in judgment of another. Paul himself asserts with the confidence that accompanies a clean conscience, "I am not aware of anything against myself." We stand before God as servants and stewards, helpers in God's household. The Lord's coming will disclose the purposes of our hearts. May we be the recipients of God's commendation.

Dear Lord, make me a keeper of your secrets, a steward of your mysteries. Give me the opportunity to serve. Amen.

This little piece of Jesus' Sermon on the Mount reminds us of the choices before us if we are to help usher in the reign of God. And the choices are tough and pretty clear-cut: serving God or chasing wealth; trusting God or dwelling on life's needs; seeking God's rule or worrying about tomorrow.

Media and our surroundings condition us on a daily basis to want more: more love, more money, more friends. But the "more" we get requires even more time to manage our unnecessary abundance. The more time we spend managing wealth, the less time we have to manage our relationship with God. We often cheat ourselves of the fullness of God because we focus on the fullness of materialism. And as Jesus tells us, we can't serve God and money; we have to choose. When we obsess over "more," we rob ourselves of God's faithful provision.

When I was a child, I didn't understand the sacrifices my mother made to provide a hot meal and clean clothing for me. Her constant and loving provision made a difference in my life. Because of my immaturity, I am sure I requested "more" from time to time. Being the selfless parent that she is, she probably gave me more than I ever needed or deserved. So it is with God. This passage twice refers to God as Father, the parent who tends to birds and clothes the fields and who knows our every need and provides. Striving for God's righteousness brings the realization that our desire for "more" often leads to "less" where it really counts.

Dear Lord, help me fix my eyes on your reign and not on the immediate satisfaction this world offers. Amen.

SUNDAY, FEBRUARY 27 ~ *Read Matthew 6:34*

The unknowns of tomorrow cause distress in our souls. We often believe that if we obsess about tomorrow, we will unlock its mystery, foresee the future. Yet, when our tomorrows become todays, we realize that the time spent worrying over them was futile. Being prepared for tomorrow is important, but dwelling on it can waste our time. When we waste time, we never actualize our God-given gifts to the fullest.

This verse reminds us that God provides not only for our todays but for our tomorrows as well. We can easily forget this promise, especially when we attempt to control every moment of our existence—a big task for fallible humans. We cannot foresee failures and victories. The good news is that the One who can foresee them takes care of our todays and tomorrows, freeing us to choose a life of joyful discipleship.

Donald Miller, author of *Blue Like Jazz*, says that God used to be "a swinging speck in the distance; now He is close enough I can hear His singing. Soon I will see the lines on His face." Allowing God to take control of our todays and tomorrows brings us one step closer to seeing the "lines on [God's] face" and to engaging in God's work in the world.

How will the reign of God come in our world, in our lives? Perhaps it begins when we strive for righteousness and put away our worry about what we can't control. When we give our lives to God, the gap between our life and God's plans lessens, and we find ourselves one step closer to the kingdom.

Dear Lord, help me to lay my tomorrows in your hands. May I learn to live obsessed with your work rather than with the worries tomorrow may bring. Amen.

Eyewitnesses to Majesty

FEBRUARY 28–MARCH 6, 2011 • JASMINE ROSE SMOTHERS

MONDAY, FEBRUARY 28 ~ *Read Exodus 24:12-18*

Most people I know have a hard time waiting. Our fast-paced society makes waiting an annoyance. Yet we spend much of our time waiting. We wait in traffic; we wait on hold; we wait in line; we wait for our next appointment to arrive; and we wait for someone to call, text, or email us back. We're usually hurrying up to wait! The problem is that we are in such a hurry that we miss what passes us by while we wait. We miss the children laughing; we miss the flowers blooming; we miss the stars shining; we miss the clouds rolling; we miss the whisper of the wind; and if we're not careful, we miss life!

Growing up, I remember hearing the phrase, "Good things come to those who wait!" This saying certainly proves true for Moses and the Israelite people. God commands that Moses come to the mountain and "wait." So Moses goes up the mountain alone and waits in silence. "The glory of the LORD" envelops the mountaintop and Moses, after six days of waiting, meets God.

I wonder what would happen to us if we settled in to wait? What might be revealed in our lives if we slowed down long enough to respond to the Lord's request for a meeting? Might we then possibly hear the voice of God in the laughter, the blooming, the shining, the rolling, and the whispering? Moses waits and then walks away with life-altering instructions for the Israelites. I wonder if we would walk away with solutions for our worries, healing for our pain, peace for our chaos, joy for our sorrow, and hope for our despair.

Glorious Lord, teach us how to wait, so that we might have our own life-altering, mountaintop encounter with you. Amen.

Associate pastor, Atlanta First United Methodist Church; Atlanta, Georgia

TUESDAY, MARCH 1 ~ *Read Psalm 99:1-5*

I turned on the news today and faced disturbing headlines: shootings, fatal car accidents, stock market dropping, home invasions, institutional failures, church fires, poverty, disease, dysfunction, meanness, homelessness, helplessness, and sadness. Layoffs, foreclosures, and cancer are forcing humanity to come to grips with the fact that we are merely human, only helpless creatures. We know that we can control very little in life. In a society that expects us to be superhuman, we must face the fact that we are not God.

The psalmist affirms a God who is sovereign over *all* the earth: people tremble and the earth quakes! This God is in control, setting forth a new world order of justice, equity, and righteousness. We serve a God who knows how many hairs are on our heads. Our God formed us in our mother's womb and cares more about us than we can fathom. We serve a God who holds our yesterday, today, and tomorrow preciously close in hand. We serve a God who does not stand idle but works on our behalf.

"Holy is he!" This God is beyond challenge, beyond resistance, beyond explanation. The divine purpose will be worked out in the earth; no one can block it.

We must learn to praise and trust God when we understand why life is the way it is and when we don't understand at all. We begin to acknowledge that it is not up to us to fix everything. Revenge is not our business; regret is not our dwelling. What we can affirm is that God rules over all as "Mighty King, lover of justice" who works on behalf of us and all creation.

Mighty King, we praise you! Help us to yield to you and to trust you. Amen!

I love the people of God! I value their differences and flaws, and seemingly God does too. The folks God chooses to use as instruments are not superhuman but people with real problems, real stories, and real lives. Today's passage mentions three who interceded with God on Israel's behalf: Moses, Aaron, and Samuel. You may recall that Moses had a laundry list of excuses, and Samuel's very existence was nothing short of a miracle. Yet God called them to serve.

We are not that different from them. All three were going about their own business when God called. Yet, at critical times in their nation's history, they voiced the concerns of the people God had called them to serve. They "called on his name" and "cried to the LORD," giving voice to the oppression and injustice the people were experiencing at the hands of other countries.

Because the three intercessors called out to a God of justice, God "answered, . . . spoke." God listens for the needs of people in desperate situations and avenges wrongdoings.

Moses, Aaron, and Samuel all knew something about this God. This God is to be worshiped. This God hears the cries of the needy and responds. This God forgives and requites wrong deeds. "Extol the LORD our God."

What has been your experience of a sovereign God who listens and is involved in your life decisions? What cries have you voiced—and on whose behalf? When has God heard, answered, forgiven, and avenged? What causes you to praise God?

Holy God, I praise you for your listening ear and involvement in my life. Amen.

"Mommy, Mommy! It's Jesus!" I remember it like it was yesterday. I stood in the aisle at the grocery store with my dad and my younger brother as a stunned little boy proclaimed loudly enough for the whole store to hear that my dad was Jesus. Now, Dad was his pastor and was the one who told him the stories of Jesus during children's time. Dad had baptized this boy, and Dad even wore a long robe on Sundays—just like the pictures of Jesus on his Sunday school class walls.

How could the child mistake his pastor for Jesus? This child had taken what he knew to be true about Jesus and translated it into something that made sense to him.

Our passage today alludes to an event in which Peter, James, and John saw Jesus talking with Moses and Elijah, and he then was transfigured before their eyes. For the three disciples, this event as recorded in the Gospels was largely one of sight: they *saw* Jesus in dazzling clothes. But in these verses from Second Peter, the event focuses on hearing: "This is my Son, my Beloved, with whom I am well pleased." And what happens by virtue of these words, according to this epistle? "[Jesus] received honor and glory from God the Father when that voice was conveyed to him." These words mark Jesus as Son of God, the Christ.

Today I challenge you to stand in amazement as "eyewitnesses" to the majesty of Christ. Take what you know to be true about Jesus and translate it for your own living. Honor God with your life, your time, your thoughts, and your gifts. Share the glory of the Beloved Son with those around you. Perhaps one day you too might be mistaken for Jesus!

Majestic God, we praise your holy name! Having experienced your glory, let us not remain silent about your goodness and majesty. Give us "eyewitness" faith so that we may go and share your majesty with the world. In the name of Jesus we pray. Amen.

These days everyone has an opinion about everything, everywhere you turn: radio, television, Twitter, Facebook, and bloggers. Many of these opinions come attached to some prediction. Too often we treat the word of God and the prophetic message of God like everything else—an opinion for debate and manipulation.

Yet today's text enforces the understanding "that no prophecy of scripture is a matter of one's own interpretation." Real prophecy comes through humans "moved by the Holy Spirit." The validity of God's prophetic movement in our lives comes when we seek the Holy Spirit's direction. Rather than allowing opinion or circumstance to sway us, we are to "be attentive"—discerning the Holy Spirit's movement.

Easier said than done? Not really—if we first seek the Son in whom God is well pleased. Listen to that nudging from the Spirit that says go this way, not that way. Hear God's direction. Witness God's hand at work in your life.

People will always have opinions. But the author of Second Peter bears witness to a firsthand experience of the divine, the "stuff" of authentic prophecy. We serve a God who will guide us if we will pause long enough to hear God speak and see God act. Facts are always better than opinions. What better source than the living God?

Spirit of the living God, fall afresh on me. Help me seek you first in all things. May I set aside distraction and focus on your leading. Amen.

Can you imagine the thoughts of Peter, James, and John as their friend and teacher leads them up on a mountain and is transfigured before them? What must it have been like to see the heroes of your faith, Moses and Elijah, appear before you and talk? The three disciples want to celebrate the moment. They want to memorialize it and keep it forever. Traditionally, monuments marked places of meeting with God.

Peter moves us from the sublime to the ridiculous, and only the overshadowing of God's presence interrupts his taking action on his tent making. God has something else in store for the threesome this day: not a rock to mark the spot, not a temple to commemorate the Lord's presence. God's plan involves something better than they can imagine. A voice from heaven affirms and confirms what is essential: Jesus is indeed God's unique offspring. God has a point to make on the mountain that day, and they are to listen to Jesus' words as teacher as well as "listen" to his life and its instruction.

The Transfiguration gives a glimpse of Resurrection glory, But the path to glory will entail pain and suffering. Sometimes, our well-intended actions and outbursts cause us to miss the point of what is essential. We miss the majesty of the moment.

Don't miss the majesty and glory of God in your life today. Do not erect memorials and miss out on the essentials. Don't try to respond to everything; just listen. I wonder what you will hear.

Glorious One, help us not to miss the Light in our lives today! Amen.

SUNDAY, MARCH 6 ~ *Read Matthew 17:5b-9*

TRANSFIGURATION SUNDAY

We fear what we do not know. We fear heights because we might fall. We fear small, closed spaces because we may get trapped. We fear people who are not like us because we do not know how they will respond to us or how we should engage them. We fear life itself because of its unpredictability.

In today's passage, the three disciples, some of Jesus' closest friends, are "overcome by fear" at the confirmation of Jesus' majesty. They fall "facedown to the ground, terrified" (NIV). What about this declaration creates such a reaction? The scene before them and the heavenly voice seemingly overwhelm them.

When in your life have you experienced such a cause for fear? How many times have you allowed fear to paralyze you? Yet Jesus comes and touches them and says, "'Get up and do not be afraid.'" With their gaze on Jesus alone, they arise.

We encounter life as people of God who have experienced a transfigured Christ, a moment of dazzling glory that may move us to fear. We must learn to live beyond the fear by feeling Jesus' loving gaze and touch and hearing his words. Christ calls us to "get up" and engage the world, not as fearful people but as persons driven by the light and love of the transfigured Christ. We arise and go down the mountain, holding the vision in our hearts and minds.

Gracious and holy Lord, we praise you for the gift of your Son. We praise you that we no longer have to live in fear but can live the life that you have promised. In Jesus' name we pray. Amen.

Living with Limits

MARCH 7–13, 2011 • MARTIN E. MARTY

MONDAY, MARCH 7 ~ *Read Genesis 2:15-17; 3:1-7*

Limits: we cannot live with them; we cannot live *without* them. Without boundaries we would be victims of trespass. Without lines, the child would color "all over the place." Without limits set by law, conscience, or neighbor-love, we would be barbarians. Were not this Lent limited to forty days we would not have Easter joy. On the other hand, Lenten observance reminds us that we cannot live with limits, at least not without chafing. We like to think that we are in command of our destinies and can use our faculties to press beyond boundaries. We naturally resent limits set by parents, employers, teachers, or friends.

We go no farther than page two of the scriptures before running into the story of God's setting boundaries. Eden, the first location on our mental maps, is bounded, as Adam and Eve learn when they are expelled. God generously states, "You may freely eat of every tree of the garden." God limits that good offer by only one command: avoid a single tree, at pain of death. Wouldn't you know, eating of that tree became alluring: that is the one they must enjoy, no matter the command, no matter the risk. A beguiling voice of the enemy is heard: eat of that tree's delights, and "you will be like God."

The man and the woman who represent all of us ate, as we do, not realizing that letting God be God is less about limiting us than about finding our place, not in Eden but in our world of promising places, where we may freely make good choices.

Creator of the gardens of our lives, help us to find the value of good choices and then free us to enjoy their yield responsibly. This Lenten season give us the fruit of obedience. Amen.

Fairfax M. Cone Distinguished Service Professor Emeritus, The University of Chicago

TUESDAY, MARCH 8 ~ *Read Psalm 32*

Limits measured by chalk marks, traffic lanes, or barriers at ledges of cliffs have positive purposes. We welcome them when they make it possible for us and others to follow the rules of a game, drive safely, or prevent falls. The limits that really count, though, are those set by the very nature of what it means to be human. Each of us is but one among many, and to transgress— literally meaning "to violate boundaries"—hurts others.

The Psalms and other scriptures picture the Lord internalizing the hurts we cause. Cheating, victimizing, or speaking ill of another are forms of such acts of hurting. We find it hard to go through this Lenten season, which begins tomorrow, without knowingly violating the rights and the good of others—and thus transgressing the limits set by the Lord.

If we had to awaken each morning and carry the burden of guilt for every misstep inherited from yesterday, we would be paralyzed and unable to meet the opportunities of a new day. Christians need to carry nothing, to be unburdened, to be free of guilt thanks to the forgiving that Jesus effected and which God recognizes. Of course, we must repair what we broke before today, including relations to those close to us, or far away, for that matter. Yet a new reality is ours, as line one of Psalm 32 has it: "Happy are those whose transgression is forgiven, . . . and in whose spirit there is no deceit."

The psalm further sings that "steadfast love surrounds those who trust in the LORD." The experience of that "surrounding" therefore has no other limits. In its context and settings we are called "upright in heart" and also licensed to shout for joy.

O Righteous One, whose boundaries enclose large places, help us to be free to leave the past behind and greet a new day. Amen.

WEDNESDAY, MARCH 9 ～ *Read Joel 2:1-2, 12-17*

ASH WEDNESDAY

Limits to costumes and gestures of mourning were necessary long ago. They seem hardly necessary now. In eighty-plus years of living among Christians and others, I have never once seen people in a congregation at worship tearing garments off their bodies. Perhaps we have glimpsed a child in a tantrum tearing his or her T-shirt, but that is not in lament for sins. Some medieval (and modern?) monks wore hair shirts, but they do not model the repentant life among most believers.

So when the prophet Joel prophesies doom—unless the people forsake evil ways and turn back to the Lord—he utters a commandment that we are not tempted to break: "do not rend . . . your clothing." Joel, in the name of the Lord, is asserting that such a gesture achieves nothing. In the subsistence economy of ancient Israel, to tear a garment that might, untorn, cover or warm another was a flaw. Lepers were to tear their clothes to warn others to keep a distance from their contagious diseases. They did not do so as a mark that they wanted to be right with God. The prophet ruled out the external act of ripping clothes.

If rending garments went beyond limits, another act of rending fit into the divine plan. It was a call for the unlimited: "rend your hearts." We still speak of something being "heart-rending." This spiritual rending achieved good purposes. Joel has things to say about the heart, with its limitless possibilities for doing evil, limitless need for good, and potentially limitless experience of divine love. The "torn" or opened and expectant heart, we read, experiences God as "gracious and merciful, . . . abounding in steadfast love"—and awaits our turning.

Gracious and merciful God, move us to respond this Ash Wednesday by returning to you in sorrow and being ready to welcome the occasions for joy. Amen.

Limits to the good that humans do and even to the good that humans are capable of doing trace back to one of two figures on whose story the apostle Paul trades in a letter he wrote to Roman Christians, with a copy forwarded to us. "Adam" is all but lost in the mists of ancient time and the mysteries of untraceable space. Now Adam gets lost in Christian arguments over "original sin" or "total depravity," used to describe the human condition.

For today let's find a word for the limits. Catholic theologian Karl Rahner at one point simply asserts that "things are not as they ought to be." God's great "ought" pronounced creation "good." We were to live in harmony with God and others. Yes, we were to *live*; but Paul says "death came through sin," the great ought-not. Pin it on Adam if you will, as Paul does, or hang it on all of us, as he also does. In daily prayer and devotion, with repentance in Lent or anytime, and with forgiveness every time, we get to move beyond sin in the eyes of God who looks at us "in Christ."

Death is also a legacy. Dr. Lewis Thomas, noticing what was called "the denial of death," advised that we moderns learn to talk about death: "There is a lot of it going around these days." Paul does talk about it, but he talks about its limits. Death signals limits; indeed, it is the limit of our earthly lives. The next word from Paul is that "death exercised dominion," but—good news—that was long ago. It remains a reality, but its dominion is limited, thanks to the "New Adam," Christ, who has brought about that change.

Free us, forgiving Lord, from the dominion of sin and death, and grant us the gifts of freedom and new life. Amen.

Limits bind and constrict. They are not the end of the story that Paul implied when he referred to Adam and his burden. Instead, he urgently makes a point that should stick in our minds all day—and all of life. He speaks not only of a "gift," which is something we can appreciate any day, but of a *free* gift of grace. Many of us are suspicious of gifts that have strings attached or are peddled in misleading ways. They have a catch.

Not only do we read once of a "free gift," we note it five times in three verses of the letter to the Romans. We get the point or begin to get the point or should get the point. If we were tempted to fault God for letting "Adam" burden us, we are now in position to thank God for the "free gift." Paul also uses the phrase "much more surely" twice. Let's pause for a moment this Lenten Friday and let the reality soak in as we quote the rich text: "Much more surely have the grace of God and the free gift in the grace of one man, Jesus Christ, abounded for the many." The many? Literally millions, literally billions "receive the abundance of grace and the free gift."

Paul—let's admit it—may be, and is, an inspired biblical writer, but he can also cram some difficult and crowded lines into his letters. They are at times obscure and abstract enough to keep professional scholars busy with them all their lives. Whether or not we are scholars, whether or not we have our entire lives to devote to study, we do have this moment of this day to clear our heads and focus our minds and prayers.

At such a moment we find good reason to revisit something so important that it gets said five times: God's grace through Jesus is a free gift!

Christ, open our hands and hearts so that we may hold God's free gift today. Amen.

Limits often exist to be tested—within limits! None of us would want to be tested by sparring with a world champion. Few would test their mastery of physics against an Einstein. But some testing comes in forms that delude us into thinking we can handle it on our own. Then temptation comes with such spiritual force that we find ourselves unprotected—and we lose. Something in most of us says, when less than cosmic testing comes, "I can beat that!" As long as "beating that" works to my attention, one thinks, *I can safely give in.* Many a tempted spouse feels sure that he can stop sinning after having only *sampled* the lures of adultery; or an alcoholic, that she can stop with one drink.

Jesus voluntarily responds to the call of the Spirit into the wilderness, there to be put to the test himself. And his tests do come. If he is the Son of God, he hears, he should do a magic act and turn stones to bread. He triumphs by responding with a scriptural body-blow that any Jewish boy would have known to use, as might we.

A more dramatic test of his limits comes with the call to do a cosmic daredevil act by jumping off the Temple and letting God's angels catch him. Jesus responds, "'Do not put the Lord your God to the test.'" What Jesus commands his Enemy, he can advise his friends. Our tests may seem and may be less than cosmic, but they are real. We are not alone when facing them.

God of wisdom, at week's end as we prepare for worship in community, let us draw strength from you, asking your protection when we do not know how to protect ourselves. Amen.

SUNDAY, MARCH 13 ~ *Read Matthew 4:8-11*

FIRST SUNDAY IN LENT

Limits to divine patience can serve to teach us how to put an end to attacks on our spiritual health and integrity. The end of today's Gospel story shows Jesus growing impatient and dismissing the tempter. As we read, we consider what it means for us.

Something of what it means occurs on a scale with which we cannot identify but leaves clues about what it is with which we can identify and contend. When the devil asks Jesus to bow down and worship him, a dramatic exchange occurs that is so vast that only a mad egotist would fit herself or himself into the conversation. Jesus has just let himself twice be called "the Son of God," even if the one who names him is taunting. When "the Son of God" contends against the personification of evil, more is at stake than any of us have a right to imagine about ourselves.

However, we *are* in the story. The battle against all that works against the purposes of God is faced and won in billions of little encounters around the world and through the ages. The devils we are called to worship may be material or political, searches for fame and acclaim, or simply ourselves. The temptation story ends when, having learned from Jesus, we use the brisk brush-off: "'Away with you, Satan!'"

Better than that, the test really comes to an end when something positive replaces all the negatives we face. That one thing is the presence of the only one worthy of worship, "the Lord [our] God," whom we get to serve.

O God, when believers gather for worship, help us focus only on you, who calls us to service. May we draw strength and hope from each encounter, giving thanks to Jesus the Victor. Amen.

Standing on the Promises

MARCH 14–20, 2011 • F. DOUGLAS POWE JR.

MONDAY, MARCH 14 ~ *Read Genesis 12:1-4a*

Uncertainty is a part of everyone's life. The difference for Christians is that we deal with uncertainty by standing on the promises of God. In this text Abraham learns what it means to stand on God's promises. God instructs Abraham to leave a familiar place and go someplace yet to be named. Wow! Imagine being asked to leave all that is familiar: home, friends, comfort of knowing the area and all those things that ground a life—to go someplace yet to be named.

If we willingly stand on God's promises, then, like Abraham, we go. The good news for Abraham is God's assurance that in his going not only will Abraham experience God's blessing, but so will others. In fact, Abraham will become an instrument of God's blessing to those who are hospitable to Abraham on his journey. Those who are inhospitable to Abraham will not experience God's blessing.

We can take at least two lessons from this text: first, God expects us to move out of our comfort zones so that we can be a blessing to others. Second, we extend hospitality to others because as we do so, God blesses us—not in a material sense but in a holistic manner. As you meditate on this Lenten text today, reflect on the uncertainty in all of our lives, acknowledging that Christians stand on the promises of God, and that is enough.

Holy One, may you continuously call us out of our comfort zones so that we can experience your blessings anew. Amen.

Assistant Professor of Evangelism, Saint Paul School of Theology; Kansas City, Missouri

When we are having a bad day, week, or month, we tend to hang our head. We often do not even notice our posture because our particular situation has so enthralled us. It rests, like a gigantic weight on our shoulders, forcing our heads to look down. When we find ourselves in this situation, we can easily feel that no one understands what we're going through. We feel that we are all alone!

The psalmist tells us that in those very times, we must lift up our heads and look to God. This remedy has worked for him: "I lift up my eyes to the hills." The point is that if we can change our outlook, then we can begin to come out of our valley experience. The psalmist makes it clear that our ascent out of the valley is not of our own doing but a work of God's grace. This God who has spun out galaxies in creation will come to help us and keeps us in both good times and difficult times.

During this Lenten season as we move toward Resurrection Sunday, we remain mindful of God's grace at work in our lives. In our prayers and reading of scripture, we remember that God always goes before us; we simply respond to God's work of prevenient grace. This grace allows us to affirm the promises of God as true in good times and bad times.

Think about what has been burdening you the past few months. What gigantic weight are you carrying? Whatever the weight, meditate on this text. As you move toward Resurrection Sunday, allow God's grace to give you assurance.

We often do not think about safety until something happens in our lives: someone breaks into our home or car or in some way violates our sense of safety and well-being. Many of us take safety for granted because we rely on home security systems, car alarms, and other products to protect us. We feel safer when we depend on the promises made by those products to keep us from harm. We feel free to focus and think about things other than our safety because we believe the claims of the product.

The psalmist reminds us that God promises to protect us. Verse 7*a* seems to go even farther by claiming, "The LORD will keep you from all evil." Most of us buy into the idea of God's protecting us at a certain level but find it more difficult to believe God protects us from *all* evil. Every day we face challenges in our lives or know someone who is struggling. The reality we experience does not seem to match the promise made by the psalmist related to God's protection.

During this Lenten season if we move on to read verse 7*b*, then the promise is not that far-fetched. The psalmist does not claim that God will keep us from experiencing evil; the promise is that God will be with us and maintain our lives *even while* we are experiencing evil. You may argue that I am playing with semantics, but I perceive an important distinction in how we understand God's promise of protection. God's promise does not isolate us from what is happening in the world but maintains life in the midst of a sometimes challenging world. This is God's promise to us.

Gracious God, may our journey with you continue to provide the resources for life. Amen.

THURSDAY, MARCH 17 ~ *Read Romans 4:1-5*

This passage begins the debate that continues in Christianity today between works and faith. Paul answers the question: "How is one made right before God?" Anyone who spends time in a faith community will quickly see two sides of this debate. We can readily observe those who constantly work around the church; often their expectation is that *everyone* should be working like them. We can also spot those who are extremely "spiritual" and perceive their role as nourishing the spirituality of the congregation, which does not involve the mundane tasks necessary to keep the church operating. This split between works and faith can lead to conflict within a congregation.

I actually support a third option that remains true to the text and Paul's interpretation of the Abraham story. As I mentioned in Monday's meditation, Abraham is willing to stand on the promises of God, to leave the comfort of familiarity and go forward as God directs him. Paul interprets Abraham's radical obedience to stand on God's promises as the ultimate act of faith. Part of this act of faith requires Abraham to do something—go. When Paul states, "Abraham believed God, and it was reckoned to him as righteousness," he is arguing that believing and doing are inseparable. We need not fall into the trap of either faith or works but support the thought that faith informs our works, just as works shape our faith.

Our responses to God's "reckoning righteousness" will include the integration of our spiritual lives with the everyday activities of congregational life. This integration is not about our individual righteousness or even the church's righteousness but about a willingness to be in covenant with God through Christ.

Holy One, help us to respond daily to your act of reckoning through Christ by our faith and our works. Amen.

Many of us have read or heard about messy inheritances. Someone dies without a will, or the will is contested. In our society this is a legal issue. The court ultimately decides who has a right of inheritance. In today's text, Paul argues against what in Abraham's day would be considered a legal structure for inheritance. Paul states, "For the promise that he would inherit the world did not come to Abraham or his descendants through the law." Paul signals to us that what we consider normative related to inheritance is not the way God's promises work.

God bases the promise of inheritance to Abraham and his descendants on the righteousness of faith. They do not inherit because of a particular bloodline or family relation. Paul connects inheritance to God's promise and that promise extends to all who are willing to live in covenant with God.

How is this possible? We all descend from Abraham, our parent—our parent in the faith. As Abraham's descendants, we are heirs of God's promise. This sounds wonderful; we must, however, continually remember the word *faith*. To be an heir requires faith, and *faith* is not a passive word. Abraham's faith meant giving up all that was familiar to follow God.

During this Lenten season this text reminds us that as heirs of God's promise we must give some things up. We must be steadfast in our faith even when things around us pull us away. No one can take our inheritance from us, but we can fail to live faithfully into our inheritance.

Meditate on those things that pull you away from living faithfully as you move toward Resurrection Sunday.

SATURDAY, MARCH 19 ～ *Read John 3:1-10*

Have you ever said, "I just don't get it!" You hear, but the speaker's words make no sense. You may even ask a question in an attempt to gain a better understanding, but in the end it still makes no sense. Welcome to the world of Nicodemus, a teacher of Israel. He compliments Jesus and ends up in this conversation about being born again. Nicodemus did not intend that the conversation go in this direction, but Jesus has a way of cutting to the chase and focusing on our real issues.

Let's be honest! Like Nicodemus we have talked to the Lord at night out of public view. Like Nicodemus we too are searching for something. Nicodemus wants to know if Jesus is the real deal and coyly uses the language of "no one can do these signs that you do apart from the presence of God." Jesus does not let Nicodemus off the hook and notes the necessity of being born from above to really understand the signs of the coming reign of God. This response confounds Nicodemus; Jesus does not provide a gift-wrapped answer that will make his life easier.

During this Lenten season as we meditate and pray for clarity in our lives, we too often seek ready-made, gift-wrapped answers. We hope that Jesus will make life easier for us. But Jesus' honest replies can confuse us because they are not what we expect. We often base our expectations on what we seek rather than truly discerning Jesus' guidance. What do we bring to the table when we come searching for answers? What is our background? When has Jesus asked you, "Are you a [fill in the blank], and yet you do not understand these things?" How do you respond?

Loving God, be patient with me as I learn to discern your word and its meaning for my life. Amen.

SUNDAY, MARCH 20 ~ *Read John 3:11-17*

SECOND SUNDAY IN LENT

Many of us have seen persons hold up signs that read "John 3:16" at a sporting event or some other public function. No matter what their motives, at a certain level these individuals affirm God's ultimate promise for the world: eternal life with God through Jesus the Christ. What makes this promise so unique and special is that God has already fulfilled the promise.

Christians believe in and stand on the promise of eternal life through Jesus, which means believing that God's kingdom is a reality toward which we are moving right now. We cannot bring God's reign of our own accord, but we can participate in God's work of making the kingdom real for others here on earth. This is our calling as Christians—to participate in the work begun by Jesus until it culminates in a new heaven and a new earth.

But we, like Nicodemus, must shift perspectives: from fleshly life to the eternal, and that requires action from God. We "must be born from above." Flesh engenders flesh, but Spirit engenders spirit. We become recipients of God's promise right now as we open ourselves to the Spirit—even as we move toward God's ultimate act of reconciliation through Jesus in the future. We become prayerful about discerning God's word and become an embodiment of the Word for others. Standing on the promises of God recenters our living around the gift of new life, and our faith draws others to Jesus.

O God, during this Lenten season may we stand on your promises as we are renewed daily in our walk with you. Amen.

Streams of Living Water

MARCH 21–27, 2011 • BRIAN THORNTON

MONDAY, MARCH 21 ~ *Read Exodus 17:1-7*

I suspect that many present-day politicians have echoed Moses' cries of anguish as they have attempted to do the best for the people they represent, and they now face the danger of losing office. For Moses has no democratic escape clause, no committee to analyze where things had gone wrong. In the desert, the Israelites grumble about the lack of water and seem willing to relinquish their freedom for servitude in Egypt in exchange for food and liquid refreshment.

On a two-week mission trip, I worked in Belize to build an outreach center in a poor district of Belize City. At work's end, several of us rewarded ourselves with three days on one of Cays (keys) with a basic camp setup. We were allowed one small bucket of "sweet" water a day. Needless to say, a fair amount of grumbling ensued. As we returned to the mainland, we forgot our irritation with the conditions when dolphins came alongside our boat. They accompanied us for most of the hour's journey.

This experience reminded me of the God who, in spite of all our complaining, comes alongside us, accompanying us on the journey. When we have reached the end of our limits, God responds to our cries with a command and a promise: "I will be standing there in front of you." Water comes, and we drink.

Father, we pray that we might always see your hand in all that we experience and know that all that you offer to us is given out of love as an opportunity for us to grow in grace. Amen.

A layperson with pastoral oversight of three Methodist Churches in Durham, England; before retiring he was Chief Executive of the British Methodist Publishing House, Editor of the UK edition of *The Upper Room* daily devotional guide

When did you last make a decision after much prayer and reflection that hasn't worked out as you'd imagined? Recalling that time may make you more generous toward the wandering tribes of Israel. Today's passage records the first of the many times that they question the wisdom of their decision to follow Moses out of Egypt. Seemingly, time and time again, they will view that decision as "out of the frying pan and into the fire." Furthermore, their memory, like that of most of us, plays tricks on them as to just how much better it had been in the past! Those were the good old days.

On whom will the Israelites depend? They rebel against Moses, their understood leader, not perceiving God as their guide. In their despair, they cannot imagine the land flowing with milk and honey. They are so thirsty that their tongues stick to the roof of their mouth. And later in this journey, they will not have eaten for days. These conditions make it hard to see divine wisdom at work in the everyday happenings of life.

But God responds to Moses' plea, and water comes from a most unlikely source in an unlikely place. For the Israelites, as for us, the gushing out of God's concern—in this case water from the rock at Horeb—brings only temporary relief and renewed faith. We journey on, confident in faith until the next crisis. Then we, like them, build our golden calves of secondary security as examples of our dubious personal insurance.

But the underlying theme is God's persistent love and insistent concern as they are guided to the Promised Land.

When have you complained to God about a situation, only to discover a clear rationale through God's guidance?

WEDNESDAY, MARCH 23 ~ *Read Psalm 95*

Psalm 95 is a hymn to the sovereignty of God, recited and sung at the New Year festival when the pilgrims bearing the ark of the covenant approach the Temple. The rock mentioned in this psalm is not the water-giving rock of the desert but the dependable, solid love and concern of God for all creation.

The psalm attempts to explain just why the journey in the wilderness took so long: God's anger with this people who have gone astray. They are a people who "do not regard [God's] ways." What a surprising statement to make about a people who have so often experienced the power, might, and care of God.

I wonder sometimes if the modern church is not guilty of getting things out of balance, of allowing egotistical self-interest to inform our obedience to God. We too have received God's gracious provision. We, as Christians, bear witness to the nature of God in Jesus and the extent, in Christ, to which God will go to show divine favor for and to us. And yet, we often put God to the test, even though we have "seen [God's] work." Another side to God is that of righteousness; God can be no other, and out of that sheer goodness the Holy One desires the best for all God's children. "O that today you would listen to his voice!"

We live in a universe where cause and effect are building blocks of creation; the God who pronounced all things good at creation's dawn gives a new perspective to this principle. We, like the Israelites, praise our Maker. The joy of relationship with God results in wholeness for the individual and the community. May we listen.

Creator God, we see the universe, a staggering reminder of your creative genius, one that has sustained all matter from the beginning of time. As a redeemed part of that creation, may I care for it as lovingly as you care for me. Amen.

Paul speaks powerfully of new hope through his incredible assertion that God is willing to relate to sinful humankind. This willingness serves as a mark of God's love; as a result, we can all know as a certainty that God's grace provides a lifeline to those in danger of self-destructing. This hope encompasses all of life's experience; Paul claims that this concrete hope enables us to rejoice no matter what life throws at us. He claims that the experiences we might shun, like suffering, improve our character.

We in developing countries use the word *hope* rather loosely. "I *hope* you are all right," or "I *hope* it doesn't rain today." But what kind of hope looks at an empty cupboard and still talks of hope?

I am writing this within months of being widowed. Since my wife's death, the hope that Paul describes has become a daily reality. The presence of the person with whom I delighted in sharing the past fifty years is palpably real, as is the belief that one day we will again see each other through the grace of him who not only declared me sinful but through his intervention, acceptable.

I once owned a secondhand Austin A40 that I bought from a titled lady who had never driven it above thirty miles an hour. For ages it just wouldn't go any faster. But eventually I managed to blow out the engine dust, and the car reached the maximum speed limit of seventy miles per hour. I often think that we live our lives a little like that: never demanding more of ourselves, failing to push ourselves into experiences that would enhance our character and make us more useful disciples.

We are physically and spiritually programmed to do our best when we experience all that life can throw at us. Let us live in that hope and dare to experience the vulnerability of true Christian expectation.

Do something daring that bears witness to the hope that does not disappoint.

FRIDAY, MARCH 25 ~ *Read Romans 5:6-11*

I have just had to decide whether to attend the District Synod or to join a rally in London that seeks to highlight global injustices. At the Synod I would be among like-minded people I know and many of whom I admire. At the London rally I would be with all manner of people whom I don't know and whose motivation for being there differs greatly from mine.

I decided to go to the rally, and verse 6 of today's reading strongly influenced my decision: "while we were still weak, at the right time Christ died for the ungodly." The suggestion that I am "ungodly" makes me feel quite uncomfortable, even while I acknowledge its truth. The fact that some of my fellow demonstrators will challenge my comfort zone illustrates just how far I am from representing Christ as I should. Christ's nonjudgmental manner toward all he met powerfully demonstrates the love of God.

Just as there was no prerequisite to Jesus' reaching out to each and every one, I am asked to adopt the same attitude and approach to those that I might consider a little more "ungodly" than I am. Oh, the sin of self-satisfaction and pride! For all, for all, my Savior died.

Paul asserts that God saves the ungodly, those who merit salvation in no way whatsoever, and that God pours out an excessive assurance of that salvation on those who recognize their reconciliation, accomplished by God alone. I look for God in Christ out with the crowds in London among the unbeliever and the spiritual skeptic, perhaps feeling more at home there than in the more religious atmosphere of the District Synod.

Father, it is so easy to do the thing that we feel most comfortable with. Show us the opportunities you offer to go into the world and there make disciples of all people. Amen.

On the face of it, today's reading seems to recount a chance happening. The disciples might well have come back a little earlier, and they and Jesus have gone on their way without ever meeting the woman.

I have lived long enough to believe that what some people call coincidences are more likely to be part of the divine plan. On one occasion, while preaching in Antigua, I noticed a church member singing with the aid of a Braille hymnbook, but he did not sing all the hymns. After the service I learned that he only had part of the hymnbook in Braille. When I returned to England and my office desk, on top of the enormous pile of mail was a letter from a father whose sight-impaired daughter had recently died. "Could," the letter asked, "these volumes be of use to someone?" The next time I went to Antigua I had the joy of handing over the *complete* hymnbook in Braille.

This passage records the second instance in the Gospels that the Samaritans get good press. In today's story, a woman experiences a dramatic life-changing conversation by "coincidence." She speaks with the one who comes from heaven, who "speaks the words of God" and "gives the Spirit without measure" (3:31-36). No way will the Samaritan woman's life be the same after this meeting. As so often happens in the scriptures and indeed in real life, the most unlikely person becomes the channel of salvation for many others.

Though salvation comes "from the Jews," Jesus offers salvation to all: women, men, first-century Samaritans and twenty-first-century rally attenders. Jesus' presence breaks down barriers and brings salvation to all.

Lord, make me conscious of the ways you work in my life. May coincidences become occasions of your mighty presence. Amen.

SUNDAY, MARCH 27 ～ *Read Exodus 17:1-7 and John 4:5-42*

THIRD SUNDAY IN LENT

Both scriptures beautifully illustrate living water: the water that flows from the desert rock and the water that Jesus offers the Samaritan woman. How often have you looked at a picture of a landscape that included an expanse of water? Maybe you've sat beside a lake and marvelled at the mirror image of the surrounding scene reflected in the still water. Compare that scene with the same element but in the context of a mighty waterfall. Here water is far from tranquil as it rages and rises in mists. Its progress over the centuries wears away the solid rock.

While we feel peaceful as we reflect on the tranquillity of the lake scene, the water that flowed out of the desert rock and that Jesus offers seems more akin to "living" water. The languid waters of the lake can soon become stagnant and lifeless without the infusion of oxygen.

The water that tumbles over the rocks to plummet great distances to the base of the falls takes on the risk of falling or becoming mist, and I believe that is what Jesus offers us. We receive the same option that he gives the woman at the well: she, and we, can stay as we are. You might have managed, like the Samaritan woman, to find a formula without confrontation, to let the questions lie idle. Only when we ask the risky questions and internalize the life-changing responses do we receive the living water. This man knows everything about us too; it's no chance happening. So we go to tell others, to chatter the good news of God's kingdom and relay word about the living water that Jesus offers.

God, as we move through Lent may we possess the living water that both cleanses and infuses us with the Holy Spirit. Embolden us to be the rushing water of life for those who travel along with us. Amen.

In Plain Sight

MARCH 28–APRIL 3, 2011 • M. GARLINDA BURTON

MONDAY, MARCH 28 ～ *Read 1 Samuel 16:1-3*

Spiritual movements erupt from a well of deep hunger for a closer encounter with the divine and the passionate desire to put dreams into action. When the passionate people create institutions, they often lose their flexibility and heart for risk taking.

John Wesley, founder of global Methodism, was already an Anglican cleric when a Damascus-road-type encounter with God fired him anew with a passion for seeking God's will and living it out in life-changing ways. New praise songs by Wesley and his brother augmented traditional worship; ministries to transform social constructs such as poverty and hunger replaced former norms of class divisions and condescending charity for the poor. Wesley upset the institutional agenda to live out God's changing agenda.

Samuel too had been God's faithful servant and a part of the institutional church all his life. He had anointed the current king, Saul, according to God's instruction. Yet God suddenly calls for a new movement with David as king. But Samuel, so invested in the current institution, balks—even with God's direction to anoint a new king. He fears releasing what has been, even on direct orders from the God he'd served all his life.

We often find the key to spiritual rejuvenation right before our eyes. God in Christ calls us from the safety of our sanctuaries and routine discipleship to new levels of faithfulness, new expressions of creativity and risk. In that newness, blessings, signs, and wonders await. Where do you perceive and receive God's new thing?

God of sweeping change, I'm available to you. Amen.

Member of Hobson United Methodist Church, Nashville, Tennessee; general secretary of the General Commission on the Status and Role of Women in the United Methodist Church

My granddaughter, Sierra, weighed eighteen ounces when she was born nearly four months' premature. She looked more like a baby kitten than a human being, tiny and weak in the incubator that was her home for five months. I remember vacillating between my fear that she wouldn't live to see her first birthday and fearing she would face severe physical and mental challenges if she lived.

Today, Sierra is nearly my height. Poised, affable, smart, and sassy, she's my favorite travel companion. Never would I have imagined nearly ten years ago that that tiny, frail preemie would grow to be tall, headstrong, athletic, and fearless. She is a walking miracle, and her life alone is reason for me to praise God on my knees every blessed day.

Samuel, already doubtful about anointing a new king, arrives on Jesse's land. And despite God's warning not to be swayed by appearances alone, Samuel can't help himself. *A king*, he thinks, *will certainly look like a king: stately, older, and confident.* Samuel examines and culls, using his own limited imagination. But for God's prodding, Samuel would have missed him: the youngest son, David, the ruddy shepherd. David is the one called by our God of surprise and wonder. "This is the one," God tells Samuel.

When we invite God into our hearts and nurture the Holy Spirit fire in our souls, we begin to see what God sees: potential in all people; beauty in unlikely places; God's anointed shining through the eyes of those we dismiss; the tenacity of human spirit thriving and responding to love from inside an incubator: miracles hiding in plain sight.

Open my eyes, loving God, that I may see more clearly your will for my life. Help me see your light in the eyes of sisters and brothers I might otherwise overlook. Amen.

WEDNESDAY, MARCH 30 ~ *Read Psalm 23:1-4*

In 2003 I stopped speaking to God for six months; my husband was dying of lung cancer. There had never been a time in my life when I was not a dutiful daughter of the church. Whenever the doors opened, I was there; when volunteers were needed, I was the first to say yes. And now, the one time I needed a miracle from God—namely my husband's life—God said nothing.

So I stopped praying. God would try to enter my thoughts, but I didn't want to hear. I would recall my late grandmother reciting the words of Psalm 23 at bedtime. It had always been a source of comfort. But after Larry's death, when I seemed to hear her saying, "Surely goodness and mercy . . . ," I shouted aloud to God, "Shut up! I don't want to hear it! You let Larry die."

Then, about three months after Larry died, a friend called and made me laugh for the first time in a long time. We shared funny stories about Larry without my crying. I even recalled those last nights of his life when Larry would lay his head on my lap, and I would stroke him until he slept. Those last days were, in fact, among our most intimate.

Suddenly I realized that, instead of abandoning me, God had carried me through the worst days of my life. More wondrous still, God had allowed me the space to be really angry and even to walk away but still waited for me to come back.

The psalmist wrote, "Even though I walk through the darkest valley, . . . you are with me." I'm a living witness that nothing in this life is too difficult for God to help us handle.

Make a list of at least five challenges you've overcome with God's help. Read it each day of Lent, and give daily thanks for God's grace in your life.

Cindy, now fifty-two, has struggled with cocaine addiction since she was seventeen. Shortly after joining my church seven years ago, she relapsed and prostituted herself for drug money while living on the streets.

Since then, I have watched Cindy wrestle her demons and claim her anointing as a daughter of God. She has been clean more than a year. It hasn't been easy. Addiction is an illness, and relapse is part of the recovery process.

More challenging, Cindy's role as a "screw up" was so deeply entrenched that friends and family felt less than supportive of her new life. Yes, she has done things that caused them to lose trust in her; but a part of them needs a Cindy to kick around and to be the family's cautionary tale about wasted youth and bad company. With each relapse, they say, "I knew she couldn't kick the habit." And every day she stays clean, they say, "It's only a matter of time before she is back out there."

It's not that they are bad people, but they have made themselves Cindy's enemies in a sense. They have lost faith in her at a time when she needs it most. They have failed to see a miracle of God's transformation and healing right before their eyes.

We all need someone to believe in us, to hold us up in prayer, to see the Jesus-light in our eyes, and to believe that we can live out the promise of resurrection that is already present in our lives. So, as her prayer warrior, I join Cindy in prayers of celebration of the God who prepares a table before us in the presence of enemies and who gives grace and newness of life each day.

As of this writing, Cindy is still clean.

Loving Savior, I pray this day for all those who struggle with addiction and for those who have lost faith (often for good reason). Anoint us all with your grace and mercy. Amen.

FRIDAY, APRIL 1 ~ *Read Ephesians 5:8-14*

My friend Tanya died recently after a valiant battle with cancer. Family and friends surrounded her bed as she lay dying, her husband holding her hand. At one point, Tanya's first husband—with whom she had remained friends—stepped behind her current husband and laid a comforting hand on his shoulder. Tanya's husband reached back and squeezed the hand. It was a holy moment of understanding, reconciliation, and unity beyond anything I had ever witnessed.

Later, when I asked her husband about the moment and about the fact that Tanya's first husband had sat with the family at the funeral and had come to the house for dinner afterward, her husband replied, "He was the only person in that moment who knew exactly what I was going through. He was the only person who had ever loved her like I loved her. It meant the world to have someone there who understood my heart."

The writer of Ephesians addresses his letter to a church divided by tradition, culture, and clan. Jews and Gentiles struggle with a new concept: that God in Christ calls us to put aside old divisions and strife in order to dance on the common ground of God's grace, love, healing, and reconciliation.

The writer challenges us to move from the darkness of sin, striving, and mistrust into the marvelous gift of light that comes when we claim Jesus Christ as Redeemer and Savior. This newness of life can change enemies into friends, strangers into a beloved community, and "husbands-in-law" into brothers who share each other's sorrow. Thinking of Tanya still moves me to tears, and I am grateful to have witnessed the godly moment between two men who loved her. Praise be!

God, thank you for Holy Spirit-fired moments at unlikely times that make your peace and reconciliation known to us. May we become instruments of healing, even in difficult times. Amen.

Even the people closest to Jesus didn't really understand him. From his disciples who saw miracles and heard parables to the well-read religious leaders who resented a self-styled messiah who seemed to flout church tradition, Jesus is constantly having to explain himself to people who should have known. They ask themselves, one another, and people who encounter him, "Who does he say he is?" "Who do you think he is?"

Neighbors and Pharisees put these questions to the man whose sight Jesus restores. This man has been afflicted by a physical disability, which, in those days, was understood to be a punishment for sin. Being blind and an outcast reduces the man to begging for his daily bread. Likely, he cannot afford the luxury of engaging in theological discourse.

But when asked about Jesus, the man speaks with conviction, not from what he'd been taught or heard preached, but from his personal encounter with the living Christ. When the religious leaders try to trip him up by calling Jesus an imposter, the healed man declares, "One thing I do know, that though I was blind, now I see."

The answer to our fears, our doubts, our hunger, our longing, our confusion is often that simple. Yoking our lives with the resurrected Savior assures us that God is working for good in our lives. God is with us in our sickness and in our healing. God tosses out a lifeline and holds on to us when we feel cast out. God speaks hope to us in times of despair. God says, "Yes, you can," even when we can't yet find our way.

Oh, yes, I know
 Oh, yes, I know
 God is good and loves us so!
 Oh, yes, I know.

O God, may your deeds of yes overcome our words of no. Amen.

SUNDAY, APRIL 3 ~ *Read John 9:26-41*

FOURTH SUNDAY IN LENT

This story relates two tales of blindness: the man physically blind from birth and the spiritual blindness of the respected religious leaders. They of all people might have recognized these signs of God's grace in Jesus the Christ. However, their notions and preferences about who the Messiah will be, blind them to Jesus' possibility. God will reveal the true Messiah first to the religious authorities, they believe. He will fulfill the very letter of Old Testament law, they assert. Instead of seeing the signs and wonders among those who have encountered Jesus the Christ, the religious leaders waste time discrediting Jesus' teaching and miracles and recounting and dissecting God's acts from the past.

So the religious authorities miss a life-altering encounter with the Word incarnate. What transformation might have occurred if the Pharisees had accepted that while God's past blessings were wondrous, the best is yet to come?

In Eugene H. Peterson's biblical translation, *The Message*, God declares through the prophet Isaiah, "Forget about what's happened; don't keep going over old history. Be alert, be present. I'm about to do something brand-new. It's bursting out! Don't you see it?" (43:18-19).

God calls us this Lenten season to be attuned to the new things God is doing in our lives, to wait with hope for the new revelations that come with a daily walk with Christ. We stand on the firm foundation of God's past and present blessings, but something new and wonderful is about to break forth! Thanks be to God!

God of signs and wonders in every age, I am grateful for your blessings. I wait obediently and breathlessly for the new thing you will do in my life. Amen.

Life *after* Death

APRIL 4–10, 2011 • GWEN PURUSHOTHAM

MONDAY, APRIL 4 ~ *Read Psalm 130*

Many years ago I participated in a twenty-four-hour fast to raise awareness about world hunger. No one explained how to fast properly; I simply stopped eating. In the early hours of the fast I felt hungry. As the hours passed, I began to feel a little weak and queasy. Finally I had no appetite at all. Before the fast ended, I had to force myself to sip some broth until I began to get my strength and my appetite back.

We all know about the sin of greed, the insatiable desire for more even while we have much more than we require. We acknowledge that our obsession for material things gives root to injustice and causes disillusionment. But I wonder if an even more pitiable state is that of having no hunger at all, of settling for too little. Might our trouble stem not from being too hungry but from a loss of appetite? Might the greatest challenge we face as First-World Christians be our poor appetite for eating fully and drinking deeply of all that God wants to give us? Does our neglect of the Lord's Supper stem from our willingness to walk away from abundance? What prevailing spiritual malaise is due to a lack of appetite for what God wants to give us? In what ways have we deprived ourselves—gone without eating for so long that we no longer cry out from the depths for God?

The psalmist expresses a need for God from the depths of his being: "My soul waits for the Lord more than those who watch for the morning, more than those who watch for the morning." Oh, that our hunger for God might increase and this prayer rise up from the depths of our being.

God, deepen my hunger and thirst for you. Amen.

Pastor, Main Street United Methodist Church; Nashua, New Hampshire

Years ago my friends gave me a book for my birthday titled *Magic Eye: A New Way of Looking at the World*. The book contains page after page of colorful designs—no subject matter, just designs. At least this is the way it appears at first glance. There is actually much more on the pages than first meets the eye; if you look at the designs in a particular way, 3-D pictures emerge from seemingly abstract fields of color. What one sees on those pages is magically changed by the way one looks at them.

My Dad had magic eyes that transformed people by the way he saw them. He navigated his way through life with his yellow hat, gigantic smile, and twinkling eyes that transformed the mundane and unexciting into the extraordinary and exotic. He had no strategy for getting this done. He just looked and saw people in a way that brought them to life.

After showing Ezekiel the valley of the dry bones, the Lord asks, "Mortal can these bones live?" Ezekiel replies, "O Lord GOD, you know," which may have been Ezekiel's way of saying, "Lord, maybe you can see how these bones can live, but I just don't see it." Although Ezekiel has his doubts, he does as God commands; breath comes into the dry bones, and they live. God's vision, God's loving gaze upon the dry bones and upon the skeptical and timid prophet change everything.

Where Ezekiel can see nothing but dry bones, God sees the possibility of life. Where in your life and in our world do you see nothing but lifelessness and hopelessness? What does God see in those times and places? How might you see the world more like God sees it? Who sees you in a way that gives you life?

Gracious God, teach me to see as you see. Amen.

WEDNESDAY, APRIL 6 ~ *Read Ezekiel 37:11-14*

My friend Mike Clark recalled an experience he had while visiting India many years ago. The area had been without rain for many, many months. The earth was cracked and parched. A friend took him to a botanical garden in a city in the southern part of the country. There was nothing growing in the garden. Yet as they walked together, they paused at a series of spots in the garden. At each place, his friend described in vivid detail what he would have seen on each patch of earth had he seen it when the flowers and plants were flourishing.

It occurred to Mike that because his companion had once seen the garden the way it was intended to be—the way God meant it to be—and could remember it and describe it with heart, Mike could actually envision the flowers, even in a parched time. He commented that holding close the times when we have seen a glimpse of life as it is meant to be and being able to describe those times with passion make it possible for others to envision them in dry times.

God says to Ezekiel, "Mortal, these bones are the whole house of Israel. They say, 'Our bones are dried up, and our hope is lost; we are cut off completely.'" The people are dry, parched, exhibiting no sign of life. They cannot imagine anything beyond their dryness.

God tells Ezekiel to describe in vivid detail what God will do: "I am going to open your graves, and bring you up from your graves, O my people; and I will bring you back to the land of Israel. . . . I will put my spirit within you, and you shall live."

Where or to whom is God calling you to speak words of life? How do you describe God's actions in such detail that others can see life where there seems to be none?

God, help us to hold up your vision even in hard times. Amen.

Mike Clark currently serves as pastor of St. John's United Methodist Church; Watertown, Massachusetts

My mother died in June of 2008 at the age of eighty-seven. Her health had been gradually declining over a period of time, and my family anticipated her death. I remained at her bedside the last five days before her death, a time in which she progressed from consciousness and awareness of my presence to a state of unconsciousness and an inability to communicate. I was with her one hour before she died.

My father died nine months later. His death came suddenly and quite unexpectedly. I was not with him for days preceding his death. I spoke with him briefly on the phone the day before he died. By the time I reached the hospital, he was in the intensive care unit under heavy sedation; I can only hope that he could hear my final words to him.

In the weeks and months of grief following the deaths of my parents, I remember hearing myself saying these words to friends and acquaintances: "My mother died. My father died." I heard myself speaking them in a way that I do not hear myself in normal conversation. It was as if I needed to speak and to hear these words in order to absorb the reality of their deaths.

Jesus tells his disciples plainly, "Lazarus is dead." The path to resurrection leads through death. Death becomes the first phase of life. We think about life preceding death, but life springs forth from death. The disciples cannot experience the miracle of Jesus' raising of Lazarus from death until they comprehend that he has *really* died. Life comes after death. We die and rise with Christ every day. Death is the first word; it is not the last.

God, even as we grieve the death of our loved ones, help us to see death as the way that leads to eternal life. Amen.

Jesus receives an urgent message from Mary and Martha: their brother, Lazarus, is ill. But Jesus stays put for two more days. By the time Jesus shares the news with the disciples, Lazarus has died. When Jesus arrives in Bethany, Lazarus has been in the tomb for four days. Mary and Martha, heartbroken over their brother's death, are upset that Jesus has not come sooner. Both of them say to Jesus, "Lord, if you had been here, my brother would not have died."

Throughout this scenario and in the midst of their grief, Jesus utters confusing words. First he responds to Mary and Martha's panicked request for help by saying, "This illness does not lead to death." Later he tells the disciples plainly, "Lazarus is dead." When he gets to Bethany he tells the sisters, "Your brother will live again." Unlike Martha and Mary, Jesus seems to have no sense of urgency about this situation. In fact, he tells his disciples, "I am glad I was not there, so that you may believe." What does Jesus mean by that comment? What does Jesus want them to believe?

Perhaps Jesus wants them to believe that the way to life is through death. There is no other way. He wants those who witness the raising of Lazarus to know that he can only raise us if we are willing to die. Death precedes life. Life comes after death, not before.

What in you, in the church, and in the world is dying and needs to die before God can give new life?

God, help us to believe that death is the way that leads to life. Amen.

After Lazarus's death, Jesus goes to the tomb and asks that the stone be removed from the opening of the cave where Lazarus's body lay. Martha objects saying, "There is a stench because he has been dead four days." Opening the cave will be dreadful and disgusting!

What places in our own lives, in our communities, have been dead for so long that the stench is too much to bear? What things do we find too terrible to look at? Jesus wants to open those places; Jesus wants us to look at those things, to see them for what they are, and to believe that life will rise from death.

So people remove the stone; Jesus offers up a prayer, and cries with a loud voice, "Lazarus, come out!" The dead man comes out alive, with hands and feet still bound with strips of cloth. Jesus says to those gathered, "Unbind him, and let him go."

Though we have been given the gift of new life in Christ, we sometimes remain bound by bands of death: old scars, regrets, shame, anger, pride, greed, prejudice. We sometimes remain bound by people and circumstances that benefit from our being less than the whole persons God intends us to be.

Who or what keeps you from being fully alive? What are the strips of cloth that bind your feet and hands? What cloth covers your face and prevents you from being who you really are? Name these. Feel how they keep you bound. And then hear Jesus say, "Unbind him [or her], and let him [or her] go."

God, give me courage to come out of the places that prevent me from embracing the life you give me; use me to untie the bands of death wherever I encounter them. Amen.

SUNDAY, APRIL 10 ～ *Read Romans 8:6-11*

FIFTH SUNDAY IN LENT

A young boy came to church with his mother for the first time. The little boy and his mother had talked about church before attending. I don't know what information they exchanged, but clearly the child came to church with great expectations. When I asked the mother about her son's first day at church, she told me that upon entering the building he looked up at her and asked, "So, Mommy, where is God?" That young boy fully expected that he would meet God at church! Do you expect to meet God? Where do you expect to find God? Where does God live?

Paul says, "If the Spirit of him who raised Jesus from the dead dwells in you, he who raised Christ from the dead will give life to your mortal bodies also through his Spirit that dwells in you." When Paul says, "*If,*" he is not suggesting that the Spirit might not dwell in you. He is saying: *Since* the Spirit *does* dwell in you, *therefore*, the One who raised Christ will give life to you also! In other words, he is asking us to live into the reality that God dwells in us.

We who have lived long enough to have experienced brokenness and failure find it difficult to imagine that the Spirit that raised Jesus from the dead could or would dwell in us. But the biblical witness and the heart of the gospel is the story of God's choosing to dwell in us and among us in whatever condition or circumstance we find ourselves. We don't make it so; God makes it so. The good news is that the same Spirit who raised Christ from the dead can indeed dwell in us. And where the Spirit dwells, there is life!

God, fill us with a childlike expectation of meeting you where you have chosen to make your dwelling—both in us and around us. Amen.

WDJWUTD?

APRIL 11–17, 2011 • RAY WADDLE

MONDAY, APRIL 11 ~ *Read Philippians 2:5-11*

The other day I spotted a WWJD—What Would Jesus Do?—bracelet. The WWJD movement was big in the mid-1990s among young people who were trying to exert moral seriousness by wrestling with the gospel in their own way. Then somewhere along the line, WWJD became a line of jewelry, a merchandising juggernaut. It soon became a passé fashion relic.

If the WWJD campaign was flawed, I think that's because it posed the wrong question. WWJD? That's a tough one. Jesus was unpredictable, always confounding people's expectations. He challenged conventional wisdom, speaking with startling authority. Sometimes he said little at all; instead, drawing in the sand while others debated the fate of an accused woman—then shocking everyone by forgiving her with, "Go and sin no more."

The better question might be WDJWUTD: What Does Jesus Want Us To Do? That question preoccupied Paul in his letters to the struggling young churches of his time. In Philippians, Paul outlines some answers: strive for sympathy for others, unity among yourselves, servanthood to all. Paul adds another question: WDJD? What Did Jesus Do? Answer: In the form of God, he humbled and emptied himself and became obedient even unto death, creating a new, divine connection with human life.

WDJWUTD is easier to answer than WWJD—but harder to honor, harder to live out. Yet Paul's letters, and the existence of the church itself, testify every day to the conviction that we can; and now is the time.

God, may I both ask and respond to WDJWUTD? Amen.

Regular columnist on religions and spirituality; editor of *Reflections*, the journal of Yale Divinity School

TUESDAY, APRIL 12 ~ *Read Psalm 31:9-16*

This psalm invites the reader to visit the darkness, the shadow, the sorrow—face it, take the measure of it, own up to it. The darkness might be a deep gnawing personal regret or various misdemeanors, heartaches, destructive actions. In the darkness lurks brokenness but also yearning for wholeness.

Jews admirably provide a framework for admitting sins and making amends with people they have hurt or have failed. It happens annually during Rosh Hashanah, the New Year, a communal and individual festival of forgiveness and renewal. The Christian timetable differs. The door stands always open for divine reconciliation through the person of Jesus, if we are up to it. But we can easily take a standing invitation for granted. The urge is always there to postpone the painful moment of truth.

This psalm offers a way back to the moment of truth. It serves as a vehicle for pain and loss: "I have become like a broken vessel." Jesus knew it well. He spoke from Psalm 31 even in his torment on the cross: "Into your hand I commit my spirit" (v. 5), he cried.

Contemporary forces—the sheer pressure to look busy and successful—conspire against a visit to the room of spiritual anguish. This psalm gives permission. It links the reader to the Bible's great language of struggle and hope. It also connects us to Jesus' travail and triumph. It ends by proclaiming, "My times are in your hand"—a declaration of ultimate trust in the divine embrace, God's providence.

These coming days of Jesus' passion and trial reestablish the hidden truths of our own turbulent spiritual condition. The gospel stands ready as a moment of truth to reconnect.

How does this psalm connect you to personal brokenness? What possibilities for hope and healing does it open?

The first shall be last. Lose your life to save it. A powerless carpenter becomes the world's savior.

In the Bible such paradoxes abound. Elderly Abraham and Sarah start a family. Great prophets noisily protest God's call. But paradox stirs discomfort. Paradox implies contradiction, and nobody wants to live with contradiction without trying to resolve it and dissolve it.

Yet somehow paradox houses the meaning of life itself. Life's greatest aspects—love, soul, divine presence—are invisible, impossible to corner and label. But there they are nevertheless.

Many psalms are associated with King David. Now there's a man of paradox, a biblical hero greatly flawed—a schemer, an adulterer—yet greatly blessed by God.

Psalm 118 resounds with thanksgiving, possibly spoken by a king who had faced a severe testing time but is finally saved by God. One verse leaps out: "The stone that the builders rejected has become the chief cornerstone." Jesus himself repeats this paradoxical verse and transforms it. Suddenly the psalm does double duty. In Jewish liturgy it sings of rescue and gratitude; now it reassures Jesus' followers that God did not abandon him.

Paradox surrounds us. We are caught in a contest of flesh against spirit, mired in pursuits of material comforts though they never quite satisfy.

Yet without the curveball of paradox, we'd be sorely tempted to claim to know the pattern of all things; tempted to ignore the Creator, disdain humility, and lose a sense of humor at the strange twists life serves up.

The Son of God was tried, executed, and lived again. The Word was made flesh. Paradox prevails. Thanks be to God.

Lord, you speak through the beauty and paradoxes of this life. Grant each of us the clarity to embrace your will. Amen.

THURSDAY, APRIL 14 ~ *Read Isaiah 50:4-9*

The "suffering servant," speaking here in Isaiah, creates a startling new idea in religious history: the declaration that suffering does not signal divine indifference but serves as part of the world's big story, God's story of redemption.

That sounds terribly glib. I cannot shrug off the many horrible ways people suffer in war and in peace. The news simply is this: suffering somehow has meaning. The one true God of scripture is not a god of moody caprice but the God of all. Nothing is in vain; no detail lies beyond God's sight.

Early Christians viewed this passage as prophecy, an indication that Jesus was God's ultimate suffering servant who identified totally with God's spirit and embodied God's intimacy with human suffering. The world's pain matters. Its hopes matter. This life sets the stage for God's story.

One of my favorite quotes, by Jewish writer Isaac Bashevis Singer, says it another way: "God is an author and we are both the readers and the heroes."

Picturing God as author infers a narrative to this life, a plot written by a Creator hard at work. Singer's quote implies we have definite duties to the story. We work to honor the text that tells the story. But we are also the characters in the sacred plot line. Only people can step into the story and carry it forward.

God draws the circle of divine concern far and wide. The circle includes our suffering and doubt, forces not to be feared but transfigured. We are God's deputies on earth, God's heroes, wounded though we are, in the unstoppable story.

Eternal Spirit, make us alert to the passing moments of this life and grateful to be part of the everlasting story. Amen.

Let the same mind be in you that was in Christ Jesus," Paul urges in verse 5. That sounds like a tall order, exalted and elusive. People go to great lengths to catch up to exalted states of mind. I once spent a few days in a monastery, a powerful experience that stripped me of the usual distractions that keep me from engaging the deeper rhythms, the deeper questions and truths. I learned about spiritual discipline and mental focus. Then I drove home, back to work and responsibilities and people; home where the drama of faith had better take root and mean something, if it is going to take root anywhere.

So when Philippians says let that divine mind enter into personal thinking and identity, it sounds hard to access. But if Jesus walked this earth in full humanity, then he responded to the teeming life and turbulence around him with heart, soul, and . . . mind. His parables display great mental agility, as do his wry answers to the critics who sought to trap him with little games of logic. He made mindful choices in his teachings, his healings, his decision to turn toward dangerous Jerusalem.

Jesus' deliberateness—his mindfulness—is a sign of Jesus' humanity and a bridge to ours. But how to "let the same mind be in you"? I don't think it means trying to become little Jesuses, little messiahs. Instead, Paul talks about adopting earthly traits of Jesus: sympathy, humility, and obedience, for starters. God glorified these human values as the way of Jesus, the way of the cross and liberation too. They represent qualities of mind. And they're hard, not because they're too abstract but because we choose to resist. "Letting the same mind be in you" invites us to decide to mind the meaning of discipleship. And act.

O God, may the mind of Christ move me to a life of simplicity and courage. May the spirit of Christ make it possible. Amen.

Jesus' arrest, trial, and death—a cornerstone of our faith story—is a study in political power and Jesus' response to it. Jesus seems defenseless against worldly politics and its grim momentum, the goosestep of power. The crowd's blood lust, the wheels of justice, the mocking soldiers.

Jesus' reaction? Not a burst of physical might but an offer of bread and wine, words of prophecy and comfort; then silence, death, and resurrection truth.

Jesus' actions perform a new miracle by exposing the dirty secret about earthly power, its teetering insecurity. Discipleship becomes the new weapon of courage for facing down the preening, dangerous public world.

Notice all the powerful people in Matthew's story. They held all the cards, controlled all the options. Being so powerful, they might have moved more carefully in deciding the fate of such an important captive as Jesus. Being so powerful, they could have called time-out, slowed down the machinery of death, gotten some perspective. But no. The powerful are always powerless before their own fears. In Jerusalem, they couldn't stop the swift logic of their own violence. Their power was a prison house of prejudice, "practicality," and impotence.

Jesus refused power. He refused a political takeover and a military solution. Instead, he cleared a new path of freedom. We can choose to share in it, a liberation from the snares of egotistical nonsense and mob hysteria. The glory of simplicity, golden rule, and abundant life are the new kingdom power.

From the new vantage point, the dazzling parade of earthbound power is something to pity. Jesus' words and actions become the new durable goods. They outlast.

How does the gospel give you courage to face down the powers of this life?

SUNDAY, APRIL 17 ~ *Read Matthew 21:1-11*

PASSION/PALM SUNDAY

Many great details enliven the Palm Sunday story: the donkey and colt that Jesus rides into Jerusalem, the sudden hosannas, the disciples running this way and that, the palms softening his path. But the most striking word for me is *turmoil*. "When [Jesus] entered Jerusalem, the whole city was in turmoil, asking, 'Who is this?'"

Turmoil: It followed Jesus everywhere. His charisma stirs it, his teachings provoke it.

Turmoil: Imagine the owner of the donkey and colt, rising that morning to another day, situated safely off to the side (he thinks), suddenly finding himself empty-handed after the disciples swoop in to fetch the animals for Jesus' entry. Maybe he feels honored but maybe he panics. Why me? Will I see my beloved animals again? Will they behave for this solemn occasion? Who is this Galilean, a king you say?

The turmoil of Jesus reverberates across two thousand years every time his insistent words of peacemaking and righteousness confront our fretful daily routines and schemes.

At this time of year, I experience turmoil within as well, where my citadel opens its gates and lets Jesus pass through. I join the hosannas, but I also have to count the cost of the welcome. His presence is a rebuke against cozy religious habits and business-as-usual. From my doorstep I can see him coming. He passes by in the dust and turmoil of the moment, trailed by followers. I can see the road he is taking. From here I can see a hill called Calvary.

And so it is decision time again—either to go back inside or step forward and follow, no matter where the turmoil leads.

Consider where you might be found in the Palm Sunday story. As disciple? soldier? onlooker? follower?

The Grace of a Hard But Holy Week

APRIL 18–24, 2011 • ROBBINS SIMS

MONDAY, APRIL 18 ～ *Read Psalm 36:5-11*

Holy Week can be a hard week. Jesus moves toward inevitable crucifixion. Those around him allow rage and cowardice to consume them. Friday brings sadness beyond measure. We tend to shy away from Holy Week; we follow at a distance, shaking our heads and maybe our fists at what others do to Jesus. It would seem to be the only safe way to approach this unusual week.

Holy Week only works, however, if we put ourselves in the thick of it, which involves more than a grim determination to face the worst. It requires courage born of the knowledge that God's sovereign grace surrounds this week and our lives within this week. The psalmist says exactly what we need to hear:

> Your steadfast love, O LORD,
>   extends to the heavens,
> your faithfulness to the clouds.

There is no time, place, or circumstance beyond which God's grace does not extend. In the paradox of that grace, the deepening darkness of Holy Week proves to be a manifestation of divine light. Thus we can say with the psalmist: "In your light we see light." The illuminating grace of Holy Week enables us to see and accept ourselves in our struggles and failures. It brightens the cruciform sanctuary in which we confess both the tender affections of a Mary and the maniacal possessiveness of a Judas.

Lord, you sanctified these days before the foundation of the world. Therefore, I enter them with full confidence in your grace. Amen.

Pastor, First United Methodist Church; Eufaula, Alabama

TUESDAY, APRIL 19 ~ *Read Isaiah 49:1-7; 1 Corinthians 1:18-31; John 12:20-36*

Spiritual honor often comes by way of dishonor. God's servant Isaiah admits profound failure with the words, "I have labored in vain, I have spent my strength for nothing and vanity." Speaking in the aftermath of the nation's exile, the servant embodies the pathos of a people upon whom catastrophic judgment has fallen. Having endured such disgrace, imagine the servant's surprise when the Lord says, "I will give you as a light to the nations, that my salvation might reach the end of the earth." Israel's humiliation becomes central to the restoration of its mission: to be a beacon people through whom the radiance of God's countenance is lifted up with blessing upon all peoples.

Paul embraces the enigma of a suffering savior, saying, "We proclaim Christ crucified, a stumbling block to Jews and foolishness to Gentiles, but to those who are the called, both Jews and Greeks, Christ the power of God and the wisdom of God." Paul's words reflect Jesus' own understanding. When Greeks come seeking him, it signals the expansion of his message into the Gentile world in fulfillment of Isaiah's prophecy. It marks the arrival of the "hour" when he will manifest his identity decisively. Rather than reveling in this apparent breakthrough, Jesus turns and speaks of the necessity of his passion, noting that it is only through death to its old form that the prolific potential of a seed is released to new life. Likewise, the universality of Jesus' mission will be realized when he is "lifted up from the earth" on a cross. From that scandalous position Jesus will "draw all people" to himself. Such is the nature of the light in which Jesus urges us to walk and believe.

Lord Jesus, I yield to your will. Reduce to nothing the things that are, so that you become for me all wisdom, righteousness, sanctification, and redemption. Amen.

WEDNESDAY, APRIL 20 ~ *Read John 13:21-32*

The farther we go into Holy Week, the more undeniable the evidence that God's glory shines amid the shameful realities of human depravity. In today's passage, Jesus sits at table with his disciples, deeply troubled. He declares, "Very truly, I tell you, one of you will betray me." Unable to accept that this word could be directed at themselves, each of the disciples looks at the others, wondering which one of them it might be.

Impetuous Peter gets the attention of the beloved disciple who asks Jesus outright. The Lord's answer comes as a warning—the guilty party will accept bread that Jesus is dipping in a dish. Jesus offers the bread to Judas Iscariot, and he receives it. Is Judas more concerned with this sop than with the deadly peril of an evil he can still decline? Is he, as some suggest, trying to provoke Jesus into taking some kind of stand? Does he just not care? Whatever his thinking, Judas disappoints all who wish that his life might turn out well. Reaching and taking, he opens the door to the devil. Knowing that Judas will not turn back, Jesus urges him to move quickly. The betrayer wastes no time and bolts into the darkness.

"When he had gone out, Jesus said, 'Now the Son of Man has been glorified, and God has been glorified in him.'" Where is this glory? Clearly Jesus and the Father are glorified by the fact that Judas's betrayal moves Jesus toward the cross. If, by the eventual logic of that cross, God is glorified in the outpouring of love, might the glory of this scene be found in the sadness with which we ponder it? Could an aching desire for Judas's redemption foreshadow a glory yet to come? Might the telling of Judas's betrayal be not merely a word of caution but an invitation to an even deeper grace?

God of light, I thank you that in your compassion you sanctify even the dark grief of lost innocence. Amen.

THURSDAY, APRIL 21 ~ *Read 1 Corinthians 11:23-26; John 13:1-17, 31b-35*

MAUNDY THURSDAY

Four images define the spiritual contours of Holy Thursday. Because two of them represent the core of Jesus' passion, we identify most intimately with the bread and cup. The towel and basin manifest a similar grace, however. As Jesus washes his disciples' feet, he condescends to a level of humility that corresponds most closely to cross-bearing. His admonition that we do likewise calls us to participate in the essence of his sacrifice.

Jesus engages in this act of extreme servanthood from a position of strength. Confident in the Father from whom he has come and to whom he will return, Jesus accepts the lowly route by which his journey is to be accomplished. Doing so, he sets an example of what it means to follow him, not merely in ritual or moral imitation but in the actual experience of divine grace. By washing his disciples' feet, Jesus enters fully into the realization of their worth, not so much as men who will continue his mission but as human beings whom he and the Father love for their own sake. This compassionate valuing of them lies at the heart of the "justification" Jesus will achieve for them and for us on Good Friday and Easter.

To have our feet washed in the name and spirit of Christ is to know something of the tenderness and respect with which God regards us. Alternatively, washing the feet of our brothers and sisters puts us in a position to recognize the sacred nature of their otherness and vulnerability—to see them, albeit in small measure, as Christ sees them. In these ways, washing one another's feet in obedience to Jesus becomes a means of grace for us.

Lord Jesus, having loved me in my worldly presumptuousness, love me to the end that I may enter into the heart of your humility and thereby know the grace that transforms me into your likeness. Amen.

GOOD FRIDAY

The day finally arrives in which fortune and caution fail. Deepest dread becomes a brutal reality. A shattering statement is made. Violence runs its course. The shock is sickening, the sorrow unimaginable. John's Gospel reports that only the beloved disciple remains at the foot of Jesus' cross. All the rest have fled.

We find it hard to be here. A popular understanding of atonement says that in the hour of darkness, God looks away. Yet it is not God who winces but we. The sight of our individual and collective sins seems too much for us. See them we must, however, for acknowledgment of sin is essential to salvation. However horrifying, we are called to linger here and make our confession. This is at last the place where, by God's grace, we can come clean.

John's passion narrative makes it clear that Jesus dies to save us. We would make him a victim, but Jesus moves through the maelstrom of crucifixion as the victor. We rant and rail. We conspire and kill. He remains Beloved of his Father. We compromise, deny, and fall away. He declares, "It is finished." He is the Suffering Servant whose bruises heal us. Upon him, God lays the iniquities of us all, and he bears them, not in anger but in forgiveness. He exposes our weakness and wickedness, not with condemnation but with utter compassion. We stand empty-handed before his cross. Jesus reaches through all that is wrong with us and touches us at that deep center where God's mangled image still exists. He loves us here, and that is that.

Lord Jesus Christ, keep me near your cross, not for your sake but for mine. Amen.

SATURDAY, APRIL 23 ~ *Read Exodus 14:10-31; Matthew 28:1-10*

Caught between Pharaoh's approaching army and an impassable sea, the Hebrews can only wait—a waiting of necessity, not hopelessness. Though they tremble at the prospects of impending death, the people are told they need only "stand firm, and see the deliverance that the LORD will accomplish for you today."

So it is on the day before Easter. As we go back in imagination to that first Holy Saturday, we join the remnant of Jesus' disciples as they keep a quiet but restless sabbath. Like them, we find ourselves in an in-between time when, unable to do anything else, we must wait. Our stillness does not signify the same paralysis as theirs, however. For them it brings deadening uncertainty. For us, it is an Easter vigil. We know that this day stands between two absolutes, both of which declare the finality of grace. Having accepted the fact that Jesus died for us, we await word of his resurrection. So confident are we of Easter's coming that we read of it before it happens.

In many respects, every day in this world is like this day. We live always between Jesus' victory over sin and death and his specific victory over *our* sins and *our* death. Having been baptized into his death, we wait to be united with him in resurrection. At one level, we must get on with our lives, including a future necessity of death. Even so, a potent stillness remains at our center. There Christ does his work. There we yield to grace. There the Spirit confirms our hope. There we are formed into people prepared for resurrection.

As those who wait for the morning, so my soul waits for you, O Lord. Amen.

SUNDAY, APRIL 24 ~ *Read Psalm 118:1-2 and John 20:1-18*

EASTER SUNDAY

Easter arrives with a measure of bewilderment, but the confusion cannot last. Having journeyed in darkness, the women stumble upon the inexplicable. Mary misunderstands completely, and the disciples fare but little better. It does not matter. They are not there to grasp Easter but to be grasped by Easter. For Mary, awareness of Jesus' resurrection begins when she hears her name and realizes that she is known by him, so too with the disciples. They do not go looking for Jesus; he appears to them. The clarity that comes is not their doing. They see in the dazzling radiance of an inexorable dawn. It is all grace and all from God. A worship refrain becomes the steady, unstoppable heartbeat of the risen Lord: "His steadfast love endures forever!"

Any problems we have with Easter are not ours to solve but God's. We have only to grope along in darkness until we confront the unfathomable. At the end of our understanding and strength, we die; and our life "is hidden with Christ in God." There the Lord speaks our name in the clearest, gentlest, and strongest voice. The iridescent mystery of divine light shines about us.

Realizing that we are fully known and fully loved finally relieves us of the burden of trying and always failing to get our hands around life. In the power of his resurrection, Jesus bids us enter his life. Overcoming our sin and death, he lays a future of eternal possibilities before us. Now we begin to get it! Grace extends in every direction, even to the bearing of crosses. It is the irrevocable basis of God's relationship with this world. What joy! This is truly the first of all our days.

Risen Lord, you are my life. Set my mind on things above so that when you are revealed, I may be revealed with you. Amen.

Faith or Fear?

APRIL 25–MAY 1, 2011 • GARY HOLLOWAY

MONDAY, APRIL 25 ~ *Read Psalm 16:1-8*

Protection, safety, security. Where does our security lie? Do we put our trust in the government? in a better home security system? in the safety of a bank account? in our own wisdom and plans?

The psalmist trusts in God who offers safety and gives refuge—communal refuge. God's refuge encompasses all the "holy ones in the land." Perhaps our culture's emphasis on individualism encourages us to look for safety in all the wrong places. This psalm calls us back to genuine community, where we live together under God's protection, an enchanting inheritance that God provides.

The words of the psalm go beyond mere safety and protection. Life under God's care is a delight, a pleasure, a joy—genuinely good. God offers the good life to us as a gift.

God's refuge is both communal and intimate. We cultivate our trust in divine provision through time-tested practices of prayer and meditation. In the stillness and solitude of the night, we never find ourselves alone and vulnerable. Instead God gives counsel and instruction to our hearts.

Trust in God involves risk and often makes little human sense. Yet by placing our trust in God we opt for true security, safety, and protection. We, in relationship with one another, choose to keep the Lord constantly before us and beside us.

God of love, calm our fearful hearts. Turn our lives away from those things that promise false security. May we find our refuge in you alone. Amen.

Minister at Natchez Trace Church of Christ, Nashville, Tennessee; professor of spiritual formation, Lipscomb University; author of over twenty-five books

For many years I led a disembodied faith. I believed God was concerned with our souls, not so much with our bodies. Nothing could be farther from the biblical picture of the body. God made our bodies and pronounced them good. God took on human form in the Incarnation, thereby affirming our way of being in the world. We serve God in and through our bodies, which are temples of the Holy Spirit.

This psalm reminds us that in God our hearts are glad, our souls rejoice, and even our bodies rest secure. God wants *all* of us. Christianity does not promote a disembodied religion, promising that souls will go to a shadowy heaven. It represents a full-bodied trust in a God who will not abandon any part of us to the realm of the dead. And so, at the graveside of my friend, I spoke these words:

> We gather here today to lay to rest the body of Jack Tyner, a body that has suffered through these last days but lived a full life in the previous years, knowing that we commit to the earth only that which is of the earth. The scriptures teach us that our bodies are made of the dust of the ground and to the dust we will return.
>
> But we are more than dust. God breathed into human nostrils the breath of life, and humans became living beings. We therefore commit this body to the ground and this soul to the Lord. Earth to earth, ashes to ashes, and dust to dust, knowing full well that Jesus promises resurrection and life.

Yet we seek not merely everlasting existence but to see God face-to-face. Psalm 16 says in that embodied relationship we will experience unimaginable pleasures forevermore.

God of love, increase our trust that as Jesus was raised from the grave, we also who die in Christ shall gain life. Amen.

Tt's a miracle!" We hear these words frequently, particularly on the lips of some Christians. For them, miracles, from finding the lost car keys to the healing of inoperable cancer, happen daily.

For other Christians, such a statement does not sit well. Yes, we believe God answers prayer. Yes, we believe God works in our world. But what many call miracles—finding a parking spot at the supermarket, getting a phone call from a friend you're thinking of, finding the lost airline tickets—seem beneath the dignity of the Almighty, so we hesitate to use the word *miracle* in some of these instances.

To begin to understand the miraculous power of God in our world today, we return to the world of the early disciples who saw the power of God at work in a man, a man named Jesus. "Jesus of Nazareth was a man accredited by God to you by miracles, wonders and signs, which God did among you through him" (NIV). A human being, but more than a human being—the Son of God.

Christians bring many different perspectives and understandings to their faith. But most agree that Jesus' works are more than just startling, unusual events. They point as signs to the God who loves us. In the miracles of Jesus, believers focus on the divine presence who loves us and saves us, not just in these extraordinary events but in every event of life.

The Bible invites us into the world of Jesus' miracles where the blind see, the lame walk, the demon-possessed are freed; where we drink miraculous wine, walk on water, and even rise from the dead. By entering this world we come to see that it is *our* world, that the power that worked through Jesus still works in our lives through faith. We find that God still heals the sick, comforts the grieving, defeats evil, and rules the winds and waves.

Lord Jesus, open our eyes to the wonders you are doing. Amen.

Wind, fire, and speaking in tongues—what could be more exciting? Yet the climax of Pentecost is a sermon. Disappointed? Perhaps, because we see sermons and speeches as boring. They are only words, and talk is cheap. But these words at Pentecost have power. Peter's talk is not cheap; it is the story of the gospel.

Peter outlines the life of Jesus, including his death and Resurrection. This is the greatest story ever told—the old, old, story of Jesus and his love. But it is a new story to these listeners, especially the part about resurrection. Why should the crowd believe Peter?

Peter convinces them using scripture, by quoting the psalmist. He tells them that he and the disciples are eyewitnesses of the resurrected Jesus. His "clincher" argument is that Jesus has poured forth what they have seen and heard that day. The people in the crowd may doubt Peter, but they cannot easily doubt what they hear with their own ears. Those speaking in tongues say this amazing ability comes from Jesus. If he can send tongues, he must be alive; if alive, he is no blasphemer and charlatan. He is what he claimed to be, Lord and Christ. And this crowd has killed their long-awaited Messiah.

How in the world can they make that right? They can't, but God can—through the very one they killed. This is good news indeed! Do we still feel the power of Peter's sermon, or has the story become too old to us? Are these empty words? What can we do to recover the power of the gospel story in our lives?

Perhaps we can do nothing. But God can! And that is good news for us.

Lord Jesus, open our hearts afresh to your good news! Amen.

Many of us know the thrill of bringing a new baby home from the hospital. We lavish affection on that newborn. Although new, the baby is certainly not a stranger in the family but the center of attention and love. He or she is at home.

God has given us all a new birth into God's family, lavishing love upon us and making us feel at home. The Holy One tenderly cares for us as newborns.

The new birth springs from God's great mercy. We cannot spiritually birth ourselves. That new life comes solely through God's grace and mercy.

The new birth through Christ's resurrection gives us a living hope. "Living" means our hope is not just wishful thinking. It is real. Sure. Certain. "Living" also means our hope shapes our life. This assurance, this hope, lives in us and gives us joy in the midst of trials. We are not *optimistic* people, mindlessly believing the world is getting better and better; we are *hopeful* people who trust the world is in the hands of a merciful God.

We are born into a wealthy family, the wealthiest of all. Our Father owns everything. We therefore share in an inheritance that no one can destroy, that is not subject to natural decay, and that is perpetually new. Moth and rust cannot destroy it, and thieves cannot steal it. (See Matthew 6:19-20.) Our home with God is permanent. No one can make us homeless again. God's power protects us through faith until we finally arrive safe at home. That final home, our salvation, waits in the wings, ready to go on the stage of history at any moment. We wait patiently for that grand entrance.

God of hospitality, we give you thanks for opening your home to us. Amen.

Suffering can be good news. Not in itself, of course. We do not enjoy suffering for suffering's sake. But when facing ridicule and pain, a disciple of Christ can experience "an indescribable and glorious joy." How? How can we rejoice when those around us treat us like strangers?

First, we rejoice because suffering tests the authenticity of our faith. We can easily serve Jesus when everything goes right, when we prosper and everyone speaks well of us. True faith comes when all turn against us, and we rely on God alone. When faith, like gold, stands the test of fire, it shows itself to be the genuine article. Such faith receives praise, glory, and honor from Jesus himself.

We also rejoice because we focus on Jesus, not on the pain of suffering. Our faith while suffering praises the Jesus we believe in but do not see. In him even suffering becomes an unspeakable joy. Through Jesus we receive salvation as the goal of our faith.

The present tense here is significant. We can say, "Jesus saved me," when we remember our conversion. We can say, "Jesus will save me," when we anticipate the new heavens and earth. But when we suffer, it's important to remember that salvation is present. Even in the worst of pain, Jesus *is saving* us. The author of First Peter calls us to more than a "pie in the sky when we die" or "farther along we'll understand why" type of faith. He calls us to a faith that embraces the present reality of salvation in the midst of suffering. That salvation gives us joy.

> *God of all comfort, give us courage in our suffering. Increase our faith so we might even now receive the salvation you promise. Fill us with your indescribable joy! Amen.*

They meet at night. In secret. Behind locked doors. Afraid of the Jewish authorities. After all, the disciples have seen what happened to Jesus. None of them wants to be crucified.

Suddenly Jesus stands among them. He is no ghost! They see his wounded hands and side and are beside themselves with joy. The Lord is alive! Jesus even breathes the Holy Spirit upon them. Then he disappears.

Now they have seen him themselves, and the Spirit rests upon them. Now we expect them to have faith and courage, but a week later they are in the house again behind locked doors.

Why? Have they learned nothing? Do they still fear? Being an eyewitness to the Resurrection doesn't prevent their fear. The Holy Spirit seemingly does not give them the confidence to leave the doors unlocked. We marvel at their lack of trust. Have we more faith than they?

How many of us claim to be Christians, believers in a risen Lord, and yet continue to live our lives in fear? We lock the doors of our hearts to anyone and anything that might threaten. We put our trust in safety and precautions, not in the God who raised Jesus from the dead.

What's the worst that can happen to us? We might be hurt, abused, taken advantage of, cheated, robbed, unjustly imprisoned, beaten, killed. Or perhaps the worst that will happen is that we'll live feeling unfulfilled, unappreciated; facing midlife crises and a slow end in a care facility. God delivered Jesus from death. Can he not deliver us from our fears?

God can and does. We dare not live like these fearful disciples. We believe in this great miracle of Resurrection. Jesus lives! He lives for us. We live now and will live again through him.

God of love, increase our faith in you. Free us from our fears, great and small. Amen.

Faith or Fear?   133

Table Talk

MAY 2–8, 2011 • SONIA E. BRUM

MONDAY, MAY 2 ~ *Read Psalm 116:1-11*

The word *love* has multiple meanings in English. I may say that I love my children, I love to walk, I love tomatoes, and I love my job. Obviously I don't love my children in the same way or to the same degree as I love walking, tomatoes, or my job.

In Portuguese, my native tongue, the concept of love involves a *strong* emotional relationship. Both with friends and with things, we use the word *like*: I like Emily; I like to walk; I like tomatoes. When I moved to the United States nine years ago, I experienced confusion when one friend would say to another, "I love you," because for me it means more than friendship. It is like saying, "I am in love with you."

Psalm 116 is one of thanksgiving. The psalmist expresses his great suffering and anguish that almost drove him to despair, but God responds to his cries. Therefore, he goes on to affirm: "I love God because he listened to me, listened as I begged for mercy" (THE MESSAGE). The psalmist experiences God's goodness in answer to his prayers.

The psalmist speaks of an intimate, grateful love of God, a love of strong emotional connection. He goes on to promise continued love of God, a love backed up with action: vows and sacrifices.

Understanding the Lord's love, presence, and nearness will lead us to service and ever deeper commitment to God. Today we claim our love of God defined by intimate relationship.

I invite you to pray and declare your love to God: "Lord, I love you because. . . . " Amen.

Congregational Specialist and Coordinator for Hispanic/Latino Ministry, South Carolina Conference of the United Methodist Church; born and raised in Brazil

TUESDAY, MAY 3 ～ *Read 1 Peter 1:17-23*

Young people eagerly plan and organize their future and move toward hoped-for dreams. Their desire for control starts early, so they grow impatient with the unforeseen or unexpected situations that interfere with future plans.

In *Turn My Mourning into Dancing*, Henri J. M. Nouwen wrote the following: "Hope is willing to leave unanswered questions unanswered and unknown futures unknown. Hope makes you see God's guiding hand not only in the gentle and pleasant moments but also in the shadows of disappointment and darkness" (page 60).

Hope is not simply a wish for the future; it implies a desire for fulfillment, which may include some fear and anxiety. Hope involves an openness to whatever will come—today or a year from now.

The author of First Peter addresses new Christians as exiles, believers who no longer feel at home in the world. This audience has discovered that the Christian faith has heightened the tension between themselves and others in their culture; Christian believers in the early centuries did not share the same perspective as the Roman authorities or the Greek schools of philosophy. So the author offers encouragement and conveys hope that rests in their being part of a *new* household. The members of this household display genuine mutual love and their "faith and hope are set on God."

We may place our hope in money, career, education, position, or power. Such hope will not last and may become meaningless. Our hope issues in an obedient trust in God. That hope will never fade; it is living and eternal.

An old saying states, "As long as there is life, there is hope." How will you demonstrate hope today?

WEDNESDAY, MAY 4 ～ *Read Acts 2:36-41*

After the Pentecost experience, Peter feels the need to explain to the crowd what has just happened. Today's verses present his conclusion. He proclaims Jesus "Lord and Messiah." The term *Lord* is the same term used by early Christians to translate the name of Israel's God YHWH. Peter proclaims that the crucified and resurrected one is both God *and* the kingdom bringer.

Feeling "cut to the heart" with remorse, the crowd asks: "Brothers, what should we do?" What action can they take to remove their sense of shame and guilt? Peter challenges them to repentance and forgiveness, stating that they are to be baptized.

The crowd repents by acknowledging Jesus' messiahship, and then Peter baptizes them "in the name of Jesus Christ." Faith leads to baptism and then to inclusion in the body of Christian believers.

Peter's shared knowledge indicts the crowd's passive "unknowing." Their action is one of response, not initiative.

The crowd's question to Peter and to the apostles is one I often raise as I reflect on my passive inaction in matters of faith. My questions give voice to my sense of guilt that focuses on my own well-being, but then I fail to take further steps to transform guilt into action as an expression of my desire for repentance and forgiveness.

What actions will our repentance, forgiveness, and baptism take? What shall we do in the face of hungry children, the statistics of war, the abuse of women? What shall we do?

Consider the opportunities you have to transform your acts of response into acts of initiative that make a difference in the world. This is the call of Pentecost.

THURSDAY, MAY 5 ~ *Read Acts 2:14*

What is the largest crowd you've ever addressed? How did you feel just before you spoke?

A few years ago I attended a park in Atlanta to watch a concert of a famous artist. While I waited for the gates to open, I noticed a preacher who was shouting a message to the crowd comprised of all ages, cultures, and nationalities. Although his message was clear for some Christians, I wondered how many people understood the "churchspeak" he used: "Jesus' blood was shed for you"; "Jesus saves you"; or "Repent of your sins." What news did the people take home with them?

As a missionary in Central America, I learned that words have different meanings depending on the location and the culture of the people. As a result, I minister more carefully with the Hispanic population in the United States, which represents many nations and cultures.

"Let me explain this to you; listen carefully to what I say" (NIV). Peter's approach reminds us of the disciples' most important ministry after the Resurrection. Their mission is to proclaim Jesus as Lord and Messiah, Jesus as God's saving act—and demonstrate its crucial importance for the hearer and for us.

How can we make the message of Pentecost applicable to our lives? What is our table talk in the community of faith? How do we speak of God's deliverance?

Dear Lord, give us courage to proclaim the good news and the message of salvation that Christ brings. Amen.

FRIDAY, MAY 6 ~ *Read Luke 24:13-35*

I cannot imagine the thoughts of the two travelers on that road from Jerusalem heading home. I can speculate on their disappointment and loss, as well as worry about their future. I can hear them asking each other: What is next for us? Can we still believe the message Jesus taught us? Where can we start? Who will listen to us? So many questions with no answers, and no time to let the answers come. They are blinded by worry and the emptiness of the moment.

The two men, with minds clouded with concern and grief, do not recognize the stranger who joins them. They see him and hear his voice but do not recognize him. Why don't they recognize him? When have you been so focused in thought while walking or driving that you didn't see who or what was around you? When have you sat with a friend who was talking but left your time together with no idea of what was said?

When we feel stressed or confused, we may have difficulty focusing. We can hear, but we do not listen.

Noises on the streets, in our homes, and in our lives surround us. Our minds fill to overflowing with chattering thoughts. We find no respite in silence.

How do we listen in the midst of our noisy lives? How can we recognize God's presence in our lives? Jesus promises to be with us always. Jesus Christ walks with us and invites us to stop for a time of communion with him.

Consider your opportunities to enjoy family, to listen to neighbors, and to find a resting place in your life to be with the Lord.

SATURDAY, MAY 7 ~ *Read Luke 24:28-32*

The most meaningful memory of my childhood in Brazil centers on the family dinner table. Every Sunday, members of the extended family and other friends joined us for dinner. I remember the laughter, the happiness, the sharing of our lives—and, of course, the loud conversations. We discussed and disagreed, but the important part was sharing the meal together.

What is it about the dinner table? What miracle does it bring to our lives? I once asked these questions in a Bible study group. Everyone's answers differed according to her or his memories of the dinner table. One person said, "The dinner table brings togetherness"; a younger lady responded, "It helps us to learn more about one another." After most of the participants had spoken, an elderly man said, "It brings back memories of my parents and my childhood."

Eating and drinking together around the same table is an ancient symbol of human intimacy. The meal in Emmaus begins with an act of hospitality, an invitation by those who prepared the table. It is the memory of Christ at the table that transforms an ordinary supper into the sacrament.

Here after Easter, the hosts remember Jesus' words from the night before his sacrifice on the cross. The remembrance leads to recognition, realization, and understanding. The intimacy of table fellowship brings to the two travelers the memory of Jesus breaking and blessing the bread. Having experienced him at the table, they recall the amazing time with Jesus on the road.

For the disciples and for Jesus' followers, Easter begins their ministry; and we begin the Christian journey.

Recall memories of your family dinner table or the Easter dinner Communion in your church. What do the two share in common? What is different?

Table Talk

SUNDAY, MAY 8 ~ *Read Psalm 116:12-19*

The word *foreclosure* was much used in 2009. The Internet offers this definition: "Foreclosure is a legal proceeding by which a borrower's rights to a mortgaged property may be extinguished if the borrower fails to live up to the obligations agreed to in the loan contract."

Television networks aired special programs to help the public understand the situation and the options available. We could hear and see the word *foreclosure* everywhere. On my daily walk through my quiet neighborhood, I would see signs announcing houses in foreclosure.

The psalmist wonders how he will repay the Lord for all "his bounty" to him. He then makes a list of promises to pay back all he has received from the Lord. He says, "I will lift up the cup of salvation and call on the name of the LORD, I will pay my vows to the LORD in the presence of all his people." He declares himself God's servant and will offer a thanksgiving sacrifice to God.

Do you think God will foreclose on the psalmist if he does not fulfill his promises? How many times would God have to foreclose on me related to my many failed promises? Yet God is a loving God who sent Jesus Christ to pay our debts and free us of our burdens.

As a people touched by Easter, we come into table fellowship with a new community, the household of believers. We acknowledge that Jesus both lifted and filled the cup of salvation through his own sacrifice. And so we pay our vows to the Lord in the presence of all God's people.

What thank offering will I give to the Lord?

Letting God Be God

MAY 9–15, 2011 • CAROL MABRY

MONDAY, MAY 9 ~ *Read Acts 2:42-47*

We find the apostles alive—filled with awe, thanksgiving, and gladness. They can't get over what they've seen and are experiencing, and they aren't self-conscious about their joy.

The scripture says they meet together in the Temple—get this—*daily*! Every day! They eat together, pray and praise together, laugh and love together!

Think about it. How would it be if we, as believers, met together daily to focus on our love and praise of God? Could we do it? Would we do it? Would we keep it up?

We accept other responsibilities as part of our routine, but spending time with God doesn't just happen naturally. It takes determination, focus, and desire. Like deciding to exercise, it takes knowing its value before we start.

Yesterday four of us met for Bible study. We spent about forty-five minutes together. We squeezed it into our busy schedules. At the end of our time, each of us sat back in our chairs and smiled. Barbara said it for us all, "This is just what we needed."

For the apostles, coming together on a daily basis was needed and natural. They didn't think twice about it. Jesus had opened the floodgates of joy for them, and the miracle was too much. They couldn't contain themselves. And so they gathered to eat, to worship, to share, to praise every single day. I can think of no richer lifestyle.

Dear God, push the buttons on our souls so we deeply desire more time with you. Give us a glimpse of the greatness of everyday communing with you. Amen.

Resource Coordinator and Assistant to the Senior Pastor, First United Methodist Church; Enid, Oklahoma

My local church developed its mission statement, which reads as follows: "First Church provides a compass to guide people on their journey of discovering a more abundant life as 3-D Christians." Then it quotes John 10:10: "I came that they may have life, and have it abundantly."

Our members embrace the 3-D Christian concept. They like the idea of discovering a better way of life. But what is this abundant life Jesus promises? What exactly does that phrase mean? Jesus makes this offer to us as well.

Our temptation is to define abundant life in our own terms instead of trying to understand what Jesus meant. Our own views might include some of the claims of our culture: self-help programs that promise a new start, get-rich-quick schemes, or lifestyles of the rich and famous. If you interviewed people on the street and asked them to define abundant life, you would hear an array of answers.

Jesus says, "I am the gate. Whoever enters by me will be saved, and will come in and go out and find pasture." The abundant life Jesus refers to differs greatly from the lifestyle we search for in our society. Jesus suggests a place of security, sustenance, and provision—one that nourishes both soul and body. Notice also the suggestion that we don't find this on our own; it is provided for us as we follow Jesus, who leads us there. We find pasture by entering through him.

We weary ourselves when we try to find abundant life by our own means. The promise of provision comes when we follow Jesus.

Lord, your pathway leads to safety and provision. May I enter through your open gate and find pasture with you. Amen.

The author of First Peter continues laying out the lines of right conduct in the household of God. In this section he addresses Christian slaves, and we understand that because we are "slaves," or servants of God, these instructions apply to all believers. As members of God's household, we submit to authority only for God's sake. It is to our credit to "endure pain while suffering unjustly" out of our awareness of God.

I live in the Bible Belt where believers find acceptance. I don't know when I have ever really suffered for my faith. I recall as a college student being asked to leave the room while others did and said things I would find objectionable.

Perhaps I suffered when my father told me repeatedly that he didn't need to go to church with us children, that he knew the difference between right and wrong, that he was an atheist and didn't want to be pressured about it. More so, though, I suffered when Dad died. He asked that there be no service at all, no planned family get-together. We three children, as adults, never gathered to reminisce or discuss or deal with his death in any fashion whatsoever. There were no notes to write, nothing to plan. Dad's life simply ended.

I was profoundly saddened that such a gifted man never discovered the love of God. I wondered about God's love for my father despite his disbelief. Was Dad warmly received into the heavenly kingdom—did the angels rejoice? did the trumpets sound? In his death, I pray that my father "returned to the shepherd," the "guardian" of his soul.

O Lord, give me the grace and humility to be your servant even when others wish that I weren't. Amen.

Occasionally I teach a class on stress management. Halfway through the session, I ask the participants to close their eyes and envision a place of perfect peace, a place they would like to be. After "relaxing," I gently invite them back. We remain quiet for a moment, then I encourage them to say aloud where they have been. The responses vary: a mountain setting, a sunny beach, a waterfall.

All of us can imagine a perfect paradise, void of life's tensions, filled with feelings and fragrances of ultimate bliss. Our fanciful setting allows unlimited freedom; we shed the weight of life and step into the sunshine. It's liberating and joyful.

Knowing the pain of our deepest, darkest hours, the psalmist points us to God's provisions. We wander with him into the meadow, take a deep breath, and absorb all that's before us. So much beauty invigorates us. We toss aside our inhibitions and take off running across the field, dancing freely. Gradually we still ourselves; we lie down in the clover. It's heavenly.

We see the water and walk to it. Oh, to linger here and let our soul be restored. Then we notice the table, so full, heaped high with all we will ever need. It's too much. We're overwhelmed to the point of hilarity; our fears and foes don't matter.

We are one with God's goodness, freedom, and mercy. We don't want to leave.

Father God, transport me into such joyfulness where you prepare a table for me, even me. Help my stubborn soul open to your overwhelming love, so that I can set aside my fears and step into the warmth and beauty of your tender care. Amen.

It's about time that I purchase a new car. Mine is a 1995 model. It doesn't have all the extras: no keyless remote, no way to heat the seats, only two cupholders. When it rains, I have to remember the driver's window might stick if I lower it.

But my car runs and runs well, in fact. It gets me there and back without trouble. It's a good car and after so many years of its being mine, I'm rather attached to it. I must admit, though, I still get the itch to stop by the car dealership once in a while to take a peek at the latest models.

Even with the poor economy, advertisements bombard us, urging us to buy the newest of the new: cool navigation systems and beautiful leather seats. We find ourselves wishing for and wanting more. We're so used to owning the "newest" that we feel somewhat inferior if our possessions are old.

The new Christians weren't caught in such a cycle. They were joyful regardless of what they owned. They somehow let loose of their belongings and their possessiveness. Notice what they do: they share. "Say, here's my sofa—okay, then what about this dinette set from my place. Let's use Sam's refrigerator. How about Carol's car? It still runs as well as what we'll need."

They stockpile their possessions, selling some to provide for those in need. With all needs met, they are free . . . free to focus on their newfound faith. They rejoice and praise God together. Others can't help but notice. This real joy is mighty contagious.

The new disciples busily delight in the Lord instead of delighting in what they own. Their cups overflow.

What of all you own actually "owns" you? How and where do you find joy in Christ?

This passage makes me feel uncomfortable. Jesus' suffering unjustly is one thing. That I should ever have to do so is another. I can easily agree with the Christian faith in my mind. I can grasp, intellectually, what Jesus did for us. He took on everyone's wrongdoings, and he suffered on our behalf. His abuse was not just verbal but physical. The man died a horrific death, and he did nothing to deserve it.

At first I found this fact hard to fathom, but I got it. I've accepted that Jesus was who he said he was and that he did, indeed, die on my behalf. I remember my sixth-grade Sunday school teacher drumming it home: "Substitute your own name, Carol." So I did. "For God so loved [Carol], that he gave his only begotten Son, that whosoever believeth in him should not perish, but have everlasting life" (KJV). That got my attention.

But living out our faith differs from understanding it. We're not always eager to follow in Jesus' footsteps. Life is difficult and messy at times, and we don't want to act like Jesus. Must we try to live up to that kind of forgiving behavior? On those occasions when we suffer unjustly, can't we retaliate—just a little? Can't we respond with one or two biting words? At least let us turn a cold shoulder. They deserve it.

Yet the scripture says we are to endure any mistreatment as Jesus did. He suffered despite his goodness. He did not return abuse, nor did he threaten. Then it goes on: Jesus entrusted himself to God, the just judge. Even when I feel wounded, I'm supposed to leave it up to God. We, like stray sheep, return to the shepherd and the just judge.

O God, may I accept suffering for your sake. Come into the innermost parts of my being, and transform my soul. Amen.

John Henry Woodberry was quite the man. Larger than life, good-hearted, and good-natured, he lived out his faith quietly. All of my family thought highly of him. A West Point graduate, he ended his military career as Brigadier General. Yet, as a young-ster, I only vaguely knew of his accomplishments. I thought of him simply as "Papa."

Only when I read his autobiographical sketch did I fully learn to appreciate my grandfather. An innovative man, he designed and patented many inventions for the Army. One still hangs in the Air Force Museum. After retirement he kept his creative juices flow-ing by fashioning statues and pieces of furniture out of blocks of wood. Our family learned to treasure Papa's detailed carvings.

Papa was always patient, even when we grandchildren crowded around his carpenter's bench. Once he let us carve our own walking sticks. All seven grandchildren ended up with a cane just like Papa's. We proudly "caned" around the block that evening, our giant of a man, Papa, out in front.

Like the sheep in John's passage, we grandchildren knew who was leading us, and we followed eagerly. Delighted, we gig-gled and skipped along. We knew Papa's voice so well and fol-lowed obediently. When he said, "Let's slow down a bit," we did. If he asked us to keep close together, we did. Our Papa cared for us and would keep us safe as we walked the neighborhood.

You know when someone loves you deeply. You're smitten when he's the finest of the fine. You are proud to walk beside him, yearning to make your time with him last as long as possi-ble. You want to be like him when you "grow up."

Jesus said, "I have come that they may have life, and have it to the full" (NIV). Who are you following?

A Place Prepared for You

MAY 16–22, 2011 • CATHY WARNER

MONDAY, MAY 16 ~ *Read Psalm 31:1-5*

I climbed the log-pole ladder up a cliff, onto a ledge, ducked through an archway, and sat on the grainy floor of the small room, looking down at the crumbling walls, remainders of the village that is now part of Bandalier National Monument in Los Alamos, New Mexico. Centuries ago, our Pueblo ancestors took refuge in the literal rock. Homes hewn into stone mountains brought families relief from summer heat, winter snow, and a clear view of the Rio Grande river valley, where they hunted game, drew their water, and gathered firewood. I rubbed my fingers along a window ledge, tracing the pale worn stone, nearly white, against my skin. I breathed in the calm tepid air, and felt a sense of peace, a relief from the afternoon sun and other tourists. There was a sturdy eternal nature in that cliff dwelling. It would not be flattened by tornado, shaken by earthquake, flooded by overflowing river or hurricane.

Like the psalmist, I long for security, safety, and shelter. I crave a strength and stability that other humans cannot offer. That day I was surrounded by rock, secure inside a house of stone. *This*, I thought, *is what it means to have God as my rock, fortress, and refuge.* I felt protected in powerful presence. As I stooped through the entry and headed back into the August heat, I prayed to take that assurance with me.

Think of a place where you have experienced the rock-solidness of God. Imagine yourself in this place when you need refuge from life's demands.

Master's of Fine Arts in creative writing from Seattle Pacific University; former conference lay minister to Boulder Creek United Methodist Church; Boulder Creek, California

I'm often scooping up my mischievous cat. When he's ready to pounce on a bird or batting a prescription bottle under the bed, I reach around his belly, lift him into the air, and press his back against my chest. Caught off guard, he struggles, legs flailing and neck twisting, until I turn him toward my face. Once he sees that it's me, he relaxes. Then I hug him, tell him how adorable he is, and carry him over my shoulder away from trouble.

How catlike we are when it comes to God. "My times are in your hand," we say, wanting protection from danger; yet when we're scooped up, we often struggle, unsure as to who is holding us and if we're really safe.

If we could just turn around and glimpse God's face—see it shining, beaming at us with love—then we could relax. That's part of the psalmist's prayer, at any rate. The challenge, as Jesus will later tell his disciples, comes in learning to stop struggling, to believe and to trust without seeing.

God might hold us close with our backs pressed tight against the divine bosom and never turn us face-to-face. We might look on the world with all its troubles and never gaze directly on the brilliant light we crave. Instead, we must believe that we are indeed held and look for the love that holds us reflected in everything we encounter.

My times are truly in your hand, Holy One. Help me trust in your steadfast love. Amen.

Strongly held beliefs are challenged, and those in power won't stand for it. Another young man won't keep quiet. Like Jesus, he threatens the established order, the delicate balance that keeps people compliant and God's wrath at bay. Like Jesus, he must be silenced. Like Jesus, he accepts his violent death and offers forgiveness.

This scripture frightens me as I witness the story line played out in our world again and again. And it's not just political and religious officials who create these horrible scenarios. I have been one to clench my fist when my family is threatened. I have wanted to eliminate or shout down or retaliate when I have felt deeply wronged. I have imagined the comforting heft of a stone in my hand and felt its rough texture scraping against my skin. I have seethed with the anger that holds the rock tight, just waiting to be thrown at anyone, anything, ready to cast my stone at the easiest target.

Silencing dissent, attacking those who frighten and push us, is the expedient response; but it entrenches us as defenders. We must stamp out all threats. Trapped in reactive vigilance, we can never examine our lives and motives or admit our need to change. Unless we're willing to drop the stones at our feet, we will never be able to admit our need for God's intervention and presence in our lives. Only when we refuse to hurl a stone can we say like Stephen, "Look! I see the heavens opened and the Son of Man standing at the right hand of God."

How can we remain open to God's word when it challenges our way of life?

My infant daughter was a purist. She pushed away a bottle, spit out formula, drank only mother's milk. Introducing solids, I fed her oatmeal, pureed squash, green beans. I continued to present her with healthy options, and we were both content. Then our world changed at a play group Halloween party. At eighteen months old, she was thrilled to win a Tootsie-pop, carrying the purple-wrapped orb by its stick, until someone told her it was candy and to eat it. The thought intrigued her. When she started school, she usually discarded the carrots I packed with lunch in favor of another child's chips. Choosing junk over nutrition day after day, year after year, she gained weight. Those pounds strained her teenage self-image. She decided to lose them when she grew up and began to cook her own healthy meals.

My daughter's story isn't unique—with food or spirit. We often turn away from real sustenance in favor of quick, attractively packaged empty calories. They taste good, and we think they satisfy us; but they don't really feed us, not well. At times we punish ourselves for our excesses by eating only "good" food that tastes bad, thinking we must suffer for our own good. Rebelling, we return to the junk.

A way out of this spiral involves understanding what we really crave. We find a balance in our eating habits and in our spiritual lives so that we can be truly nourished.

Scripture tells us the pure spiritual milk of God's word is not only nutritious and organic; it tastes good too. When we take, eat, and drink, we will thrive.

Nurturing One, may we taste and see that you are good. Amen.

One town founder, fond of rock walls, built a mile of them through Boulder Creek, rendering it reminiscent of the English countryside. The walls came down as lots were split and the town grew, but one still runs the length of Boulder Street right in front of my church. Rounding the corner from Main Street, it's just a few yards before the wall comes into view. Those stones, mottled with dirt, moss, and age, held in place by gravity and occasional cement, cry out, "This is God's house," as much or more so than our hundred-year-old building. The church, built on land donated by lumberman J. W. Peery is painted white and fashioned of wood and sweat. The pews have held logging men, resort-goers, retirees, baby-boom families, and commuters. The building has burned to the ground and been rebuilt twice. The wall is made of stones hauled from Boulder Creek and stacked by Chinese laborers who built railroads in the 1880s and has withstood the great San Francisco earthquake and the more recent Loma Prieta quake.

Our congregation dates back to Wesleyan class meetings 140 years ago, our name changing with each Methodist reconfiguration. This is our history but not our foundation. God is our true founder and architect. Scripture provides our blueprint and faith the nails that join us together. We stand on the corner of Boulder and Mountain Streets. More importantly, we stand on the Cornerstone—the Living Stone—Jesus Christ.

O Cornerstone, help us stand on the living stone and, in so doing, become steppingstones for others into your home. Amen.

I met a family at church who had relocated from New Jersey to California. The husband traveled out West before his wife, teenage daughter, and preschooler. He bought a three-bedroom house, enrolled Jennifer in high school, flew back East, and brought his family to their new home. He had gone ahead and prepared a place for them.

How different this was from my experience moving as a youth. My parents hadn't registered me for school, so I was sent "home" when I showed up the first day. I didn't have a home; it was still being built, and my parents were five hundred miles away packing up our old house. I'd been given a mattress on the floor of a spare room, surrounded by packing boxes, in the house of strangers who worked with my stepfather where I lived until my parents could join me. No place had been prepared for me.

Perhaps if I had known Jesus or even known *about* him, I would not have felt so alone in my transition to high school. We all long to hear the tender words of comfort, reassurance, of belonging, being loved and cared for that Jesus offers. He prepares a place for us and welcomes us with open arms. Wherever he goes, there will be room for us; wherever we journey, he will accompany us. It's hard to understand or embrace this unconditional welcome, especially for the disciples as the blood-and-bone Jesus they know prepares for death. Thomas asks how he can find the place Jesus is going, so that he can bridge the separation. I am the way, the path of life, Jesus answers. Following the path of and to Jesus requires that we examine our lives, inside and out. Choosing the way, we make room for him to dwell within us, inviting the Spirit to take up residence in our lives, so that we ourselves might become one of the many rooms in God's house.

How have you prepared a dwelling place for Jesus in your life?

In calculus, I frustrated my teacher continually with questions about derivatives, the illusive end to all our equations: $f'(x)=$ __. "But what is a derivative?" I would ask. "If I just knew what it was, I could find the answer." "You don't have to understand derivatives. It doesn't matter what it is. Everything you need to know is in the equation, just solve it," he told me. I lasted two weeks in the class. I never did find the $f'(x)$.

Poor Jesus, his disciples are as challenged as I was. "Show us God," they say, "and then we'll be satisfied." They just don't get it, despite the metaphors, parables, and careful explanations. "Haven't you been paying attention?" Jesus responds. "Everything I am and say and do comes through God who lives in me and works through me" (AP). Still, they scratch their heads. And when he tells them, "If you believe, then you will do even greater works than you have seen from me," they stare uncomprehending. Jesus finally says, "You don't have to believe me, or understand. Look at my works. Everything you need to know is in them" (AP).

Jesus' students have discovered with their own eyes and ears what they need to know. They have watched Jesus act out God's claim on his life in speaking truth, healing the sick, offering compassion, engaging in prayer, discerning in solitude, and living in community. Let this be the proof, the answer to the equation, the divine $f'(x)$ that at first encounter seems unattainable. Jesus assures his dear friends and followers that they have been given a formula, one to adopt and use in their own lives after he is gone. As Christ's followers throughout history, we strive to repeat that formula, patterning compassion, justice, faith, hope, and love in endless permutations that point toward God.

Thank you, Divine One, for allowing us to glimpse your true nature by your works. Amen.

Presence

MAY 23–29, 2011 • MATTHEW W. CHARLTON

MONDAY, MAY 23 ~ *Read Acts 17:22-25*

God has made Godself known. Paul, speaking to a group of philosophers for whom matters of religion may be irrelevant, acknowledges in a backhanded fashion an interest in God. He states that the god the Athenians worship as unknown is indeed "the God who made the world and everything in it, he who is Lord of heaven and earth." So this God is creator, independent of need for human support but evidencing a desire to be in relationship as parent to child.

Despite Paul's testimony, in many ways we continue to believe in an unknown God who is shrouded in mystery and whose designs are made of even more mysterious stuff. To the contrary, God is knowable and present, and we can know God's plans and God's ways. As Christians, we acknowledge that the incarnation of Jesus makes known God's fullness, and Jesus' teachings make known God's plans. God's ways are made known in the resurrection of Jesus. God shrugs off veils of mystery through our knowledge of the person of Jesus Christ.

This does not mean that we always avail ourselves of God's presence and of the knowledge of God. At times we may feel abandoned by God. Yet this God is known in ways laid out before our gaze on the cross of Christ. We come to know this ever-present, overflowing-with-love God in our own pilgrimage of discipleship, drawing ever nearer to the God of all creation.

Ever-present God, help me to know your ways more fully by giving me the grace to follow Jesus Christ. Amen.

Ordained elder in the United Methodist Church, serving in the Tennessee Annual Conference

TUESDAY, MAY 24 ~ *Read 1 Peter 3:18-22*

Christ is present with us. We would be mistaken if we read this text to mean that Christ left this world behind after having suffered for the sake of the unrighteous (and that includes all of us). While the text indicates that Jesus Christ is in heaven at the right hand of God, the author wants us to understand that Christ is present now. Having brought us to God, Christ now reigns at God's right hand, which is a metaphor of presence and of God's ongoing creative and restorative power.

Many biblical texts indicate that the position of God's right hand is the hand of strength (Ps. 45:4) and of blessing (Matt. 25:33). Other psalms speak of God's right hand as being supportive (Ps. 18:35) and upholding (Ps. 63:8). To believe that Christ sits at the right hand of God is to believe that God remains interested and present in what God has made. Christ at the right hand of God supports the downtrodden, upholds the weak, pursues justice for the "crucified people" of the world, and seeks righteousness in the midst of our desires for decadence rather than holiness.

God's right hand has the power to free us from all that seeks to overwhelm us. The condition of our modern world is one of "multiple overwhelmings." Every day, any number of seemingly important things clamor for our attention. Awareness of Christ's presence may seem difficult when the words of faith are so easily overwhelmed by the noise of modern life. In the midst of all that seeks to interfere in your life, remember that Christ is present, supporting you, upholding you, and seeking to give you a "good conscience" so that you might live in this world as a person of deep faith.

Lord Jesus Christ, help me to know your presence in every moment. Amen.

Faith Ringgold has written a children's book titled *Bonjour, Lonnie*, which tells the story of a mixed-race orphan named Lonnie who is reconnected with his parents, grandparents, and caregivers through the magical tricks of the Love Bird (who speaks largely in French, by the way). Lonnie finds comfort and peace as he learns about his family of origin and becomes part of a new family that loves him, even as he learns about the racism and hatred that his parents and grandparents endured. The story of the Love Bird is one of advocacy, of watching over in love the ones a busy and chaotic world can easily reject and leave behind.

In today's passage, Jesus addresses the twelve before his departure. The disciples know and love him, and the reality and extension of this love through the Advocate will keep them from being orphaned. The Advocate does not come as a reward for good behavior but as the gift of God's grace.

Through the Advocate, whom Jesus sends in his name, we also experience God's presence in the special capacity of loving caretaker of our lives and souls. Jesus sends the Holy Spirit to be present in the midst of real life so that no one is orphaned or left behind in a busy and chaotic world.

How many of us live with fears and disconnections of various kinds? How many are truly orphans in this world? How many live in this world finding joy in every day?

The Holy Spirit's presence as Advocate invites us into a life with God. The Holy Spirit abides with us in good times and bad, offering the affirmation of God's love and guidance.

Holy Spirit, whenever I feel alone and spiritually desolate, support me and guide me with the love of Jesus, a divine love-gift for all God's children. Amen.

THURSDAY, MAY 26 ~ *Read Psalm 66:8-20; 1 Peter 3:16b-17*

These two texts address a common question: why do faithful people suffer? The psalmist writes out of an ancient cosmology where God is purposefully engaged in the world, if not the direct cause of all events. So God is to be praised because the sufferings of life are tests and trials brought on by God. God ultimately will bring the faithful out of suffering into "a spacious place."

For the author of First Peter, suffering can be, but is not always, God's will: "It is better to suffer for doing good, if suffering should be God's will, than to suffer for doing evil." For the author of First Peter, suffering for the good may be God's will (much like Christ suffered for the good of all), whereas suffering for doing evil is attributable to the evildoer alone. A faithful person may suffer for doing good either as a result of evil in the world or as a result of divine discipline. It is therefore always better to seek to do good than to engage purposefully in evil, because with the evil one we will definitely suffer, but by pursuing the good we may or may not suffer. Indeed, suffering for the good is positive discipline for the soul.

These words offer shallow comfort to those who actually suffer *now*. It is infelicitous to say to those who suffer that they simply bear with it now because it might get better later—and that this suffering is good for the soul! Baloney, I say. Let us recognize that our common human condition resonates between comfort and pain. A strong faith helps us deal appropriately with both and faces its strongest testing in times of trial. Let us recognize that a strong faith conditions our response to the realities of human life, marked as it is with joy and hope as well as pain and anguish.

God, strengthen my faith, so that I may face times of testing in good stead. Amen.

FRIDAY, MAY 27 ~ *Read 1 Peter 3:13-22*

The theologian Jürgen Moltmann is known for his theology of hope. "The Christian hope is directed . . . towards a new creation of all things by the God of the resurrection of Jesus Christ" (*Theology of Hope*, page 33). We may direct our hope toward this new creation, but we also hope in the present, thereby nurturing goodness. This is no small thing, to nurture goodness in a world seemingly gripped by continual fear. Multiple channels of twenty-four-hour news feed us the same bad news over and over. We can easily become convinced that nothing good is going on.

So how do those whose hearts "sanctify Christ as Lord" live outside of fear and the fear of suffering? How do we daily testify to God's goodness and to the beauty of God's creation?

The scripture says that we are to mount a defense of "the hope that is in you" doing so with "gentleness and reverence." Christianity seems to operate best when it is in a defensive posture; that is, we live in the spirit of the apology: that gentle and reverent explanation of the good that orders our lives and of the hope that is within us. The resurrection of Jesus Christ and God's promise of the new creation are excellent places to begin our defense against fear with God's counternarrative of hope.

I met a man once who declared, "I can't wait for summertime! I just love summer because I get to eat my weight in fresh tomatoes and watermelons." This is precisely what it means to live a life of hope: to live in the present with a joy that looks forward to the amazing things God is doing.

God of hope, help me testify to your goodness. Show me a reason to hope in the presence of fear. Guide me daily in the ways of your new creation. Amen.

SATURDAY, MAY 28 ~ *Read Acts 17:26-31*

This week's theme of "Presence" has focused on God's presence as a God who is known rather than unknown; who is present in Christ for our sake; and who is present as the Advocate, the Holy Spirit. We are present to others who need the experience of goodness and hope. Today's text suggests how we are present with God. Paul writes, "'In him we live and move and have our being.'" For Paul, this is a familial presence: we are God's children. We have being because God has given us existence, and we never stray far from that connection—if we are capable of straying at all. We honor this connection with God by seeking a penitential and spiritual life.

"How is it with your spirit?" This question evokes a response about how we live in the presence of the One in whom we "live and move and have our being." Do we seek the presence of God daily? How do we honor God with our work and vocation? How do our lives testify to the good news of Jesus Christ? I can honestly answer these questions more clearly on some days than others.

The good news is that we are being made perfect in love. Through the power of God in Jesus Christ, each of us is empowered to live in the presence of God, to praise the Creator through our work and vocation, and in every moment testify to the good news of Jesus Christ. Some people call this discipleship. Following Jesus means we learn to live fully in God's presence, the God who gives us life and does so in the midst of all that life throws at us.

How is it with your spirit?

I intentionally keep my study small. When I sit at my desk (which is an old pub table I found in my grandmother's attic), bookshelves surround me on three sides. When I work, I can feel the closeness of the ideas bound up in those books. I can reach out and open up Walter Brueggemann's *The Word Militant* or Rosemary Radford Reuther's powerful *Sexism and God-Talk.* Hovering over me, near the ceiling, are the works of John Wesley, Martin Luther, John Calvin's *Institutes*, Thomas Aquinas's *Summa Theologica*, bunches of Saint Augustine, multiple volumes of early church saints, and the books of scripture in various translations.

I have surrounded myself with books so that when I go into my study, my thoughts are quickly drawn to the scripture and its interpretation. This is what I believe theology is, after all—the interpretation of scripture. In this sense, every time we sit down to read the Bible, we are engaging in theology.

Jesus invites us to keep his commandments. Those who keep his commandments are those who love him; those who love Jesus are loved by God; and God will be "revealed" to them in Jesus, who will love the lovers. A rather oblique text, to be sure, but I think in a way this is what all of the thinkers on my bookshelves are after: keeping the commandment of love so that they might experience the revelation of God's love.

In doing theology we attempt to unravel and understand all the ways we love and do not love God, hopefully to the end of opening ourselves more fully to Jesus. That openness affords the healing by the One revealed to us in love. Whether you surround yourself with books, with symbols of the church, or with the beauty of God's creation, "read" those things as interpreting the scriptures and seek in them the love of God's presence.

On this day, God of love, I seek to praise you and give you thanks for the gift of love, Jesus Christ. Amen.

Never Alone

MAY 30–JUNE 5, 2011 • KIMBERLEE CONWAY IRETON

MONDAY, MAY 30 ~ *Read Psalm 68:1-10*

Psalm 68 speaks of God's presence in all of life. God rises to scatter enemies, and the righteous rejoice before him. God rides through the desert and marches through the wilderness to lead God's people to a fertile place of abundance. God protects the widow, acts as father to the fatherless, and creates community for those who live alone. God pours out rain on the parched land and provides for the needy. God, this psalm declares, is not distant, unmoved by human pain and need. God is with us. God goes before us and walks beside us. God provides for us out of love.

Sometimes, though, we find it hard to see God's provision. Sometimes, our circumstances overwhelm us, and we wonder where God is. In such times, I lean hard on faith and gratitude. I count daily graces, even if they seem silly or primitive. Thank-you, God, for air to breathe, for a heart that beats, for fingers able to type. Thank you for your presence with me right now.

I do not always feel God's presence, especially when life is hard; but this psalm and countless other Bible passages promise that God is with us, and I cling tightly to those promises. I rely on faith that I don't feel to keep my heart grateful, my eyes open to any way that God may reveal the divine. And amazingly enough, the more I look, the more I see; the words of gratitude slowly become less an act of the will, a sacrifice of praise, and more an act of the heart, an outpouring of heartfelt worship.

Loving God, in Jesus you promise never to leave us or forsake us. You promise to restore and redeem us. You promise to be with us always. Help us to believe your promises. Amen.

An elder, worship leader, and lay preacher at Bethany Presbyterian Church (PCUSA); Seattle, Washington

The past few days, my own small demons—self-pity, anxiety, fear—have loomed large in my heart and mind. Their fierceness has taken me by surprise. I confess I'd let myself think I'd finally gotten the better of them as days and even weeks had gone by without their fretting me too hard. But we are fragile creatures and slip so easily from okay to not okay; and when the voices of our demons whisper and shout in the ears of our hearts, the darkness can be very dark indeed.

These past few days, I have had to fight hard to keep my eyes on the Light. Having enjoyed a period of relative calm and contentment not so many days ago, this sudden return to a place of battle, of weary fighting against the fear, the self-pity, the anxiety, has taken me aback.

The author of this epistle tells us that we need not be taken by surprise. "Beloved," he says. (I love that word, *beloved*, because it takes us straight back to our fundamental identity: I am one who is loved; you are one who is loved.) "Beloved, do not be surprised at the ordeal that is taking place among you to test you, as though something strange were happening to you. But rejoice insofar as you are sharing Christ's sufferings."

I have not yet learned to rejoice on those days when the battle against my personal demons rages fiercely, but I have learned to count the graces God pours out and to be grateful that I do not fight alone. Always, Christ shares the battle—and he will always win.

Jesus, on those days when the darkness encroaches too close and we must fight to see the Light, you are with us, fighting beside us, fighting for us, giving us grace sufficient unto the day. Help us to be faithful, not to surrender to the darkness, and to seek your Light, however dim it appears in our dark-struck eyes. Amen.

When my son was a baby and wanted to nurse in the middle of the night, I sat in the rocking chair in his darkened room and stared out the window at the greenbelt across the street. Mostly it was too dark to see much more than the outline of the trees. Night after night I sat in the dark room, nursing Jack and staring out into the darkness.

I felt so alone.

Then, one night, I realized that somewhere out there beyond the greenbelt other mothers would be sitting up alone, nursing their children. I thought of my friend on the other side of the country whose son was only one day older than mine. Perhaps she was up too. I began to think of all the women I knew who had nursing babies and all the women around the world whom I didn't know but who were part of this community of nursing mothers. I began to pray for these women—some by name, others nameless—and slowly, I began to feel less alone. Yes, I still sat in my rocking chair in the dark by myself. But out there, other women sat too, and, though we were apart, we were not alone.

In his letter to a persecuted church, the author of First Peter reminds his readers that "your brothers and sisters in all the world are undergoing the same kinds of suffering." Remembering others who may be experiencing the same difficulties we ourselves are experiencing reminds us that we are not alone. We are part of the body of Christ, and we are children of the God who is always with us, the God who cares for, restores, strengthens, and establishes us.

Loving God, when we feel alone in our pain, remind us that you are with us, holding us. Remind us that others feel alone too, and strengthen us to pray for them, that they also may know you hold them in your arms of love. Amen.

THURSDAY, JUNE 2 ~ *Read Acts 1:6-14*

ASCENSION DAY

Today is Ascension Day, the day we recall Jesus' return to the Father after his resurrection. On the day of the ascension, Jesus' friends and disciples journey with him to Mount Olivet. There he leaves them as he is lifted into the clouds and out of their sight. But, though Jesus has returned to heaven, his disciples are not left alone. Even before the coming of the Holy Spirit on Pentecost, they are not alone: they have one another.

There on the mountain as they stand staring into the sky, they have one another.

When they return to Jerusalem and gather in the upper room and with one accord devote themselves to prayer, they have one another.

In the days of waiting for the promised Comforter, they have one another.

How much more, then, do we, who live after the outpouring of the Holy Spirit, have one another? We are the body of Christ, filled with the very Spirit of God. We are to minister to one another and to the world as such. We are to bear one another up through prayer and exhortation, through physical acts of service—a gentle touch, the gift of a meal, a ride to the doctor or the airport. As members of Christ's body, we have one another. We bear Christ to one another. We love, live, and serve in Jesus' name as Jesus' physical body in the world.

Jesus is lifted from our sight, it is true. But we see him every day in one another. We mirror him every day to one another. He is with us still.

Jesus, may I live this day aware of you in me, your Spirit indwelling me. May I seek to see you in, and reveal you to, each person I meet this day. Amen.

FRIDAY, JUNE 3 ~ *Read Psalm 68:32-35*

As I write these words, my house is in the chaos of a "small" remodel; my body is ill from an unexpected pregnancy; and my children are shrieking in their room, even though it's a half hour past their bedtime. My back aches, so as soon as the kids are ensconced in their beds, I heat water on the stove. As I pour the steaming water into my pink hot water bottle, words of praise and thanksgiving spontaneously spring to my lips: "Thank you, God, for your love for me. Thank you for my life."

These words surprise me. I am not feeling particularly grateful for anything at that exact moment. I am, in fact, feeling rather grumbly about my messy house, my upset stomach, my rambunctious children. And yet, those words come. I smile in surprise and think, *Yes, I do have a good life.* I am grateful that these words have come, as it were, out of nowhere, to bless me and remind me of the goodness and grace that surround and fill me.

Sometimes, I can pray the words of Psalm 68 gladly—"Sing to God, O kingdoms of the earth; sing praises to the Lord"—with joy in my voice and my heart. Other times, I must pray such words as an act of the will, an act of obedience to God.

And then there are moments like tonight, when those acts of obedience catch up with me, and I find I am praising God from a place that is deeper than mere emotion, from a heart that is not controlled by circumstance. In those moments, I know I have listened to the voice of God and heard it and been transformed by it. And I rejoice.

God of power and might, you speak your word, and it does not return to you void. May we hear that word. May it sink deeply into our lives. May it transform us into the people you created us to be. Amen.

*G*lory. It's not a word I think about a lot. But Jesus uses it (or its verb form *glorify*) five times in these five verses, which makes me pause and ponder. *Glory.*

Glory is beyond us, beyond our senses, beyond our comprehension. Even the keenest, clearest human eyes are dim, and we can only behold so much glory. We do not understand it, and it frightens us. This is why every angel, every messenger of the Most High, had to say, "Do not be afraid." This is why Jesus came in the flesh. He cloaked his eternal glory that we might know him without fear; and, in knowing him, know God.

Still, Jesus' glory leaked through his fleshly frame. How could it not? He was very God of very God. All that he said and did whispered God's name, accomplished God's purposes, heightened God's glory.

And now, just before his final accomplishment, Jesus voices his longing to return to the Father: "Glorify me in your own presence with the glory that I had in your presence before the world existed." The Father will answer yes to this prayer, but it will be many weeks before Jesus experiences the glory he knew from before time—and he will first endure the cross and the grave.

I wonder if our lives follow a similar pattern. We long to experience the glory of God. We long to manifest that glory. But we must first pick up our daily cross (a cross Jesus bears with us) and walk under it, one foot in front of the other, until darkness falls at the end of the day, the end of our lives. Then we will know God and finally see the Holy One in divine glory.

Lord Jesus, you know what it is like to long for the Father's presence, to seek the Father's will, to yearn for the Father's glory. May we be faithful as you were, following in your steps. Amen.

SUNDAY, JUNE 5 ~ *Read John 17:6-11*

Even in the closest of my relationships—with my husband, my children, my sister, and dearest friends—I do not know all there is to know; even here there are surprises, some delightful, some not. The human soul is too deep for us to know ourselves fully, let alone to know another.

And yet Jesus prays that we, his followers, may be one as he and the Father are one. It is more than I can imagine, but it is what I want, this union with another who knows me intimately and loves me in spite of myself. It is what I sought in romantic love, what I hope for in marriage and friendship and childrearing. But I only catch glimpses of it in moments of shared laughter over a meal, of understanding and empathy, of beauty made more beautiful because it is shared, moments of union that I wish would never end but always do.

It will not always be so. The time is coming when Jesus' prayer will be answered, and we will be one with each other and with God as Jesus and the Father are one.

Like an hors d'oeuvre at an elegant meal, these moments of intimacy, of union, that we experience now whet our appetites, letting us taste the smallest bite and promising us, there is more where this came from—and the more is even better than what you just tasted!

Jesus is Emmanuel, God-with-us, and that is wonderful beyond words; but us-with-God, as Jesus prays in this passage, will be thousands upon thousands of times richer! Now we see in a glass darkly, but then we shall see face-to-face. Now we taste union, but then we will soak in it—and we will soak it in. It will envelop us and fill us and we will be satisfied, sated, so full that our cup runs over.

Jesus, may we taste each day the goodness and grace of intimacy with others and with you, and may those tastes awaken our appetite for your coming kingdom. Amen.

Breathing Out . . . Breathing In

JUNE 6–12, 2011 • NED HILL

MONDAY, JUNE 6 ~ *Read Psalm 104:24-34, 35b*

Life is far more than breathing in and out. Yet there is no life apart from it. Breathing, a constant in our life that we rarely think about, is essential to our earthly existence.

More than forty years ago, when I was taking a water safety course in preparation for a summer job as a lifeguard at a local swimming pool, I received instruction in mouth-to-mouth resuscitation. Should the day ever come when I had to pull someone from the pool, I needed to be prepared to breathe back into them the breath of life. I would only be giving back what the psalmist clearly understood as the breath that had been first given by God.

The psalm hints at the creation story in Genesis 2:7: "Then the LORD God formed man from the dust of the ground, and breathed into his nostrils the breath of life; and the man became a living being." God is clearly understood as the one who creates physical life and the one upon whom all life depends for its sustenance.

As we prepare to celebrate the coming of the Holy Spirit on the Day of Pentecost, we recall that the words *spirit* and *breath* are both translations of the same Hebrew word *ruach*. God not only breathes physical life into us but is the source of life's entirety. As the psalmist rejoices in God the creator, we join our voices in praise and thanksgiving to God who bestows far more than the flesh and blood of life. We rejoice and give praise to God in whom we live and move and have our being.

Divine Breath, fill me with life that I may breathe out songs of praise and glory to you in all that I say and do. Amen.

Senior minister, Edenton Street United Methodist Church; Raleigh, North Carolina

TUESDAY, JUNE 7 ~ *Read John 7:37-39*

The Jews had long expected the coming of the Messiah. Yet when Jesus comes he is, for many, the unexpected Messiah. That observation reflects less on God's timing than on the kind of Messiah Jesus proves to be. His humble birth, his life among the poor and dispossessed, his violent death and resurrection—all were "unexpected." Even among his followers, as he nears his death, there is confusion as to his identity. Jesus continued to say the "unexpected," giving rise to frequent misunderstandings. The verses that frame today's reading give ample evidence of the uncertainty among those who hear him. Jesus says, "I will be with you a little while longer, and then I am going to him who sent me. . . . You will not find me" (vv. 33-34).

As the drumbeat of Jesus' approaching death grows louder, he makes a promise. There is more to come; even after his death and resurrection, the story will go on. Not even his ascension into heaven will signify the end. The story will continue in his followers' lives.

Jesus, who came in an unexpected way, lived an unanticipated life, died as a common criminal, and was raised from the dead, tells his believers to expect more: "It will happen as I tell you that it will."

Jesus calls to those who thirst for more, offering refreshment to all believers. By the power of the Holy Spirit they themselves will become rivers of living water. That is what believers were to expect; that is what *we* are to expect!

Promised Spirit, come upon us and among us. Come as the expected One! Amen.

WEDNESDAY, JUNE 8 ~ *Read Acts 2:1-6*

What sounds like the rush of a violent wind and looks like tongues of fire resting on those who awaited the fulfillment of Jesus' promised Spirit is just the beginning! Every bit as miraculous as the sights and sounds of the Spirit's coming is the fruit of its coming. Suddenly, these Galileans, known for their lack of linguistic abilities, can speak in other languages. Filled with the Spirit they have such inexplicable power and authority that some attribute their words to drunkenness.

People who have come to Jerusalem with their own words and phrases hear what is being told them in their own language. It is not enough to say that the Galileans could suddenly find the right words and put them in the right order at the right time among the right people. The Galileans are able to speak as the Spirit gives them ability. Their words are the work of the Spirit.

As a preacher I am often surprised by what people hear in a sermon. They occasionally receive a blessing beyond anything I intended and remember sermons far longer than I would imagine. The words I speak are so ordinary, words spoken by someone well aware of his limitations and inadequacies. However, somewhere between my lips and the listeners' ears something happens. The mystery of the Holy Spirit breathes a transforming power into a string of ordinary words.

This doesn't happen only in the pulpit. Anyone who has stood at a graveside or at a hospital bed and wondered what to say knows this. Our words need not be profound or original. When words fall from the lips of one upon whom a tongue of fire has gently rested, the words breathe power and authority beyond our wildest imaginations.

Give thanks to the Spirit for giving power and authority to your words.

THURSDAY, JUNE 9 ~ *Read Acts 2:7-13*

I find it easier to tune out what is being said when I don't understand the language. It is far easier to read a book in Rome's airport than in New York or Chicago. I am amazed at how quickly I recognize my native language when I suddenly hear someone speaking English in Angola. After several days in the land of a foreign tongue, I cannot help but be drawn to words that I understand.

It is hardly surprising that "foreigners" in Jerusalem were amazed and perplexed when they heard in their native language about God's deeds of power. That same news is as likely to be spoken today on the streets of our cities as it was on the Day of Pentecost. The message may come in word or in deed. It is as likely to be proclaimed in ordinary conversation as it is in a sermon. It may even come in silence.

Each of us hears what God has to say to us in a unique way. You may hear it in the hymns of Charles Wesley and I in the music of a Christian rock band. You may hear about God's deeds of power around a table as you study the scripture with fellow Christians, and I may hear it in the silence of a retreat or as I serve hot chocolate to the homeless. Each of us hears in our unique God-given way.

That people heard the same message but in different languages was perplexing to those who had gathered in Jerusalem from places near and far. It is still perplexing today. But it is how the word came to people on the Day of Pentecost, and it still comes to us that way.

Lord, teach me to cherish the ways that you have chosen to speak to me and to respect the ways that others hear you. Amen.

FRIDAY, JUNE 10 ~ *Read Acts 2:14-21*

Peter has the unenviable task of trying to explain what had taken place on the Day of Pentecost. The devout Jews who have gathered in Jerusalem from every nation are amazed and perplexed by what they have seen and heard. Perhaps in exasperation or simply to discredit the disciples of Jesus, they suggest drunkenness as the answer. How else do you explain the multitude of languages being spoken by the Galilean followers of Jesus?

Peter wants all who hear him to know that the Spirit, when poured out upon the people, makes prophets of sons and daughters, visionaries of young men and women, and dreamers of the elderly. Prophets, visionaries, and dreamers comprise an odd lot. They are the ones who seem out of step because they are one step ahead of the rest of us.

Jesus had lived, died and been raised from the dead. He had now ascended into heaven. No longer is he a physical presence on earth. Who will carry on? How will they carry on?

Ordinary men and women will become the transforming presence of Christ. The outpouring of the Holy Spirit will empower and equip those Galileans for the missionary effort that will change the world as they become the prophets, visionaries, and dreamers.

Even today, people filled with the Spirit often look odd. The people who love their enemies, turn the other cheek, and walk the second mile will seem strange to the rest of the world. However, we know the truth about such people. They are not drunk; they are just one step ahead of the crowd, and they are marching toward the kingdom.

Come, Holy Spirit; save us from the fear of looking odd. Amen.

SATURDAY, JUNE 11 ~ *Read 1 Corinthians 12:3b-11*

Internet shopping and catalogues are fine for some purchases. However, sometimes I want to see the item and feel it in my hand before I buy it. I want to see what it really looks like.

Since early childhood I have wanted to know what God looks like. I have happily dismissed some of my early images of God as an old white man. But giving up that image has not lessened my desire to see God as God really is.

To see what God looks like I have to go no further than the church. By church, I do not necessarily mean a building. For example, I saw what God looks like one Saturday morning when four hundred people worshiped together and then went out into the community to serve others. Using the diversity of gifts given by the Spirit, empowered by the Spirit, and intended to prosper the whole, these people showed our community what God looks like.

Those who chose to serve others that Saturday morning were young and old, skilled and unskilled—but all gifted by the Spirit. The gifts were very different, with no single gift being more valued than another. As Paul notes in First Corinthians, all have been given gifts; not one person has been left out. The gifts are given not based on worthiness but as a gift of God's grace.

The church, people like you and me, manifest the Spirit for the common good. We are the means by which the world comes to know what God looks like.

What is it that I can do only because the Spirit has uniquely gifted and empowered me to do it?

SUNDAY, JUNE 12 ～ *Read 1 Corinthians 12:12-13*

PENTECOST

The diversity of people who gather in Jerusalem on the Day of Pentecost seems staggering. Acts 2:5 states that devout Jews from every nation under heaven come to Jerusalem. Therefore, the church has exhibited great diversity from the day of its creation when the power of the Holy Spirit brought it into being.

Paul will affirm the diversity as well as the interdependence of the church members. But he will do this only after his listeners understand that the church, like a human body, is one with many members. The body draws strength from the diversity of its members.

Time and time again, I find that in our desire for oneness in the church, we mistakenly believe that we must all be alike. We have a hard time with people who have "other" gifts, "other" understandings of the scripture, and "other" ideas about what it means to follow Christ. We tend to think that we will become one when the others become like us.

As I reflect on my faith journey, I realize that I have learned valuable lessons about following Jesus from people who see things differently from me. I have learned from them what I could not have learned from those who always nod in agreement. Only by the power of the Holy Spirit does the church, with all of its diversity of worship styles, differences in theology and doctrine, and multicultural influences, remain one body.

We do not simply tolerate our diversity; we affirm and value it for what it gives to the one body, the church. On this Day of Pentecost let us thank God that we are not all alike. Let us give thanks that we, by the power of the Holy Spirit, are one with God and one another.

Breathe on us, Holy Spirit, that in our diversity we will find strength, not strife. Amen.

Evening and Morning

JUNE 13–19, 2011 • L. JOSEPH ROSAS III

MONDAY, JUNE 13 ~ *Read Genesis 1:1-31*

The writers of scripture do not attempt to prove God's existence. The Hebrew Bible opens with the simple claim: "In the beginning God. . . ." God is. God moves. God speaks. God acts. The Creation account unfolds in scenes of order and sequence identified in six days. The refrain "evening and morning" tells us that God is at work even when God's work cannot be seen or understood. During each day of creative activity, God speaks the cosmos into existence. The seventh day has no beginning or ending, which reminds us that Genesis provides a much grander account than mere chronological history.

This account saves the greatest revelation about God for the last creative act: "Let us make humankind in our image." We can read this "us" as a plurality of majesty; the creator God is above all other would-be gods. It does proclaim that the image of God is relational. When God creates, both male and female are required for a manifestation of God's image. This is not a deity of philosophical speculation: a first cause, prime mover, or divine law giver. The God of revelation is first and foremost a God in relationship to the whole of creation.

When we realize that God is love, we affirm both the relationship within God known as Trinity and the essential relational nature of God to us and ours to God and with one another. Only after relationship is possible does the divine benediction on all creation come: "it [is] very good." And indeed in communion with God and one another, it is.

Creating God, may we rejoice in being your children, reflecting your image in the world around us this day and week. Amen.

Author, teacher, and Southern Baptist pastor; Nashville, Tennessee

TUESDAY, JUNE 14 ~ *Read Genesis 2:1-4a*

The verb translated "create" is used only of divine activity: something only God does. Only God pronounces benediction upon life; it is good. Only God can come in human form. Only God can die and rise from the dead. Only God can be *with* and *in* us while also remaining ever present throughout the cosmos.

This uniquely creative being takes time to rest and enjoy creation. But most of us lead lives of quiet desperation. Even as we sing the praises of "Amazing Grace," we live and work for the kingdom of God's success and survival in the world as if that success depends upon us and our efforts.

God has created, called, and gifted each of us as an expression of divine character and love. But our service to God grows out of relationship with God. Sabbath reminds us that all things are not held together by us or through our efforts. Sabbath reminds us that God is our first priority. Sabbath reminds us that we are created for God and, as God's children, for relationship with one another. Sabbath is learning to say no. Sabbath is taking time away. Sabbath is seeing that all God's work is very good.

Our very busyness keeps us from the holy task of being still and remembering that God alone is God. Our Lord invested daily time in solitude and communion with God. We can do no better than to follow Jesus' example.

Take times of sabbath at the beginning, during, and at the end of each day in ways appropriate to your life. Observe at least one day of sabbath every week. It may have to be one other than the time you spend in the all-consuming activities of the church. Allow the Spirit, through the discipline and yoke of obedience, to give you rest.

O Lord, may we allow you to teach us to order our days so that we always have time for rest with and in you. Amen.

Apopular worship clip features a model in which everything the church does centers around the schedules, felt needs, tastes, and temperaments of would-be worshipers. Everything from an oil change to Super Bowl tickets are promised to those who come to be embraced by the church where "it's all about you."

By contrast, the psalmist celebrates the majesty of God's name. In the ancient world a name revealed something about that person's essential identity or nature. God displays power in creation. As the heavens seem so limitless to the naked eye, God's power inspires awe. So what is humankind that God takes interest in us? That's the question the psalmist raises. Why does God care for us? These questions affirm that God does indeed take interest in and care for us. Out of God's majesty and the greatness of God's grace and power humankind is created.

We are endowed with a spiritual identity that allows us to reflect the image of God because God is in perpetual relationship within the Godhead as Trinity. We are invited to be part of this divine dance of relationship.

Enemies of our spirits will ultimately be overcome. Division, violence, and death will be no more. We will join the chorus of that never-ending song giving thanks to the Lord because of God's righteousness. We are emboldened to praise the Lord, the Most High.

The praise and telling are all about God; but in the paradox of grace, the telling engages all of us. Ultimately "his" story (God's love in the man Christ Jesus) becomes our story as we are woven together in the divine tapestry of love.

O God, I stand in awe of the glories of your creation and the reminder that we share in your divine majesty and love through Christ. Amen.

THURSDAY, JUNE 16 ~ *Read 2 Corinthians 13:11-13*

The church did not agree on a formal theological statement of the doctrine of the Trinity until the fourth century at the Council of Nicaea. But the earliest Christians of Jewish background first bore witness to evidence of the Holy Trinity in the entire canon of scripture.

At the dawn of creation the Spirit of God broods over the abyss. God's breathing into humankind the breath of life constitutes the emergence of personhood and personality. The Hebrew scriptures are chock full of references to the Spirit of the Lord. The birth narratives of Matthew and Luke depict the Spirit of God as the active agent in the conception of the Christ Child.

Jesus' baptism has definite trinitarian witness with the Spirit of God appearing in the form of a dove and God's pronouncement: "This is my beloved son in whom I am well pleased." In the Great Commission, Jesus calls for baptism in the name of the Father, Son, and Holy Spirit; one of the most straightforward declarations of the concept of God as Trinity in the Gospels.

Second Corinthians 13:13 serves as a benediction or pronouncement of blessing. Paul appears to be referring to a tradition with which the Christians at Corinth are familiar. He invokes the "grace of the Lord Jesus Christ, the love of God, and the communion of the Holy Spirit" upon these and all future generations of believers who would receive this word.

Grace has been defined as an acronym for the phrase "God's riches at Christ's expense." But God's love compelled the display of grace toward us sinners through the death of Christ on our behalf. The Holy Spirit is the animating presence of God both in the Resurrection and in the birth of the church at Pentecost. Any time believers come together in the name of God, we bear witness to the mystery of the Trinity.

May the grace of Christ, the love of God, and the fellowship of the Holy Spirit be evident in my life today. Amen.

FRIDAY, JUNE 17 ~ *Read 2 Corinthians 13:11-13*

People of faith face two extremes when speaking of God. We can err on the side of inscrutable mystery, acknowledging that we know little about the nature and character of the divine. Or we can claim too much as if we could contain God in the theological dogma of our language.

Saint Thomas Aquinas, an optimistic Christian thinker, argued that we can deduce certain aspects of God's power and majesty from reason as part of general revelation in the natural order. Classical philosophical arguments for the existence of God (first cause, order in the universe, moral and religious nature of persons, etc.) have been cited as proofs of God.

The God of philosophical speculation is not the God revealed through our Lord and Savior, Jesus Christ. Even Thomas conceded the mystery of the Holy Trinity, known only through special revelation (God in Christ, the teaching of both scripture and the church).

Mystery is a good word if we realize we are not talking about a "who-done-it." We can solve problems with more data or a new explanation of known facts. We can figure out puzzles and put them together given time, patience, and the ability to properly manipulate the various pieces. But mystery of a spiritual nature can't be solved or manipulated. It can only be embraced and lived into.

Paul hints at the mystery of the Godhead when he uses the trinitarian formula in today's passage. Everything we need to know about God we learn through Jesus Christ—this is a grace gift. Through him we learn that God is love and by faith in him we sense the Holy Spirit who binds us to one another in fellowship. This is the mystery we embrace and live into today.

Triune God, may we experience and express your grace, love, and communion this day. Through Christ our Lord. Amen.

Earlier in Matthew's Gospel, someone asks Jesus about the greatest commandment. He cites love of God and of neighbor as the sum of all the law. His response perplexes his enemies into silence. All Christians and many spiritual persons with no specific confessional identity would agree that loving God with all of one's being and loving neighbor as we love ourselves makes sense.

Most Christians would agree that we are also responsible for bearing witness in Jesus' name. The Great Commission (Matt. 28:19-20) figures into our thinking as prominently as the "great commandment." We are to go, or more precisely, "as we go," we are to "make disciples."

These verses indicate that we do not confine our Christian witness to a time or place. This witness involves no technique, program, or memorized presentation. This is a living and breathing 24/7 expression of our experience of Christ with us always. Elements of the steps will follow discipleship. Disciples are those who have been baptized into Christ. All Christians connect baptism and faith. Through baptism we bear witness to God's work in community and in an individual life. When we invite people to believe or share in the blessings of baptism, we are "teaching them to obey everything that I have commanded you."

I have been consciously committed to Christ for most of my life. Yet I continue to learn daily more and more about all that Jesus commands and what it means to follow him. A disciple is one who is a "disciplined learner." Through the spiritual disciplines we learn to discern and reflect Christ's presence in our lives into the lives of others.

Lord, may I see you at work in my life and circumstances and be willing to share and live out that reality on behalf of others. Amen.

SUNDAY, JUNE 19 ~ *Read Matthew 28:18-20*

TRINITY SUNDAY

Acts 1:8 records Luke's version of the Great Commission, which relates power for witness to the gift of the Holy Spirit (first expressed in the church on Pentecost). Instead of outlining the process as in Matthew's Gospel (making disciples, baptizing, and teaching) the author expresses the *direction* of the early church's witness. They begin where they are (Jerusalem), travel into surrounding territory (Judea), and take the message of Christ across the Roman Empire (the ends of the earth).

Lacking any of the organizational, institutional, or financial resources of the Western churches of today (particularly in America) a disparate band of would-be followers who had cowered in the face of the authorities, betrayed and denied Christ, and returned to their homes as if nothing had happened, were transformed into an unstoppable force.

The early church took the working of the Holy Spirit seriously. They believed in the radical power of prayer. Following Jesus was not optional; it was their way of life. How do we explain this transformation? One simple word: *power*. They had a keen awareness of God's power at work in their lives. In Matthew 28:18 Jesus announces, "All authority in heaven and on earth has been given to me." In the light of his "right to rule" over heaven and earth, Jesus deploys us to make disciples. We need also to remember the words of Acts 1:8: "You will receive power when the Holy Spirit has come upon you." We derive power not from *our* authority but based upon Jesus' authority.

We, by the inner dynamic of the Holy Spirit's work in our lives, live so fully for Christ that we are willing to die for him, and that kind of commitment commands attention.

Lord, may I yield myself to your rule and thereby experience and express the inner dynamic of the Spirit in all that I am. Amen.

God's Call, Our Response

JUNE 20–26, 2011 • WAYNE E. WILLIAMS

MONDAY, JUNE 20 ~ *Read Genesis 22:1-14*

Responding in faith to the call of God, Abram leaves his home to go to a strange land. God promises to make Abram the father of a great nation, and, as a sign of the covenant, changes his name to Abraham (ancestor of a multitude). To Abraham and Sarah is born the child of promise, Isaac. Now, years later, another call comes, "Abraham!" Abraham recognizes the voice of the God who has led him through the valley and mountaintop experiences of his life, and he answers expectantly, "Here I am." How else would Abraham respond to this God who has always had his best interests at heart?

God's call in Genesis 12 cuts Abraham off from his past and his family; God's call in Genesis 22 will cut Abraham off from his future. Abraham is to "offer" Isaac as a burnt offering on the altar of sacrifice, a ritual act of worship.

Abraham in trust affirms that he and the boy will worship, and that they will *both* return. Abraham carries the implements of danger: the fire and the knife, leaving Isaac to shoulder the wood. The passage then provides glimpses of intimacy between a father and son as "the two of them walked on together." We might note the tilt of the father's head as he leans to hear the questions raised by the beloved and promised son. And Abraham's words in reply to Isaac's question bear public witness to his personal experience: "The LORD will provide." Abraham's words and action convey his trust to his son, and they walk on together into God's future.

Lord, may I trust you more. Amen.

Retired United Methodist pastor; San Jose, California

The message is unfathomable. God says, "Take your son, your only son Isaac, whom you love, and go to the land of Moriah, and offer him there as a burnt offering on one of the mountains that I shall show you." Abraham obeys. He builds the altar. He binds Isaac and places him on the altar. Isaac does not struggle. What message is there for us in Abraham's response to God and Isaac's submission to his father?

As we begin reading the story, we know more than either Abraham or Isaac. The writer tells us the why. God is testing Abraham, though we may view the story as the testing of God, Abraham, and Isaac. When ordered to sacrifice his son, Abraham does not plead or argue with God. Why?

And there's Isaac. Isaac is a boy but not a little boy. He may even have been a young man. Strong enough to carry wood for the sacrificial fire, he allows his father to bind him and place him on the altar. Why? He has asked his father, "Where is the lamb for a burnt offering?" Abraham has assured him that God will provide. Facing death, Isaac trusts his father, who has loved and cared for him. Isaac trusts that he will continue to do so. Abraham trusts that the God who has promised will provide. Neither Abraham nor Isaac is disappointed. God is put to the test, and God provides.

God calls you and me, even as God called Abraham, to go through deep valleys and over high mountains. The Holy One calls us with opportunities and challenges that test us beyond what we think we can manage. We say, "Lord, I can't do it." And the God who knows our weaknesses and strengths responds, "Trust in me, for I will provide." God assures us that we can do more than we ever dreamed possible. What tests have come in your life, and how have you responded?

How do you trust that God will provide?

When our daughter, Debbie, was three years old, we lived in the Hudson River valley in New York. That's Rip Van Winkle country, and unless you have experienced thunder and lightning in Rip Van Winkle country, you have never experienced thunder and lightning!

One evening an unusually severe electrical storm seemed to center right over our house. Expressing her fear, Debbie asked a profound theological question for a three-year-old, "If God is so busy thundering and lightning, how can he take care of us?" At some time or another, most of us—probably all of us—have asked essentially the same question, "Where is God when we need God most?"

Something drastic has happened in the psalmist's life. He feels forsaken. Time has passed, and no deliverance has come. He lives in a world of ceaseless thunder and lightning.

What do you do when God has hidden God's face from you, and you have no hope? The psalmist does something that many of us are afraid to do. He tells God exactly how he feels, even going so far as to accuse God of abandoning him. He gives expression to his feelings with words like these: "How long do I have to wait?" He doesn't mince words.

The psalmist affirms our freedom to tell God exactly how we feel. The author of First Peter provides one answer, "Cast all your anxiety on [God], because he cares for you" (5:7). Sometimes the problems we face overwhelm us. We do ask, "Where is God when we need God most?" Thank God for the faith to voice our concern to the One who can make a difference.

O God, we thank you that in our darkest moments and most difficult times we are free to tell you just how we feel. Amen.

Have you ever tried to blackmail God? Maybe you haven't, but the psalmist comes pretty close. Everything has gone wrong in his life. He has prayed and received no answer. He needs help, and it never comes. Finally he cries out words to this effect, "Lord, hear me. If you don't answer me, I'm going to die. If I die, my enemies are going to say that they have won the battle. They will be happy; but just think, Lord, how that is going to reflect on you."

Now and again the burdens of life crush us—the death of a loved one, serious illnesses, broken relationships with family or friends, losing a job. We could go on and on. These experiences are not only personal. The world's brokenness troubles us—homeless people, others living in luxury; people starving, others with surpluses of food; world conflicts; the threat of terrorism; prejudice and bigotry.

When we suffer as the psalmist did, we may ask, "God, where are you when these things happen? Why do you let them happen? Why do you not come to my aid?"

The psalmist goes on to petition God to "consider . . . answer . . . give light." The first two petitions ask God to pay attention and take the situation seriously. The third request for "light in the eyes" indicates life-giving vitality. The psalmist asks the Giver of life to intervene, to restore life's fullness.

David, confronted by his own sin, beset by the failure of others, and faced by events over which he had no control, finally could say, "In my distress I called upon the Lord; . . . and my cry came to his ears" (2 Sam. 22:7). We too can cry out to a God who hears, attends, and restores.

Lord of grace and mercy, we cry to you in our distress. Grant us the confidence that you hear us and respond to us; through Jesus Christ our Lord. Amen.

We do not know the reason for the psalmist's anger and depression, but he needs help. In today's verses the tone changes radically; the psalmist has experienced reprieve or support. His prayer has been answered; the Lord has acted.

A friend was fishing on a lake in California, maneuvering his boat toward a flock of ducks. As he drew near them, all the ducks except one flew away. He steered his boat right up to the duck, picked it up, and put it in the boat. Only then did he discover that a fishing hook attached to a line and a heavy weight was caught in the duck's breast. Freedom required release from the hook and weight that kept him from doing what every duck is expected to do—fly.

Held down by "hook, line, and sinker," the psalmist cannot fly! New hope is born when his trust in God's steadfast love comes to bountiful fruition. Once again he sings because of God's goodness to him.

Let us remember that God's promise is not that life will be free from the hard places or disappointments. Rather, through all the struggles of our lives, God's love for us endures—forever.

John Greenleaf Whittier in "The Eternal Goodness" expresses that hope:

> "Yet, in the maddening maze of things, . . .
> I know that God is good!"

O God, grant us the assurance that your love never fails and the confidence that nothing—absolutely nothing—can separate us from your love and care. Amen.

SATURDAY, JUNE 25 ~ *Read Romans 6:12-23*

If you had gone to school in 1784, you might have learned to read from the *New England Primer*. Here is one of the verses you might have memorized:

> In Adam's fall,
> we sinned all.

This is precisely what the apostle Paul emphasizes in his letter to the Romans. In our natural state we are slaves to sin. The law, which the slave to sin finds oppressive, is nevertheless the schoolmaster or disciplinarian seeking to give direction to the slave to sin.

Paul states it bluntly. We are all slaves, either slaves to sin or slaves to righteousness. We serve the one we obey. It can't be both ways, and there's no middle ground. "What then?" Paul asks. God offers the free gift of eternal life for all through Jesus Christ our Lord. By faith in Christ we are no longer slaves to sin and the law. Then a remarkable thing happens: We become obedient from the heart. This represents a complete reorientation of our life. We *choose* to become slaves to righteousness. The love of Christ compels us and changes our lives completely. Even though what we do from the heart may be essentially the same as what we did under the law, there is a difference. The law centered upon fulfilling certain requirements, demanding a righteousness that could never be attained. This new obedience from the heart represents a relationship established in faith.

Our new relationship with God leads us to establish meaningful relationships with other persons. Obedience from the heart means that our work as a servant of God will not be a burden but will provide us with a sense of purpose and fulfillment.

How is obedience from the heart being fulfilled in my life?

SUNDAY, JUNE 26 ~ *Read Matthew 10:40-42*

Preparing the apostles for a preaching and healing mission to Israel, Jesus declares that those who receive the Twelve welcome Jesus and also God who has sent him. He concludes his instructions by saying, "Whoever gives even a cup of cold water to one of these little ones in the name of a disciple—truly I tell you, none of these will lose their reward."

Who are the little ones? The little ones appear to be thirsty disciples who will appreciate a refreshing cup of cold water on the mission journey. Those who respond even to the lesser needs of the Twelve will receive their reward. Since we are not one of the Twelve, nor are we apt to meet walking missioners on a journey, how can we find meaning for today in these words?

Think of the little ones as people in distress. How can we reach out to the impoverished who need wells for water in developing countries, the hungry, the homeless, victims of disaster, the sick, the lonely, the sorrowful, those in need? Is there no end to the cries of despair from people near and far? What can *we* do? Do we have the figurative cup of cold water to share?

We have a cup of cold water and, with our aid, thirst may be quenched. Yet we alone cannot meet every emergency. Through gifts and service, we can be part of the ministries of our church and community that reach out to all in need. In one of Jesus' parables, the king (Christ) says, "Just as you did it to one of the least of these . . . you did it to me" (Matt. 25:40).

Lord, thank you for the cup of cold water. Help me to share it with others in the spirit of Christ. Amen.

The Meaning of Wisdom

JUNE 27–JULY 3, 2011 • SUSIE KNEDLIK

MONDAY, JUNE 27 ~ *Read Genesis 24:34-49, 58-67*

Abraham receives God's promise, "I will make you the father of many nations with as many offspring as there are stars in the sky or grains of sand on the beach." So he sends a servant back to his father's family to find a wife for his beloved son, Isaac, Together they would begin the making of those many nations. Rebekah's willingness to leave her home and become Isaac's wife allows her to be an instrument for the preservation of the covenant. She takes those first steps into the unknown.

Our witnessing the fruition of God's covenant in our own lives requires that we, like Abraham and Rebekah, take those first steps in faith. To talk about something rather than initiating action is meaningless. Rebekah could have said no and then boasted to her girlfriends about the great offer she refused. That response, however, is of little value to God. I once went to a beautician who would never share with anyone her New Year's resolutions or what she was giving up for Lent until she had actually succeeded in doing what she promised. As she finally shared, respect for her faith and wisdom multiplied.

Now, God knew all along that Abraham would send a servant in search for a wife from among his kinsmen. And God probably banked on Rebekah's willingness to fulfill the covenant. God knew. Indeed, through this emotional story, we clearly see that God's declared intentions become a reality and that which had been in danger is now saved.

O God, grant me the wisdom to take those first steps into living my covenant with you instead of just talking about it. Amen.

Retired United Methodist pastor, weekend on-call chaplain, Children's Hospital; Birmingham, Alabama

TUESDAY, JUNE 28 ~ *Read Psalm 72*

This text offers three key words that are essential to wisdom: *justice, righteousness,* and *peace.* When righteousness becomes a way of life, a practice, and a habit, it can facilitate justice and peace. Some scholars believe this psalm was one sung at the enthronement of King David. The Israelites now look for qualities in their earthly king that have been evidenced by the heavenly King. The earthly king "delivers," "has pity," "saves," and "redeems." The success of the king's rule will be determined by the well-being of those he rules; therefore, the king fosters care for the people, especially those who need that help: the poor, the needy, those crushed by the oppressor. The king will bear witness to his faith through righteous living. Those under his rule will desire to live likewise, leading to a culture where justice and peace become the norm. The people go on to pray that this righteousness will flourish "until the moon is no more"—in other words, forever.

In the Genesis passage, God fulfills the promise to Abraham. In this psalm, righteousness is the measure of fulfillment of *our* promise to God. When we profess our faith, we make certain promises to God. For years, I feared giving myself fully to what I understood God desired for my life. When I finally gave in to God's call to ministry, my fear became my greatest blessing! Our lives, like that of the king, require righteous living if we are to ensure justice and peace for others. If we desire to be truly wise, we will always be moving our lives in that direction.

Lord, guide me into righteousness. Direct my footsteps so that in my little corner of the world, peace and justice and all the other virtues of your reign might flourish. Amen.

Just because we recognize wisdom when we see it or read about it doesn't mean that we can, do, or will employ it to guide our lives. How we live and how we *want* to live can be two very different things, as Paul explains to the church at Rome.

We've reflected on righteous living and its fruits of justice and peace. But we also agree with Paul: sometimes our best efforts, our heartiest resolutions, and our inward desires do not manifest themselves in right action or behavior. Why? For Paul, even the best of us fall prey to the "sin that dwells within" us.

Often I don't understand my own actions: I say hurtful things about others; I levy judgment. Sometimes my behavior is mean and ugly, and I don't even regret it later!

Life is like that for all of us at times. We who claim to live in the light of Christ may be particularly bewildered when, despite our best efforts, we forget our Christian identity. And perhaps the label of "sin" disquiets us. Psychological terms and qualifications may suit us better: we were the middle child; our parents didn't take us to church; our neighborhood isn't conducive to strong friendships.

But let's face it: often we pursue personal whims or give way to pride or "getting in the last word." Paul acknowledges that "I do not do the good I want, but the evil I do not want is what I do."

So, how do we bolster resolve and follow through in Christian action? Perhaps we need to acknowledge the temptations, acknowledge the pervasive nature of the sin that dwells within. Only God's initiative can free us, so we ask for forgiveness—we're human, not perfect.

Help us, O God, to accept your action in Jesus Christ on our behalf. Amen.

Paul points out the battle we humans experience between our thoughts and desires and our actions. He claims to be captive to the law of sin that dwells in his body. "Wretched man that I am! Who will rescue me from this body of death?"

Now, if our body, through its action, is holding us hostage—and the actions we undertake give us some pleasure—does that mean that following our thoughts and our mind is without pleasure? Many Christians and potential Christians get caught in this line of thinking and use it to evade following God. It's more fun being a sinner. Not true!

When our daughter, Heidi, was about four, she had a friend named Annie who wore red patent leather shoes. We couldn't afford such shoes, so they were the envy of both my daughter and me. Annie was a year older than Heidi and wanted her to do everything she told her to do. Because of the age difference (and the shoe envy), Annie's directiveness worked for a while and often created a lot of fun. Then one day Heidi objected. What Annie wanted her to do was not right! Annie came stomping over to our house (in those red patent leather shoes) and said, "Heidi Knedlik, if you don't play with me you are going to lose one good friend!"

She didn't, and she didn't. Heidi's mind, best thoughts, and desires overcame the captivity of her body. She delighted "in the law of God in [her] inmost self." She won in both the short run and the long run and became a better person for having said no.

God frees us at God's initiative. It is well when we align our resolve and effort with God's will. "Thanks be to God through Jesus Christ our Lord!"

Loving God, help us to value what you offer over what the world offers. Amen.

FRIDAY, JULY 1 ~ *Read Matthew 11:16-19*

Many churches in the United States display a reproduction of Warner Sallman's painting known as *The Head of Christ*. The painting reflects what some people expect Jesus to look like. I have seen other versions of Jesus by artists whose work features their own ethnic or racial background. Each artist seems to declare, "This is my Jesus." Without belittling any artist, I wonder how often we make Jesus in our own image. This is not a modern problem!

In the larger context of Matthew 11, John has sent his disciples to ask Jesus if he is the Messiah, "the one who is to come." Jesus responds, "The blind receive their sight, the lame walk, the lepers are cleansed" (v. 5). Is this answer enough for the crowd around Jesus? The crowd has apparently questioned John's ministry. John may have seemed too somber; today we might describe John as puritanical. On the other hand, people accused Jesus of being a glutton and a drunkard.

Jesus points at the excuses made by people to avoid following either John the Baptist or himself. These excuses convey the message that because these prophets of God do not behave as the people want or expect, the people will not listen to the message of the prophets. The ancient ones want only a prophet created in their own image. We do not know the response of the crowd to Jesus' words in this passage. I suspect that they remained silent.

Jesus clearly did not meet the expectations of his time, and he does not meet the expectations of our time.

How do we follow Jesus when the path he takes through the world does not seem to be the path we want? We persevere. We hold to the vision of God's reign. We keep the Christ—crucified and resurrected—before us, and we remember that the path of discipleship remains always unique and always fresh.

O God, may I see the world through your eyes of holiness. Amen.

Jesus says, "'I thank you, Father, Lord of heaven and earth, because you have hidden these things from the wise and the intelligent and have revealed them to infants.'"

Wait a minute! Did I just read that right? God has hidden all these important things from the wise and the intelligent and has revealed them to infants? Why am I struggling so hard to become wise if it's not going to get me anywhere? As we reflect on wisdom and righteousness, it's easy to think that if we just work harder and stay focused, we'll "get it."

But Jesus explains in these words: "All things have been handed over to me by my Father; and no one knows the Son except the Father, and no one knows the Father except the Son and anyone to whom the Son chooses to reveal him." What kind of explanation is that? The relationship between Jesus and the Father goes beyond head knowledge; it is an intimate knowing. Each is known to the other, and Jesus may share knowledge of the Father at his own discretion. As human beings we cannot "know" God. Once again, despite our best efforts, God is beyond our grasp, which is where the infants come in. With no preconceived notions, they accept what is given.

As a preschooler, my youngest child, Andrew, drew a nativity picture. Behind the traditional nativity, he drew a hill with three crosses on it. In front of the crosses he placed some little people and one giant person with outstretched hands. He explained that the giant person was Jesus and the little ones were his friends. Jesus was saying to them, "And this is the place where I was borned!"

In terms of knowledge of God, perhaps less is more. And only when we realize that wisdom and knowledge come as gifts of God can we can truly move in the direction of God's desire.

Creator God, help me always to remember that there is a God, and it is not me. Amen.

To say we worry too much is an understatement. We live in a world that values accomplishment, feeds competition, and rewards overachievers. It's no wonder we worry so much.

This worry spills over into our spiritual lives. Have we done enough to please God? Has what we've done made a difference? What if we're missing God's signals for our lives?

Our questions without answers lead us to worry. So we read Jesus' words to the crowds, words to this effect: "Tired? Worried? Full of unanswered questions? Unload on me, and I will give you rest!"

Sigh. *If only that were true,* we think. *If only it were that easy.*

When I was in seminary, I drove past a sign painted on an overpass each week. It read, "Trust Jesus." That's all. As I drove my weekly route, that phrase became a mantra that helped me make it me through some tough years. "Trust Jesus, trust Jesus, trust Jesus . . . " We don't have to know all the answers. We don't even have to do battle with our bodies and our sins by ourselves. We say yes to Jesus' invitation to release and rest; it is a learning process with eternal benefits.

A mantra we recite with each breath—such as "Trust Jesus"—may free us from our worry and fear. Then, at every turn of our lives, we can learn to relax with an unburdened spirit. And, like Abraham, we can step willingly into God's great flow of salvation history.

Almighty God, may I learn to place my trust in you and your providence so that I may become a wise disciple. Amen.

Holiness: Personal and Social

JULY 4–10, 2011 • MIGUEL BALDERAS

MONDAY, JULY 4 ~ *Read Genesis 25:19-26*

I find it amazing how scripture testifies to the continuing struggles of our day. Two nations struggle within Rebekah's womb, each one trying to overcome the other even before birth. As a pastor from Mexico who arrived in this country ten years ago, I experience this struggle daily.

I came to the United States to study. One of my first professors suggested that I not worry about learning to speak English, for that would come. He emphasized that I not forget where I came from: my identity and its defining characteristics of language, tradition, and custom. Today's passage speaks to us about the history of a people, the people of Israel—the chosen people who maintained their identity in all circumstances and situations. They kept in mind their traditions and their belief in the living God, the God of Abraham, Isaac, and Jacob. This continued faith and practice, in the midst of empires that tried to eliminate them, strengthened them, and Israel has survived to this day.

When I recall my first months in this country, I remember the temptation to fit in. Society pressured me to assimilate or integrate: "forget your roots, your language, your culture." Society asks us to forget who we are and from where we come. But we are born in a particular place for a particular reason! God leads and guides us in love and mercy just as God did Israel. We discover that we are part of a great family, the family of faith in Christ Jesus!

Lord, may we never forget where we come from but ever turn to you for guidance. Amen.

Senior pastor, Oxon Hill United Methodist Church in Maryland, working in a multicultural context

TUESDAY, JULY 5 ~ *Read Genesis 25:27-34*

Competition between siblings is not a new struggle. But the struggle between Jacob and Esau in the womb is so violent that Rebekah seeks a word from the Lord. And God's response overturns the established favor for the elder child. Events move on to support this unconventional word from the Lord. Two sons with differing abilities, one willing to sell a birthright for a bowl of stew. Each son favored by one parent. Yet parental wisdom resides precisely in knowing how to educate and treat children equally, for sooner or later, favoritism creates division.

Countries, peoples, and ethnicities may also feel or experience favor; we like to believe we are the chosen, the preferred ones, or maybe the powerful ones because of political, social, or economic reasons. And based on this power, we may impose our opinions and beliefs on others in irrational and unjust ways. As a Mexican, I learned about the conquest my people suffered over five hundred years ago and the unjust way our country was "evangelized." It was done with the cross *and* the sword: either you accepted Christianity by kissing the cross or you were killed with the sword.

Jacob uses parental favoritism to his advantage, and his actions result in flight; Esau loses both birthright and fatherly blessing. Among disciples of Christ, favoritism, hierarchies, and social classes collapse. In the face of the world's affirmation of division and separation, we dare to affirm that all of us are equal.

God of all, give us the courage to understand the divisions still manifest in the human family that can be overcome through your grace. Amen.

WEDNESDAY, JULY 6 ~ *Read Psalm 25*

I enjoy all kinds of music, but I especially appreciate *corridos*. These songs from Mexico relate events that transformed the local or national community. *Corridos* are part of the oral tradition of my country. These songs help us retain our history. Often the song's pain and lament over the past invite us to reflect on a situation in daily life, but it sounds like a prayer of hope that the difficult situation will end sooner or later.

Psalm 25 reminds me of *corridos*. This song by the psalmist records a series of petitions: for mercy and deliverance from enemies, relief from distress, forgiveness, and guidance. The psalmist "sings" his lament to God. He has lost his direction and needs God's guidance.

It takes humility to ask for help and guidance. We, in our society with its technological and economical achievements, often believe that we need no one else; consequently, we do not seek God. The psalmist, on the other hand, recognizes that only God can direct, protect, and liberate him.

My parents made it clear that in facing any situation we are to seek guidance and direction from God by means of prayer. As a child, I believed God attended to *my* personal needs and no one else's, *my* pleas and no one else's. Unlike my childhood understanding of prayer, I know now that God hears all prayers and offers guidance to all who seek. Though Psalm 25 seems written as an individual lament, the psalm remains one in which all the people of Israel could unite. This prayer is nothing other than to seek the face of God in all things, to allow God to lead us in truth and teach us. It is to God that the psalmist lifts up his soul; in God the psalmist trusts. How fortunate that we also may turn to God in our need and find those needs met.

Help us, Lord, to seek you in all situations and social interactions of this day. We know that you are the source of all hope, all mercy, and all love. Let your face shine upon us. Amen.

THURSDAY, JULY 7 ～ *Read Psalm 25*

The Lord "instructs sinners in the way. . . . Relieve[s] the troubles of my heart, and bring[s] me out of my distress" (vv. 8, 17). To transform the world that surrounds us with all the challenges of daily life that affect all areas (economy, social life, politics, religion), we must pray and work. When I heard this declaration I realized that if I pray for peace, I must work for justice. We, the disciples of Jesus, see the act of asking for peace and justice reflected in concrete action. Guided by God, we walk in faith to achieve what God has asked us to do.

During my first years as a pastor, I prayed that God would send laborers to the harvest; I believed that my prayer was sincere. Then one day God clearly asked me, "Are you ready to serve me as a laborer?" At that moment, I started to move from prayer to action. I began to listen in my prayers to the personal call of God and to recognize that call in the ministry and work of the faith community.

The psalmist prays to God for help and liberation. But then he listens to God's instruction and guidance. He acknowledges the love and faithfulness of God to guide him down the right path—the path of truth and salvation.

Notice the final words of the psalm: "Redeem Israel, O God, out of all its troubles." Each of us may paraphrase that prayer for our own faith communities, such as, *Redime a la Primera Iglesia Metodista Hispana* or "Redeem First Methodist Church." We give feet to our prayers through our commitment to live with the community to which God calls us and to love it in faithfulness. God will guard our life and uphold it with integrity.

> *God, give us the courage to pray and work. Give us vision to see that you always go before us. Give us ears to hear you in community. Give us hearts of hope to know that you are redeeming the world. Amen.*

Paul clearly ties the concept of liberty to that of salvation: "The law of the Spirit of life in Christ Jesus has set you free from the law of sin and of death." Free from the power of sin and death, we live life in the Spirit and "set [our] minds on the things of the Spirit." When I also heeded God's call and became free from sin and death, I committed myself to justice and to God's reign. Through the movement of the Spirit we can follow God's call to act in the world.

In my youth I believed that Christians should separate themselves from the world so as not to be contaminated by the world. Only then could we live a "holy" life. Soon I began to wonder what would happen to everyone else who had not withdrawn from the world.

I saw Christian sisters and brothers continue to starve and suffer injustice. At that point my liberty in the Spirit became a missional calling to go beyond the salvation of souls and to proclaim the good news of justice for everyone.

Paul clearly and plainly reminds us that there is no condemnation for those who are in Christ Jesus. Our ministries, whether we are laypersons or clergy, grow out of our response to the love we experience in Christ. Our actions reflect our liberty. We do not ask permission or apologize for who we are, and we tell the rest of the world of God's freeing power through Jesus Christ. When we set our minds on the things of the Spirit, God empowers us to use our gifts to serve others and to proclaim the love of God *for* all people *to* all people.

> *Give us the courage to live this liberty, Lord, that we may be the voice of those who have no voice. Keep us open to your Spirit that the Spirit might prompt us to act with boldness, living and loving as Jesus taught his first followers and all who follow the way of Christ. Amen.*

SATURDAY, JULY 9 ~ *Read Matthew 13:1-9*

When the gospel of Jesus Christ arrived in my country, the missionaries emphasized the importance of eternal salvation; we were to accept Jesus as our personal Savior. I received and accepted Jesus as Savior, and then, like many teenagers, I thought I was done. I only had to sit back and receive the blessings that I deserved as a son of God.

Everything went well at the beginning because of God's goodness. I lacked for nothing even though my family lived in poverty. Yet I sometimes felt like a spoiled child who throws a fit when he or she doesn't get what is asked for. In my house I never had the opportunity to throw a single fit. But in spiritual terms—in my relationship with God—sometimes I did act this way. Later I recognized my immaturity. One day my mother came to me and said, "If you continue with this demanding attitude of entitlement, you will never have anything. You will only be a witness to what God does; you will never be involved, since, from a spiritual standpoint, you will always be a child!" These words cut me to the quick because they came from my mother whom I loved and respected.

When I read this parable in Matthew, I often think of myself as rocky soil: I heard the word and received it with joy. But the rooting of the faith was not deep within me. In my immaturity I remained in shallow ground. However, the seed had been planted in me, and I needed to quit resisting the natural growth process. I now hear the word and bear fruit; hopefully, thirty-, sixty-, and a hundredfold.

Lord, help us listen to the people that you have matured so that under your direction they may educate and guide us in your way. Amen.

SUNDAY, JULY 10 ~ *Read Matthew 13:18-23*

Many worldly temptations, distractions, and struggles can prevent the word of God—the sower's seed—from growing into a fruitful faith. When my mother died, I was fifteen years old. My parent and friend who had counseled me was no longer with me. I had decided to accept the will of God and that is what I declared; but I also fought with God. I did not understand how God could take from me someone I loved and needed so much.

God waited patiently and, through this experience, I came to understand that those of us who call ourselves disciples have to be willing not only to believe but also to obey God's will—in favorable or unfavorable circumstances.

Often when problems arise, we run or find ourselves seduced by economic power and the pleasures of this world. In these ways we distance ourselves from God. We may shy away from proclaiming God's justice in order to protect ourselves. The parable in today's reading reminds us of the steps of bountiful harvest: *Hear, understand,* and *bear fruit. Hear*: cultivate the virtue of listening; be quiet and listen. *Understand*: this imperative collides with our pride, our prejudices, and our personal demons, which we protect because they excuse us from obeying or bearing fruit.

Bear fruit: When we recognize our need of God, we intentionally seek to be quiet and to listen for God's voice. Then we can understand God's will and obediently do it, rather than pursuing our own agendas. We become seed sown on good soil: we hear and understand, bear fruit and yield. "Let anyone with ears listen!"

Good God, perfect in us the ability to listen, understand, and bear fruit according to your will, through Jesus, your son, we pray. Amen.

God's Ever-Present Spirit

JULY 11–17, 2011 • PATRICIA RAYBON

MONDAY, JULY 11 ~ *Read Genesis 28:10-19a*

During my college years, I ran from God, church, and family. Hard *and* fast. As a result, I made bad choices that forever changed my life. Still, like Jacob in this story—who steals his brother's birthright and flees from his family—I discovered that, in the midst of my worst situations, God was present. Like Jacob, who wearily pauses and falls into a troubled sleep, I surprisingly was able to note in my own nightmarish experiences, "Surely, the LORD is in this place, and I wasn't even aware of it!"

I look back on my darkest season and gratefully bear witness to the Lord's glorious hand at work. What a gracious reminder that God does not abandon us, especially when we're in the middle of difficult times. Our own vulnerability at those times may heighten our spiritual vision, may open our spirits to God's presence.

We can read this account of Jacob and get swept away in the dramatic details of Jacob's vision—the angels descending and ascending the staircase and the Lord standing above it all. We may be better served, however, by being willing simply to see God's glory, by sharpening our awareness of God. By opening in expectation of God's presence, we may strengthen our witness of God's love and grace, becoming able to tell others of the low times in our lives when we became aware of God's presence.

May this passage inspire us to look daily for God's presence in our ordinary lives—then, as Jacob, to celebrate our Bethel experiences. It's a perspective that changes everything.

Glorious God, thank you for blessing me with the ever-present light of your Spirit. Amen.

Journalist, speaker, and author of inspirational reflections; church usher and Writing Ministry founder, Shorter Community A.M.E. Church; Denver, Colorado

The news was the talk of the town. The city's largest church appointed a new pastor. After hitting a membership high of 10,000 and then falling to 2,500, the church had selected an innovative young pastor to guide the congregation to a rebound. But was this new pastor up to the challenge? *Was this young man the right leader for the job?*

Today's story about Jacob offers a provocative answer. That is, in young Jacob—a real failure at serving his family—we learn that God handpicks servants and territory. As God declares to Jacob: "The ground you are lying on belongs to you. Your descendants will be numerous. They will spread in all directions. And all the families of the earth will be blessed through you" (AP).

Through Jacob? All families blessed by a man who deceived his own? Only a redeeming God can make such an astounding promise—that a failed family member with amazing potential can be restored by God into a leader. Why? Because God goes with us. "I am with you and will watch over you wherever you go." What a powerful promise from God! God is able to take our misdirection and set it aright—then to put us back into our rightful place in God's plan. Jacob, whose name is changed to Israel, personifies this potential in all of us. God's sovereignty redeems. Our part of the story is to be yielded and willing, ready and available. Or as that new pastor in town described his strongest asset, "I am broken."

Redeeming God, when we fail, remind us of your redeeming love for all people. Amen.

WEDNESDAY, JULY 13 ~ *Read Psalm 139:1-12*

When I was a young journalist—and a young wife and mother—I thought I could take credit for anything I achieved at home or work. If I wrote an article, I credited my energy. If I baked cookies for my daughter's classroom, I credited my effort. No matter how big or small the project: planting a flower, teaching a class, or writing a book, I believed it was accomplished by my energy, my vision, and my output.

This psalm asks for nothing; its focus is God and God alone. God knows when the psalmist sits down, rises up, lies down at night. God is with him day and night. As I grew older and perhaps wiser, I came to acknowledge the deep truth embedded in this psalm. The Lord knows all about me, about all my actions. God goes before and after and places a hand of blessing on my head. I can never escape God's Spirit or find myself outside God's presence!

Those comforting thoughts from Psalm 139 have quieted troubled hearts across time, and they remind me that God's presence supports and sustains my efforts. Even better, if God goes before me and follows me, my work should always point to the Lord.

Thus, as I worked to write these devotions, I determined to let the Lord lead the effort. The psalmist put it this way: "Even before a word is on my tongue, O Lord, you know it completely." So it is with me. Help each one of us, O God, to let your presence speak first.

Lead and guide me, O God, even as you never leave me—today and forever, first and last. Amen.

To see our faults and also our strengths takes a sharp spotlight. The psalmist writes: "Search me, O God, and know my heart; test me and know my thoughts." A provocative request.

But does the psalmist desire God's measure of his performance personally or vocationally? (Would the psalmist differentiate between these two contemporary categories? And does it help us to draw distinctions between vocation and profession?) Or is he asking God to reveal what God alone can know? "You know when I sit down and when I rise up," the psalmist confesses. "You discern my thoughts from far away."

Godly knowledge of ourselves can move us from an idle, self-led, hit-or-miss life to one led by God. For those in ministry, that's critical, to be sure. How many well-intentioned ministers of the gospel are working in the wrong vineyard? And how many laypeople do we see toiling at somebody else's calling or neglecting a God-given gift? Could such misaligned laboring be offensive to God?

Perhaps the better choice consists of seeking God's knowledge of us. We might learn more about ourselves, not through self-help books and pop-culture alternatives but by pursuing the one who created us.

We open our hearts and minds to God, beseeching the Holy One to shine a searchlight into every dusty corner, illuminating even our anxieties. This godly knowledge draws us to follow the Lord "in the everlasting way." On that path, we recognize that we can't stray far from God's spirit. Once we surrender, then we can follow.

O God, help us to serve you this day by heeding your knowledge and going where you lead. Amen.

FRIDAY, JULY 15 ～ *Read Romans 8:12-17*

We don't pick our parents. I've heard that saying more than a few times. It implies we're all born or adopted into earthly families. But as children, either way, we can't choose.

In this epistle, however, the apostle Paul reminds us that, in Christ, we can choose a spiritual family and a spiritual life. Even better, in choosing a life in God, we "are children of God." But again, we don't pick our heavenly parent. This time, God picks us. Or as Paul writes, "That very Spirit [God's] bearing witness with our spirit that we are children of God."

This amazing statement speaks of God's great longing for us. God wants us, and we will be known to all as God's children and God's heirs.

On those days when we don't feel worthy or valued, Paul's letter reminds us that we are chosen. On days the enemy's voice drowns out the still, quiet voice of God, Paul's letter assures us that we are chosen. On days our circumstances make us feel worthless or confused or defeated, Paul's letter directs us: We are chosen. Whether or not others pick us for their groups, friendships, or families, God picked us first. Are we qualified? Of course not. We take our place in God's family totally dependent, willing to exchange our weakness for divine strength.

The rules of God's family are unworldly; we can't earn our adoption—it's a gift. We can't elevate our status; we're all one in Christ. What can we offer in return for such love? Just our little, our most, our all.

Loving God, in a world that sees us as unworthy and unready, thank you for choosing each one of us as your special own. Help us today to live so others will accept your adoption too. Amen.

In many African American churches, like the one I grew up in, worship is a joyous, musical, hand-clapping, foot-stomping, praise-the-Lord good time. No somber, sober theology appears to fit here. Today's admonition to share in Christ's sufferings would seem a piercing gospel. And the worshipers in my fifties-era childhood church—if they were honest—longed not to share in Christ's suffering but in his glory.

Then a man named Martin Luther King Jr. came along. In a speech about drum majors, Dr. King urged African Americans—indeed, all people—to deepen our sense of the gospel message. Instead of seeking personal victory, as a drum major commands the spotlight in a marching band, he urged us to serve humbly, behind the scenes: "If you want to be important—wonderful. If you want to be recognized—wonderful. If you want to be great—wonderful. But recognize that he who is greatest among you shall be your servant. That's a new definition of greatness."

His intriguing invitation helped beleaguered believers find ways to make sense of our earthly sufferings, to redeem our heartaches for lives of service and love. We would come to affirm Paul's words: "The sufferings of this present time are not worth comparing with the glory about to be revealed to us."

As servants, we in that church understood that Christ's example of giving himself up so none would perish was the model for our own lives. But is such self-denial suffering? Such service often feels, ironically, more like a gift. In fact, suffering with Christ to serve others feels like joy—a blessing, not a burden. "In hope we were saved."

O God, we thank you for your earthly example of divine suffering. Thank you for the privilege of sharing in it. Amen.

At an end-of-summer picnic, the guests mingled, introducing themselves and getting acquainted. One woman mentioned that she hailed from the southern United States, and she commented, "That's fine, if you don't mind living in the Bible Belt." My stomach tightened; I held my tongue. The woman went on to criticize TV evangelists, "crooked" preachers, megachurches with "hypocritical members," and Christianity in general. I listened without debate or defense—just trying to hear an outsider's view.

Later, I reflected on the body of Christ all over the world with its communities of saints and sinners all under one roof. Today's scripture on the wheat and tares clearly indicates that we will find good and bad seed in Christian communities.

Our task, however, is not to pluck out the bad or pull up the weeds. In the parable, the servants would eagerly grab a hoe and start weeding. "No," the owner responds. "In gathering the weeds you would uproot the wheat along with them. Let both of them grow together until the harvest."

Why such tolerance for bad seed? Because the Harvester alone judges. While we focus on someone else's shortcomings, we're likely not to see our own. Worse, while we're busy judging, we'll miss seeing God's presence in our midst. But by toiling together, all of us learn what only God can teach us: mercy, forgiveness, patience, love. Wheat and weeds together; imperfect as it seems, that's how it's supposed to be.

O God, we thank you for your wisdom that guides us through our imperfect world as we longingly seek this day's perfection in you. Amen.

There's More to Come

JULY 18–24, 2011 • KENNETH R. PARKER

MONDAY, JULY 18 ~ *Read Psalm 105:1-11, 45b*

Psalm 105 calls us to pray, trust, and share when we face hard times. We can pray our way through hard times. To give thanks and sing praise in what is now—that encourages us to seek more of God's strength and presence in what is to come.

As Frances nears the end of a life that has been strong of heart but not strong in health, Howard sits with her. Like you and me, Howard prays the liturgy of night prayer that petitions God for "a perfect end," for death to come late in life with no snags, at the ready. But here is Frances.

We can trust our way through hard times. God's word spreads to all on earth. It holds for all time. To slaves in Egypt and strangers in Babylon, it vows, "To you I will give the land." To us, it says, "There's more to come."

In pain and anger, Frances sighs, "I don't understand." Howard comes to see that this is out of his hands: "We must let be what was and is and will be." For here is Frances.

We can share our way through hard times (vv. 12-45). This sharing takes stories. Strangers can be safe and get help, for God calls a Joseph (vv. 12-22). Slaves can get strong and see signs, for God calls a Moses (vv. 23-45a). For strangers and slaves, there's more to come.

Howard sits with Frances as a friend, in silence, with no story told by those who give care. It's hard to grasp what things mean with no story. In Holy Week, Frances dies. In spite of an imperfect end, says Howard, "Frances was a great spirit among us who touched a lot of lives." Long may her story be told. So here is Frances.

Lord, help us praise you, even in hard times, as we pray, trust, and share. Amen.

Copastor, First Baptist Church; Belfast, Maine

Jacob learns two conflicting lessons in life. (1.) Trust no one: "the Lord helps those who help themselves," folk wisdom that Jacob holds to from birth and fights for through life. (2.) Trust God: "the LORD will provide," sacred truth that Jacob learns from family and grows to claim for himself in time.

On the run, Jacob stays a month with kin. Laban eyes Jacob. Jacob eyes Rachel. Laban schemes: "We're kin! Work for no pay? Name your price." There are two daughters: Leah, whose name in Hebrew means "cow," and Rachel, whose name means "ewe." Jacob smirks, "I'll work seven years for the lamb." Years race by like days. Laban throws a party. Dad brings a veiled bride. The pair slips away. Laban laughs all night.

At dawn Jacob wakes to see the cow. The bride peers back. The groom moans, "Uh oh!" He doesn't grasp that there's more to come, can't guess how many olive shoots there'll be from this vine: Reuben, Simeon, Levi, Judah, Issachar, Zebulun, and Dinah. Jacob goes back to sleep. So much for "the Lord helps those who help themselves."

Next day Jacob shouts at Laban, "Why is this? What about Rachel? You tricked me!" Laban winks at friends—whom Jacob has regaled with tales of a young twin who tricks a first twin—and says, "That's not our way. Don't spoil this for your new bride. I'll give you the lamb for seven more years." Years creep by like decades. Dad brings a veiled bride. The pair slips away. Laban sleeps all night.

At dawn Jacob turns to see the lamb of great price. The bride gazes back. The groom sighs, "Oh, yeah!" He still doesn't grasp what's yet to come, can't guess how few olive shoots there'll be from this vine: Joseph and Benjamin. Like us, Jacob doesn't get it: "The LORD will provide."

Lord, teach us to trust that you will provide.

Matthew 13 tells a number of tales of what it's like when God is in charge. God-in-charge is like a seed. It's like a mustard seed planted in a field. It starts small, Jesus jokes, but grows large. It yields an herb to heal and a spice to savor. We get it!

God's rule starts tiny but grows to more. "We can't do great things on this earth," claims Mother Teresa. "We can only do small things with great love." Or do we get it?

The plant draws "birds of the air" to nest, Jesus notes. The good news: the seed grows to an herb that heals and a spice to savor. The bad news: the plant draws pesky birds that steal our seeds and make a mess of things. The news shocks us. There's more to come.

God-in-charge is also like a cook. It's like my spouse who makes bread. Pat stirs yeast in warm water with flour, salt, oil, and sugar. She kneads the mix and lets it rise. She kneads it again and lets it rise. She spreads and rolls it with sugar and cinnamon, then seals both ends. It bakes with heady aroma. It tests by hollow taps and cuts to warm steam. It tastes like no other.

Pat hides yeast in the mix. It spreads through the dough. Without it, bread is hard, dry, and bland. With it, bread is soft, moist, and rich. We get it. God's rule adds a part that spreads to the whole. Or do we get it? Jesus jokes at the scope. Three measures, or eighty pounds, of flour with water make one hundred pounds of dough. We laugh at the stuff. Yeast spoils. The law bars what rots from the recipe for bread at the feast of Passover (Exod. 12:14-20). Jesus adds yeast, which rots, to the recipe for bread at the spread of God's rule. The rot shocks us. There's more to come.

Lord, change us all by your rule. Amen.

Matthew adds more to what it's like with God in charge. God-in-charge is like treasure hidden in a field; someone finds it by chance and hides it in haste. With joy, the finder sells all else to buy much more.

God's rule hides in an act of love or a move toward peace, a kind deed or a true friend. To find it brings joy and leads us to give up all else. Sacrifice makes sacred.

A friend hunts cans for cash with a basket on wheels. I like to stop and chat. Some days she scours a purse and hands me two dollars: "It's for the church." I do the math. It takes forty cans to get two dollars. I want to say, "You don't have to do this." Instead I say, "Thank you." From treasure hid on the streets, we feel great joy. We give up all else for much more.

God-in-charge is also like a buyer in search of pearls. With joy at finding the best, the buyer sells all else to get much more. God's best comes when we hunt for it. Once found, we give up all else. Sacrifice makes sacred.

Engaged, but with no ring or means to mark the intention, Pat and I married and moved to California with foster kids Sam and Dan. After seminary, we moved back to Maine to serve churches. Ned was born.

One day Pat and I saw a ring in a store, a thin band with slight opals set in a butterfly shape. Pat liked it. I said, "Try it on." With protests, she did. She loved it. The price was too high for us. Full of joy, ready to give up all else, I urged, "Let's do this." Over protests, we did. She cried; I cried. As shoppers finding the perfect ring, we felt great joy. We gave up all else for much more.

Lord, help us give up all else for much more. Amen.

FRIDAY, JULY 22 ~ *Read Matthew 13:47-52*

God-in-charge is like a net cast in the sea that snags a catch of fish. The crew drags it to shore. They sit and sort the fish. They save the good ones and toss the bad ones. It's like the end of the age. Angels will come and get rid of what's bad.

At age eleven I lived on Clearwater Bay in Florida. I kept a raft on the bay and fished with squid for bait. One day my friend Lloyd and I cast out lines. A fish struck, with more and more to come. We reeled in flat flounder, blowfish that puffed up, and many more kinds. With no time to sort, we filled our pails. Word spread. Friends joined us. When the run stopped, we built a fire on the shore. Adults came to sort the fish. They dumped the bad ones and saved the good ones. I can still smell the drift-wood fire, still taste the roasted fish, still see the grand sunset, still hear a strong baritone sing "Amazing Grace." With God in charge, we're busy hauling in a big catch of fish, so we leave it to angels to sort later. It's not our job. "Do you get all this?" Jesus asks. We say yes.

Jesus goes on. A scribe trained for God's rule is like the head of a home, who brings out of its stores things new and old. It's like folks in our church when they celebrated its 200th anniversary. They mixed old things from their history with new things to come for the future. So Jesus warns us not to try to judge who's in and who's out; just mix what's old with what's new. Then Jesus heads to Nazareth and wows the home crowd in the synagogue.

Lord, teach us to catch as we can without judging. Amen.

When we are weak, we can trust the Spirit to pray for us and the Lord to work in us. But last Friday, Margaret is moved to a hospice room. Now a much loved member of our church must put this long held trust to one last test: "I just want to go home."

We trust the Spirit to pray for us. At times we don't know what to do. Or say. Or think. Or pray. All we can do is to sigh. The Spirit steps in to help. The Spirit echoes our sighs and prays for us with sighs too deep for words. Not words, just sighs. Sighs with us, sighs for us. God hears the sighs of the Spirit. God hears the echoes of our sighs. No matter what we face, the Spirit will help us, weak though we may be. By Saturday, all Margaret can do is to sigh. The Spirit, we trust, prays for Margaret with sighs too deep for words.

We also trust the Lord to work *in* us. We may not know much else. But we can know one thing. All things work as one for good. They "synergize," a transliteration of the Greek. In God's love, they work as one for good. They synergize for good, at God's call.

I learned this as a child from my parents. Verse 28 was their life verse. Paul draws a flow chart of life from start to end with God's call in the center. God foreknows you and me for our good. God plans us for Christ's image for our good. God calls you and me for our good. God justifies us for our good. God glorifies you and me for our good. On Sunday, Margaret no longer even sighs. Still we trust that all things synergize for good too great to guess in God's love and call. As Julian of Norwich put it, "All shall be well, and all shall be well, and all manner of thing shall be well."

Lord, in our weakness may we trust you. Amen.

There's more to come, but does it last? As I sit with Margaret's family and wait, I find myself asking with Paul, "If God is for us, who is against us?" Paul answers this question with more questions.

First, if God is for us, what of grace? God gave Jesus for us. Won't God give all else to us? What of choice? God chooses us. Who can charge us? God says yes to us. Who can say no? What of love? Jesus—who died, rose, and is now at God's right hand—pleads for us. Who can separate us from the love of Christ? We face tough times. Are we on our own? No! With Psalm 44, as excerpted by Paul, we face hard times for and with God. In the end we win. Why? Jesus loves us, this we know, for the Bible tells us so. God is for us. There's more to come.

Then, who can be against us? What of life and death? They can't keep us from God's love in Christ. What of angels and powers? Hosts can't keep us from this love. What of present and future? Time can't keep us from this love. What of heights and depths? Space can't keep us from this love. Nothing can keep us from God's love in Christ. So we can trust, not fear. God is not against us. There's more to come.

In fact, our seats are saved. For years Margaret has believed that a beloved spouse is saving a chair at a banquet table with the lamb of great price. On Monday, Margaret took this long awaited seat. In a few days, I will read Paul's words in a memorial service with new hope that there's more to come.

Lord, let us trust at all times that there's more to come. Amen.

Who Am I?

JULY 25–31, 2011 • DAN R. DICK

MONDAY, JULY 25 ~ *Read Genesis 32:22-26*

How many times does faith bump up against "real life"? We know who we want to be, who we believe God wants us to be—but that simply isn't who we are . . . yet. The life of Christian discipleship is a lifetime of becoming, a commitment to grow and change, develop and learn. Such a commitment comes with a cost. Like Jacob's experience, encountering the living God can be a wrestling match. It forces us to use new "spiritual" muscles, and we come away exhausted. Jacob grapples with the angel of the Lord throughout a long, trying night with a determination not to let go. What an amazing illustration of the passion and perseverance required to truly know God!

Every activity that improves our lives requires hard work. No athlete, musician, scholar, or leader achieves greatness without discipline, practice, and determination. The same is true for people of faith. To grow as Christian disciples we dedicate our lives to becoming who God wants us to be. And we cannot become who God most desires us to be if we avoid God. We pray, study scripture, reflect on our beliefs, alone and with others. In doing so we will encounter God again and again, and these encounters will transform us. Are we willing to hold on with the tenacity of a Jacob, knowing that by doing so we will never be the same? Even if our faith results in a "limping through life," will we seek it with all our heart, mind, soul, and strength? This is the risk and the reward of true discipleship—a tenacity that insists we will not let go unless God blesses us.

Lord, may we hold to you as we trust you will hold to us. Amen.

Director of Connectional Ministries, Wisconsin Annual Conference; Sun Prairie, Wisconsin

Being a Christian is not a simple thing. In a complex culture of competing values, not everyone respects or admires people of faith. Many people ascribe labels and stereotypes to those who believe in God, not all of them flattering or supportive. We can easily feel misunderstood and even persecuted. We cry out to God at the injustice of being mocked; we want others to respect our beliefs, and we often resent being made to feel embarrassed to share our faith publicly. Why shouldn't we be able to feel good about our faith and to celebrate our God?

The psalmist writes a glorious poem to God, seeking God's vindication and the strength to deal with the unjust oppression of adversaries and opponents. Words written three thousand years ago could have been penned last week. The author in ancient Israel voices a modern lament. No one enjoys being misunderstood, and we don't like being ridiculed when we try to do what we believe is right.

In such a world, we may not always receive validation and support for our beliefs from others. From time to time we may find ourselves completely out of sync with those around us. At such times we cannot throw up our hands in despair; but instead, we can turn to God. We learn to trust God's promises that we will not be forsaken when we live by our deepest values and beliefs. Paul echoes this sentiment when he reminds the Romans that nothing on heaven or on earth can separate us from the love of God. We may wrestle with the question, "Who am I?" but it is always well to ask, "Whose am I?" as well. We are children of God, and, as such, we need not worry what others think, as long as we live our lives with integrity and grace.

Gracious God, may I worry less about the praise and respect I receive from those around me and be more mindful of the ways I might honor and glorify you. Amen.

From early childhood, our journey of maturing requires that we become independent. As we move from infancy to childhood to adolescence, our identity emerges as we take on more responsibility and authority. We want to make our own decisions. We form our own beliefs. We become unique individuals. This is just one aspect of maturing. If we stop at the level of our own independence, we become stuck, for only in relationship do we become everything God intends us to be. A shift from independence to interdependence keeps us moving in a healthy direction.

How much richer are our lives because of family, friends, and acquaintances? We are part of an incredible network of people with knowledge, experience, gifts, expertise, beliefs, opinions, and values. Truly, together we are greater than the sum of our parts. We are created for community. Each of us individually may be incomplete and inadequate, but together? Together we become so much more than we can ever be on our own. The answer to the question, "Who am I?" is at once "a unique individual," as well as "a member of the body of Christ."

An old tradition linked to the story of the miracle of the loaves and fishes says that the true miracle occurs when Jesus releases the gathered people from their fear and selfishness to share with one another what they were saving for themselves. In this understanding of the story, each person has a little with them to eat, but they hide it for fear that others will want it. As the small bounty passes from person to person, each tosses in a portion of what he or she brought, resulting in abundance and excess. Individually, none of us has much power to bring about great change; but together, by God's grace, we have the power to change the world.

When I become too focused on my own needs, Lord, remind me that I am part of a larger community and that together we will have more than we need. Amen.

Who Am I?

THURSDAY, JULY 28 ~ *Read Romans 9:1-5*

All too often relationships end because one person continues to grow and develop, and the other does not. The things two people shared in common that brought them together no longer matter so much. Especially in those cases where the life of one person takes an unexpected or significant turn, the bonds of friendship can dissolve. This is a terribly painful experience, but the person who is growing and changing most in positive ways often feels he or she has no choice but to move on.

This is the epiphany Paul speaks of when he writes to the church at Rome of his relationship with "the Israelites." Paul stands at a crossroads: leaving his heritage and history for a new faith. The people who surrounded him, taught him, formed him, and whom he called friends can no longer sustain Paul. Though he acknowledges them as good people, chosen of God, blessed and set apart, he realizes that they are no longer "his" people. The new truth for Paul is Jesus, the Christ. Paul is a new man in Christ, changed forever on the road to Damascus, moving in a completely new direction in his life. He would like nothing better than for the Israelites to believe what he believes, to know the Messiah he now knows; but he realizes that this is not to be.

Throughout Paul's writing, the pain of being "unequally yoked," of living as a Christian among those who do not share the same faith, is evident. Paul reminds us that growth does not come without sacrifice; what we believe and how we choose to live our lives has a cost. There is grace, however, in that we do not break from old relationships without new relationships taking their place. We do not lose more than we gain. In Christ, we find new connections, a new people, to whom we belong.

Lord, growing in faith is difficult. Not only do we have so much to learn, but we deal with the pain of all we leave behind. Stand with us, Lord, so that we might have courage to make hard decisions as we become the people you call us to be. Amen.

FRIDAY, JULY 29 ～ *Read Matthew 14:13-21*

How hungry are you for Jesus? Are you just a little hungry—willing to nibble and snack, just to get a taste of what it means to be a Christian disciple? Are you simply seeking nourishment—a sensible diet to sustain you and give you strength to deal with the ordinary day-to-day demands of your life? Are you famished—starving for substance and sustenance, needing to feast on the rich banquet of all God has to teach and offer? Are you hungry enough to follow Jesus wherever he might lead, regardless of the cost?

One of the amazing features of the story of the feeding of the five thousand is that so many people willingly wander out into the middle of nowhere to listen to a carpenter from Nazareth. Hundreds of people leave work and home on foot to pursue Jesus, seeking his wisdom and his healing. It is not an easy trek. There is nothing simple or sensible about heading into the hills without provisions and supplies. Yet the crowds follow Jesus because they know he will give them something they need.

We all know the discomforts of physical hunger. Few of us have to face real hunger on a daily basis, but we know the insistence of a growling tummy. With spiritual hunger, the "still small voice" will not leave us alone; we want to seek God with soul, mind, heart, and strength. We want to bask in the glow of holy friendship with Jesus Christ and with others who follow him. Nothing will satisfy our soulful hunger but time with God.

When we gather to worship God, it is a time of feeding our spiritual hunger. We sit together and receive nourishment, but it is never enough just to receive. Only in sharing what we receive can our hunger truly be satisfied—by letting others know what it means to be filled.

Fill us, O God, with the spiritual food that sustains and strengthens us, that we might be a source of nourishment and support to others. Amen.

BY CHOICE HOTELS

BY CHOICE HOTELS

The Hebrew people greatly valued their names. The family name was a source of honor and prestige. For a people with a history of slavery and displacement, the one thing no one could take from them was their name. More than a label, a name placed a person in community through family, tribe, and nation.

Early Hebrew names often reflected descriptions of an attribute or defining feature and a connection to the father who gave the name identity. A name located a person in community through family, tribe, and nation. All else could change in an uncertain world—as Jacob's life story illustrates—but at least one could count on his or her good name.

This makes Jacob's encounter with the angel of the Lord so incredible. Not only does Jacob receive a physical reminder of the wrestling match, but he is forever changed in a much more significant way by being given a new name: Israel. No longer is Jacob simply the son of Isaac, grandson of Abraham (another whose name was changed by God), but now he is Israel, the father of a people and the founder of a nation. The answer to the question, "Who am I?" always included not just the person but the lineage, with each person being the sum of the whole family.

We often think of our faith as a personal and private matter. God may disagree. While each of us individually belongs to a church or has a unique relationship with God, we are also members of the whole body of Christ. We are no longer "just" individuals but are joined together to be something so much more, so much greater. We are Christ for the world, transformed by God—from individuals to a people, just like Jacob.

Lord, I am humbled to be part of the body of Christ. Help me to be worthy of such honor and grace; and in all I say and do, help me to glorify your holy name. Amen.

We cannot answer the question, "Who am I?" apart from two other questions: "Who is God?" and "What is God's will for my life?" A serious exploration of these questions reveals a simple but powerful truth: I can only be fully myself when I am in a healthy relationship with God and purposefully seek to do God's will. And I can do this by maintaining a healthy relationship with all of God's children. God wills that we become the incarnation of Christ for the world, and no one can do that alone.

It isn't enough to know that God loves us and that we receive God's blessing. The Israelites knew as much, and as Paul laments, that was not enough. To be God's people requires that we change and grow, that we obey God's word and will. The Word was made flesh in Jesus the Christ and, by God's Spirit, the Word continues to be written through the body of Christ—the church. We protect our inheritance as the children of God through openness to God's guidance through the Holy Spirit.

Our faith, never limited to what we believe, includes how we behave and how we relate to one another. So much of Jesus' and Paul's teaching addresses the whole community. No man or woman can accomplish God's will alone. Only in spiritual community, bound together in Christian love, can we ever hope to become all that God intends. What is impossible to any one of us becomes attainable when we join together, guided and empowered by the Holy Spirit. In Christ, the question "Who am I?" is best articulated as, "Who are *we*?"

Make us one, O Lord. One with you. One with each other. And one in ministry to all the world. We pray humbly in Jesus' name. Amen.

Lord, Lord . . .

AUGUST 1–7, 2011 • MONTY BROWN

MONDAY, AUGUST 1 ~ *Read Romans 10:5-13*

"If you confess with your lips that Jesus is Lord and believe in your heart that God raised him from the dead, you will be saved." How often I have heard words like these put into some kind of formula—a "salvation formula" or a "Roman Road to Salvation"! But I keep coming back to Jesus himself saying, "Not everyone who says to me, 'Lord, Lord,' will enter the kingdom of heaven, but only the one who does the will of my Father in heaven" (Matt. 7:21).

How do we reconcile such words—those of Jesus and those of Paul? Clearly Jesus' words prevent Paul's words from being reduced to mere formulaic validity. "Say the right words and you will be saved" does not seem to fit into Jesus' paradigm.

Rather, Jesus (and Paul rightly construed) declares that it is the heart and the actions arising from the heart that are required. It is about relationship. Spouses professing faithfulness while practicing polygamy just won't cut it. What matters is whether the heart is changed, whether the life is transformed.

It's not always easy. Sometimes it's very difficult. Indeed, we can't do it on our own. Some of the sweetest words in the Gospels are those of the man who claimed, "I believe; help my unbelief!" (Mark 9:24). And for Jesus that was and is enough.

Help me be real with you, O Jesus. Empower me to move beyond mere words and formulas. Help me to remember when we fell in love. Amen.

Son, husband, father, grandfather, pastor, author; Charleston, West Virginia

TUESDAY, AUGUST 2 ~ *Read Romans 10:14-15*

In this passage, feet are beautiful—not because they are naked or washed (by Jesus in the upper room or by Ruth down on the threshing floor)—but because they "bring good news." I look at my own feet and must confess that "beautiful" is never an adjective I've thought of or heard anyone else use to describe them. I keep them covered as much as possible. Could anyone really think that my feet are beautiful?

It's powerfully reassuring that the "resurrection feet" of Jesus still bore the crucifixion marks. Those scars made his body and his resurrection all the more good news. When his resurrected body proclaimed the good news that God had conquered death for all eternity, a wounded body made that proclamation.

Today's scripture tells me that the beauty of my (or anyone's) feet is not to be found in conformity to some exterior standard. Rather, their beauty comes in their usefulness in carrying to others the good news borne by Jesus' wounded feet.

Many have not heard or believed the good news, that their broken and ugly lives can benefit by this good news. For so long they have heard only the words of judgment, "not good enough," so they cannot believe that the good news of salvation is also for them. They can't imagine that anything about their lives could ever be called "beautiful."

In all of our brokenness, we are particularly suitable vessels for the good news. Indeed, God seems to have a penchant throughout the Bible for using broken people as vessels of the good news. It is our brokenness that bears witness to God's good news that others need to know. It is by God's work, not our own, so none may boast.

Lord, I believe; help my unbelief. Encourage me not to fake it on your behalf. Amen.

This epic tale records not merely the story of the escapades of Joseph, an ancient Indiana Jones or biblical Luke Skywalker. Rather it is the "story of the family of Jacob."

Jacob "settled" here in this place. He is not the first settler; indeed, he is a third-generation settler of Abraham's family, Abraham who settled here as an "alien."

That sense of identity as "family" and "alien" plays an important role in the First Testament of the Bible. Even today when Jews celebrate the Passover, they remember that "a wandering Aramean was my ancestor" (Deut. 26:5). That remembrance connects them to the family story.

Our faith might be better served if we think more in terms of the good news being a family story rather than a set of moral principles. With family, it's personal. With family, we overlook one another's eccentricities and differences and focus on our relatedness.

The notion of "alien" also shaped the worldview of our forebears of the faith. The essence of law involved care for strangers, because the Israelites remembered that they too had been strangers (Deut. 10:17-19). If we would remember times when we were aliens, it might change much of our attitude and action toward the strangers, the aliens, among us. We might then remember and recover the ancient biblical custom of practicing hospitality to strangers. The first-generation settler in this land, Abraham, did exactly that.

Hospitality. Strangers. Family. Not merely hospitality for our friends, but treating strangers with the recognition that they are indeed family.

O Lord, encourage an attitude shift that leads us to care for the stranger. Amen.

THURSDAY, AUGUST 4 ~ *Read Genesis 37:12-28*

He came to Shechem, and a man found him wandering in the fields; the man asked him, "What are you seeking?"

Can you imagine the story of Joseph had not the unnamed man just happened to have overheard the brothers talking about moving on to Dothan? No bread crumbs or forwarding address would direct Joseph to them. Consider the story's end if Joseph had gone home to Jacob to report, "Not there, Dad. Didn't see any sign of them. I guess we'll just have to wait until they come back."

No Egyptian slavery for Joseph, Egyptian prison, Potiphar's wife, Pharaoh's court, salvation from famine, slavery for all Jacob's children, Moses, Passover, parting of Red Sea, Sinai, Ten Commandments, or return to the Promised Land—all of this because of the unnamed man at Shechem, who happened to overhear and pass along the word.

I do know that there was the fourth-grade teacher, whose name almost no one in my life now knows, who taught me that every day of our lives we each have a profound impact on the life of someone else.

I do know that there were people all along the way, whose names are unknown to my congregations, who shaped me and formed me and helped me hear a call to ordained ministry.

They say everyone clamors for their "fifteen minutes of fame" in life. The man from Shechem who pointed Joseph toward Dothan never got his due, not even having his name remembered and recorded. But what he did changed the course of history for the family of Jacob and for us, Jacob's descendants.

O God, today may the impact of my life on someone else be for your glory and not for my own. Amen.

Give thanks. Make known. Sing. Seek. Remember. Praise. And tell the story to others of what God has done for us.

We often find it difficult to follow Paul's admonition to "walk by faith, not by sight" (2 Cor. 5:7) when all we can see around us appear to be bad options. I heard an older fellow one time, in the midst of unfathomable sorrow, say: "It doesn't feel like God is in the midst of this at all. Luckily I don't have to rely upon my feelings. I can rely upon my memory."

Sometimes we can see God's hand in life's circumstances only when we look at them in the rearview mirror. But, when we do look and see, we need to both give thanks and remember those times. They can help us keep the faith later when our present sight and emotions fail us. Sometimes, in an attempt to make everything "user friendly" and to leave nothing to question in our worship, we may have obliterated the sacred symbols of ritual and of memory.

Our forebears of Jacob's family understood the importance of sacred symbols in terms of memory. When your children ask why this worship of Passover (Exod 12:26)? Why these rules? (Deut 6:20)? Why these stones stacked up as a monument (Josh. 4:6)? The answer is always the same: Give thanks. Make known. Sing. Seek. Remember. Praise. And tell the story to others of what God has done for us.

When we speak only in present-tense feelings that do not involve memory, we may be user friendly. But as good as Twinkies taste, we ought not make a complete diet of them.

Lord, may I spend time each day remembering and giving thanks. May I pray the psalms and know that I kneel, sit, stand, and pray in solidarity with the saints who have gone before and those who will follow. Amen.

SATURDAY, AUGUST 6 ～ *Read Matthew 14:22-27*

How often do we read of disciples stuck out on the waves? This is the second time in Matthew's Gospel. But their fear is real regardless of how many times it occurs. When I ride across a certain bridge, the railing beside me is lower than my bicycle seat, and I am sixty feet above the water. No matter how reassuring my self-talk may be or how many times I've done it, the fear that grips me each time on that bridge is real.

What interests me as I read this passage is to hear that what really terrifies the disciples is seeing Jesus. The Gospel writer tries to explain their fear by saying that they think Jesus is a ghost. But when I get afraid of Jesus, I can't claim that as my excuse. What? Get afraid of Jesus, you say. Whatever can you mean?

When I make up my lists of to-do items. When I pack my day with all kinds of activities and convince myself of how far behind I am and how I don't possibly have time today to sit quietly with Jesus, doing nothing but drinking in his presence. I can go day after day, piling leftovers of yesterday's list onto today's list, getting more and more behind, more and more frustrated.

The One who stilled the waves and fears of life then is still available to do so today. But it seems that sometimes I am more afraid of what it might mean for me to be still and turn over control to him than to fear all that faces me.

Those silly disciples . . .

Be still my soul. Let fear not turn me aside from the One who longs to gather me as a mother hen gathers her chicks. Amen.

It's that satanic *if* word. The devil used it in the wilderness: "'*If* you are the Son of God. . . . "* Then we are told (at least in Luke's version) that Satan departs from him until an opportune time. (See Luke 4:13.)

The usual thought involves the devil's reappearance, using the "*If* you are the Son of God" shtick, speaking through the mouths of those at the foot of the cross. But we also see it in this Gospel lesson, coming from Peter's mouth." "Lord, *if* it is you, command me to come to you on the water." I picture Jesus, standing on top of the waves, smiling and signaling to Peter: "Come on, big boy. Let's just see how your *if* game works."

Peter gets out of the boat. When he begins to sink, he cries, "Lord, save me!" Jesus catches his hand and replies, "You of little faith, why did you doubt?"

We often assume that Peter's doubting began when he started to sink. I think it began when Peter put Jesus to the *if* test. When Peter began going under the waves is when he threw his doubts out the window. That's when Peter didn't ask for tests. That's when Peter needed Jesus to be the Lord.

After the Resurrection, John's Gospel records one last Jesus and Peter boat-and-water incident. Peter is in the boat and sees someone on the shore. Someone says that it's Jesus. *Now* Peter doesn't need to test Jesus with words to the effect: "If that's really you, Jesus, arisen from the grave, then prove it by making me walk on the water to you." No, he just dives into the water and swims to his Lord.

Lord, I believe; help my unbelief. Let me know that you always unconditionally affirm me in your love. Amen.

Coloring Outside the Lines

AUGUST 8–14, 2011 • JENNIFER DESMARAIS

MONDAY, AUGUST 8 ~ *Read Genesis 45:1-5*

Joseph methodically puts his brothers through the paces. He uses his position and power to hold up a mirror to his brothers so that they might see what has been written on their hearts by their long-ago actions. The reflected image is clear. The brothers immediately connect their actions toward Joseph with their current circumstances.

Then it happens. While Joseph holds the mirror, he catches a glimpse of himself. Joseph looks in the mirror, and the young man he sees moves him to tears. Behind the wise eyes of the powerful man that Joseph has become is the younger brother who loves and misses his dad and his family. Joseph's heart reflects reconciliation and he releases his plans for retribution. He embraces his family and uses his position and power to help them.

The mirror never lies. It shows the wrinkles in our clothes and the lines on our faces. We give it a quick glance for approval before stepping out the door in the morning. We look for a hair out of place and tuck in our shirt.

What if we could see more? What if the mirror could look deeper and reveal what is written on our hearts and pictured in our souls? Would we have the courage to look? to face the person God sees when looking our way? God loves us regardless of what is reflected, but to see ourselves as others see us can be painful, joyful, enlightening, inspiring, and often surprising. Would you find it a blessing or a burden to see yourself through God's eyes?

God of love, help us reflect to others the love and acceptance that we know through our relationship with you. Amen.

Small-group leader, mother of three; Lancaster, Pennsylvania

TUESDAY, AUGUST 9 ～ *Read Genesis 45:6-15*

God can use to good purpose experiences and situations we wouldn't choose for ourselves. The child abandoned at birth can become the cherished son to a couple who lives oceans away. The woman who feels lonely in a crowded church can become the devoted friend who invests in and journeys with others. The brother sold into slavery can become the ruler in a foreign land who saves lives. God is flexible; God is innovative and resourceful. God sees myriad opportunities each time we veer off course.

God navigates the human experience like a GPS system. God sees the situations that befall us and watches as we make poor choices. We lose our way, and God recalculates. Tune in to the voice of the Holy Spirit, who says, "Recalculating." We may make a wrong turn, but God can recalculate, restore, and get us back on the road. Trust the leading of the Holy Spirit and God's word to lead to God's best desire and intention for our lives.

As with Joseph and his brothers, God brings good from a bad situation: a reunited family, wealth from poverty, provision in a time of dire need. God, indeed, had made the best of Joseph's detour in Egypt and recalculated.

Expect detours. Celebrate long winding roads. Send postcards. Ask for directions. Be open to the Spirit and the will of God to use you to reflect divine love and the light into that dark alley that feels like it's "off route."

It's not about you but about what God can do through you. The Lord is a God of wonders. Life may turn into a white-knuckle ride; hold on tight and pray. God is "recalculating."

Merciful and gracious God, help me to quiet my mind that I might better know your wishes. Use me for your will, and give me the strength to bring your love and light to the dark corners of people's lives. Help me embrace challenges as opportunities to recalculate. Amen.

WEDNESDAY, AUGUST 10 ~ *Read Matthew 15:10-20*

Our true purity resides in the heart rather than in outward religious observance. Disobedience to mores and norms does not defile an individual. Sin, breaking God's law, defiles the individual: What I say. How I treat others. In Jesus' time, this meant persons could eat with unwashed hands. Today, we might interpret this to mean that God doesn't care if I wear jeans and a T-shirt to worship. God cares if I murder or steal—not if I skip the coat and tie on Sunday. It matters who I am inside.

This distinction reminds me of the chocolate bunnies all wrapped up in fancy pastel foil at Easter. The bunnies come in two basic varieties: the hollow bunny and the solid bunny. I think the same can be said of Christians. There are hollow Christians and solid Christians.

The hollow Christians go through the motions of prescribed religion but do not engage in faithful living. Like the business-man who ushers on Sunday morning just to make new contacts. On the outside, he is walking the Christian walk and talking the Christian talk. However, on the inside, his heart reveals selfish ulterior motives. A thin coating of Christianity does not mask the heart of any sinner from God.

Solid Christians *look* like Christians and *act* like Christians. Their loving hearts manifest themselves in loving deeds and actions. They are the same inside and out. Their love knows no limits, and the passion with which they live out their faith fills them up. They are solid in thought and deed.

Thank you, Lord, for filling me up each day with the joy, hope, grace, and faith that makes my life so sweet. Amen.

Jesus met all sorts of people in his travels. His community was forever expanding to include people along the way: disciples, beggars, lepers, prostitutes, thieves, and widows. A collection of souls that Jesus united by "coloring" them the children of God. Jesus colored people as he healed with a touch or a word. Jesus colored people in his teaching as he met people where they were. Jesus colored people in worship as he preached God's word. Did Jesus ever color outside the lines? Yeah, he did.

The day that Jesus healed the Canaanite woman's daughter is one day that Jesus colored outside the lines. Her faith put the crayon into Jesus' hand and in a quick short stroke of healing he colored outside the line. Even the least of these, those outside the lines, deserve the Lord's mercy. Jesus never meant to stay inside the lines.

Living out our faith in community will lead us outside the lines. At the community meal where we serve. At the clothing bank where we volunteer. At the mission trip on which we work. In missions and ministry, we reach out most often to individuals outside the lines. And just as the Canaanite woman's faith moved Jesus, we too find ourselves moved by our interactions with the people who are outside our lines. We who thought ourselves the instrument of change are, in fact, the changed.

The lines shift. You can't look in just one place for God's children. Close your eyes and let faith guide your crayon to color your world as you share God's grace and mercy. Let yourself be led outside the lines.

Thank you, Jesus, for using all the crayons in the box to color our world with grace, love, and mercy. Help me share your life and your love. Amen.

FRIDAY, AUGUST 12 ～ *Read Romans 11:1-2a, 29-32*

Does God close doors and lock people out of grace and love? Some theologians lead us to think that is possible. In today's epistle lesson, God's faithfulness to Israel looms larger than theoretical debate. The question of God's abandoning Israel is a question of divine integrity. If God has cancelled or changed the covenant, we're all in a heap of trouble because then we have a God who may as readily abandon us. Paul decisively helps us know that this is not the God of Jesus Christ!

God does not abandon. God has made very great, very comprehensive, very specific promises to a people known as Israel. God chose Israel and promised to bless the nation. The blessing was not even conditioned upon their behavior. In other words, God blessed despite some of Israel's actions. Paul describes three actions: God chose a people; God made covenant with a people; and God kept the covenant.

Perhaps the most important aspect of Romans 11 comes in verse 29: "The gifts and the calling of God are irrevocable." God calls not only Israel but all of us! How do we come to know that we can trust God and God's faithfulness? The simple answer is through Jesus. God's covenant goes from being exclusively with one specific nation to universally for all people. Jesus proclaimed God's irrevocable love for the whole world. Nothing and no one can close that door and lock it.

How can I stay open to God's love and direction today? How can I guide others to stay open to God's love?

Good and gracious God, you disclosed yourself to Abraham, Isaac, and Jacob. You made yourself known through Jesus. Let us be one in the unity of your Spirit and guide us to know that your love excludes no one. Amen.

Against the backdrop of the rhythm of four square, young and old visited with one another while artists created holiday originals. Parents noted with admiration and joy that their children, who were once the little ones learning to play four square, were now the older children teaching and coaching the next generation of four-square players. For over two hours the kids enjoyed a high-spirited game overflowing with goodwill and generosity. Above the din of the activity, warm greetings rang out from all corners of the social hall and the kitchen, as a never-ending stream of members and friends from the neighborhood joined the frenzy of fun and food. To me, this scene represents the church at its best—all generations of the church family in fellowship together and embracing the community at large. Being a community in which to live and love and learn.

The sum of who we are comes from adding up how we live and how we love and how we learn. The biggest variable in this equation is the people in our lives with whom we live, love, and learn. Guess Mom got this one right: your friends matter. It matters because rubbing shoulders with people changes you and them. It matters because you can pray all you want for God to create community; but if you are doing nothing to build the unity, it will never happen. It matters because while boundaries are healthy, life is not about boundaries, and lines cross when you do life in community. When you belong to a faith community where you invest in and journey with others, your life and the life of the community is blessed. How very good and pleasant it is when kindred live together; when they live, love, and learn together.

God, we are thankful for the opportunity to be part of your community. Amen.

SUNDAY, AUGUST 14 ~ *Read Psalm 133*

When my family started attending church so the kids could go to Sunday school, I felt like a mere bystander with no connection to the people, the pastors, or God. I sensed no unity with the people of the church. I could open the doors of the church but not my heart. Serving Christ, proclaiming his message, and being in community for him made me uncomfortable. However, through the habit of attending church, I slowly grew to value and desire the blessings of being united as a church family. It is a blessing for others who can sense God's love in our midst, and it also blesses us because we sense the support and encouragement of one another.

In this psalm, the oil flows from the head down to the beard, and I trace this same trickle-down effect in my family. Our unity and relationship with the church started with my husband and me. As we allowed God's anointing to guide our thoughts, it flowed down to the kids. As a family we began to learn how to dwell in love and unity, and God's Spirit flowed more freely among us.

Like the dew nourished the mountains, unity in Christ has nourished my family; our life has grown vibrant. As a family we led a weekend-long outreach project at a local transitional living center that supports people by helping to move them from homelessness to permanent housing. What an amazing experience as together we used our gifts in Christ's service.

Be mindful today of allowing God's anointing to guide your thoughts. Remember that you are part of a body of believers and that no matter what your day brings, you are not alone.

Faithful and loving God, help me today to recall the joy and blessings of a shared journey with other believers and with you. Amen.

Faith Empowers Community

AUGUST 15–21, 2011 • TERRY J. HAMILTON-POORE

MONDAY, AUGUST 15 ~ *Read Exodus 1:8-22*

When we list the heroes of the Bible, two names don't often come up: Shiphrah and Puah, two women who help other women birth babies. *What could be more nonthreatening?* And that's what Pharaoh must be thinking as the two of them stand before him, summoned to explain why he still sees boy babies around after he's given orders for them to be killed at birth.

"Oh," the midwives tell him, "the Hebrew women aren't like the Egyptian women: they're so strong and healthy that they give birth before the midwife can get there." As they know, Pharaoh considers the Hebrews as inferior, perhaps even subhuman, like livestock; so Pharaoh has no trouble believing them. Just as he'd believe that only the boys matter and that a girl can certainly pose no threat to him. Meanwhile, these harmless looking women have been quietly bringing to birth a revolution.

This passage offers us a lesson when we feel powerless, with no way to challenge oppressive structures. With so much wrong in the world—war, terrorism, famine, homelessness, and climate change—how can everyday people like us have any effect at all? Shiphrah and Puah didn't have to become something they weren't in order to make a difference. They simply went about their daily work with integrity and refused to allow that work to be used for evil. And that's all that's required of us, as well. When we live and work with integrity and courage, we too erode the powers of oppression and lay the groundwork for a revolution of goodness.

God of all goodness, help us to live and work each day as those who are bringing your gracious reign to birth. Amen.

Presbyterian minister, pastor of Christ Lutheran Church; Fairfax, California

TUESDAY, AUGUST 16 ~ *Read Exodus 2:1-10*

This past winter my church took turns with a number of other congregations as part of a rotating homeless shelter. Every Wednesday evening a small group of women would arrive at our church, eat dinner with us, and sleep in our sanctuary. As we ate with them we learned their stories, and they learned ours. Soon we could no longer think of homelessness as an issue but as a real experience faced by people we actually knew. That personal connection—the realization that Gloria, Amanda, or Christine might be sleeping on the street the next night—gave us a sense of urgency to continue to help these particular people in tangible ways.

I imagine something similar happens to Pharaoh's daughter when she opens that basket and sees the crying baby. She has certainly seen needy children before; but when we observe suffering in large numbers and when we ourselves are simply passing through, it's easy to distance ourselves. Here, though, lies a particular baby in a basket that the princess herself holds. She recognizes that it is a Hebrew baby—one of those that her own father has ordered to be killed; but this close, personal encounter makes the baby and his needs real to her, and she feels responsible for his well-being.

As worshipers of a God who chose to live among us and encounter people face-to-face, when we too open ourselves to face-to-face encounters with those in need, we find ourselves changed. We can no longer act like objective observers because God places their needs squarely in our hands.

Gracious God, guide us toward those who need us, and open us to them in humility and compassion. Amen.

WEDNESDAY, AUGUST 17 ~ *Read Psalm 124*

If it had not been the Lord who was on our side . . . " We read here the praise of a group that has come through terrible danger—a people who have been attacked by an enemy, beset by the powers of nature; a people whose very survival has been in question, and yet here they are: whole and alive. They ascribe this survival to God's being on their side.

I can't help but notice, however, that having God on one's side does not keep trouble away. Enemies still amass; flood waters still rise. How often have we, when faced with excruciatingly difficult circumstances, felt that those disasters signaled God's abandonment?

Throughout scripture, the people of God find themselves beset by famine, by slavery, by the trials of the wilderness, by sometimes unspeakable suffering. If that's the case, then what good does it do to have God on one's side?

The good that it does is to help us get through it. Knowing that God is on our side gives us courage to face our troubles— whether those troubles come in the form of an army or a flood or an illness or some other form of danger or suffering. Knowing that God is on our side helps us hold our heads high because the outcome of our situation matters not only to us but to God. And knowing that God is on our side gives us hope, because even though all ordinary forms of assistance may have failed us, there is still One who will not let us go under.

Blessed be you, O God, for standing by us in trouble and for bringing us safely through. Amen.

THURSDAY, AUGUST 18 ～ *Read Romans 12:1-2*

At the birth of each of my children, I gratefully acknowledged how whole their bodies were. They were beautiful. And it wasn't because they conformed to some artificial, "buns of steel" standard (thankfully, the cookie-cutter template for beauty isn't usually applied to babies), but because their bodies worked. Tiny though they were, they arrived fully equipped to do the things babies need to do in order to grow and thrive. They could sleep, eat, digest, hear, see, and cry—all abilities geared toward bonding them into relationships. Only with others relating to and caring for them could they survive and flourish.

Our media-saturated culture tends to value our bodies according to how decorative they are. So when Paul says, "Present your bodies as a living sacrifice, holy and acceptable to God," it can come as a revelation to us to think that our bodies could be acceptable to anyone, let alone God. It's a revelation, and also a reminder that the beauty of our bodies lies in what they were made to do, which is to connect us with the world and with others. Vision, hearing, touch, taste, smell—these are all relational abilities.

The "sacrifice" Paul speaks of comes in our decision to use all of our senses and abilities to build and nurture relationships and to contribute to the health and survival of the whole living, breathing, interconnected body of Christ. And since we are part of that same body, what may begin as a sacrifice (whether of pride or of a misguided sense of worthlessness) results in building us up as well.

Loving God, help us to appreciate the goodness of the bodies you gave us and to use those bodies for the health and wholeness of the body of Christ. Amen.

Michael, a faithful member of my congregation for years, was a quiet man (who, suitably enough, worked in a library). He preferred not to serve in positions of church leadership. He was not yet sixty, so his sudden death after a short illness shocked the membership.

In the weeks that followed Michael's death, the congregation seemed a bit ragged around the edges. Much of this "frayed" feeling was related to the grief of his loss; but there was another reason as well. Things just weren't getting done.

I and others would arrive for church and realize there was no coffee. The ushers would reach for the plates at the time of the offering and realize that the plates weren't there. Small thing after small thing fell through the cracks. Why? Because Michael had always done them! These tasks didn't appear on a list anywhere because they had always magically happened, quietly, with no one's having to think about them. Now we have to think about them, list them, and assign them.

"Don't think too highly of yourselves" (AP), Paul admonishes the church. His words serve as an important reminder for those who believe the church revolves around them. But I hope that Michael didn't think too lowly of himself; that he had a full awareness of how vital his simple actions were to the healthy functioning of the congregation. "As in one body we have many members, and not all the members have the same function, so we, who are many, are one body in Christ." One body. Not a conglomerate of individuals vying for power and importance, but one body. Separate, we are just fragments; together, we are whole.

For making us part of your living, breathing, interconnected body, O God, we give you thanks. Amen.

When Jesus asks, "Who do people say that [I am]," the disciples offer several answers, all involving dead prophets. When Jesus asks, "Who do you say that I am," Peter responds, "You are the Messiah, the Son of the living God." This is the "right" answer, and its rightness lies in the adjective *living*.

When we try to articulate our own understanding of Jesus, we sometimes fall back on the language of creeds or doctrines—language that is often framed in the past tense ("born of the Virgin Mary, suffered under Pontius Pilate," etc.). While these words can provide a framework for faith, that framework still requires flesh. Where do we encounter Jesus? How do we experience his presence in a living, breathing way?

It's worth noting that his own disciples don't have a single, clear, fixed understanding of who Jesus is and what he is about in the world. Peter may give the right answer in this passage, but just a few verses later his understanding will be so wrong that Jesus will rebuke him and call him Satan.

Because Jesus is the embodiment of a *living* God rather than a dead philosophy, our understanding of him is always growing and developing (and, as with Peter, sometimes bears correcting).

So, where have you witnessed Jesus' healing? How has he fed you? When has he opened your eyes? And, most importantly, when you are asked, who do you say that he is?

Don't be concerned if you aren't entirely sure. Because we serve a *living* Lord, we don't have to have the complete answer. Instead, we trust that he will continue to teach, encourage, and correct us along the way.

Living Lord, walk alongside us and guide us toward a fuller understanding of who you are and what you ask of us. Amen.

SUNDAY, AUGUST 21 ~ *Read Matthew 16:13-20*

I was a latchkey kid. At least I was when I remembered my key. On the days that I didn't, I was a locked-out kid. My childhood experience makes me a bit nervous when Jesus announces that he is handing to Peter (and, by extension, to the entire church) the keys of the kingdom of heaven. What if we lose them? Or what if we have the key, and we know it's the right key, but we just can't get it to work? We stand there jiggling it back and forth in the lock to no avail.

The bigger problem with Jesus' handing the keys to us is that if we lose or mishandle them, we are not the only ones affected. "Whatever you bind on earth will be bound in heaven," Jesus says. "And whatever you loose on earth will be loosed in heaven." That's a frightening responsibility for anyone with a history of bobbling keys.

So what are these keys that Jesus is handing us? They are the ways in which we discern God's will. In a rapidly changing world, how do we interpret God's word to us and declare with confidence what is good and acceptable for God's people in our particular time and place? This is no small task, and, with so much at stake, we approach it with a healthy dose of humility.

But while it is a big task, it's not impossible, because we don't do it alone. As Peter affirmed earlier in the passage, we serve a living Lord who continues to act and speak in our lives and in our world. Besides which, Jesus didn't hand the keys just to an individual but to the church as a whole. If we get stuck, chances are someone else will step forward and, in one smooth motion, turn the key.

God of love, give us discerning hearts so that together we can know your will for us. Amen.

Burning But Not Consumed

AUGUST 22–28, 2011 • S. THEVANESAN

MONDAY, AUGUST 22 ~ *Read Exodus 3:1-15*

A bush blazes but is not consumed, and a voice tells Moses, "Remove the sandals from your feet." Through sight, sense, and touch, Moses feels the glory of God. This experience of God completely differs from everyday ordinary events. When have you felt God's glory?

Our experience of God shows up in our relationships with other people. After his experience with God in the midst of the wilderness, Moses becomes a different person. He no longer runs away from problems and people. He sees the terrible burden of the Hebrew people in Egypt, and he acts on God's direction. How does our awareness of God's love guide us in a world of uncertainty and ambiguity? How does God's love shape our understanding and our feeling for a world with terrorism and other attacks against humanity? God's love can shape our perception and experience of the natural order, involving floods, tornados, and hurricanes. When we take off our shoes to experience God's holiness, our perception of life changes.

In many ways, even as a pastor I am insensitive to people's pain, as well as to the injustices of the system. How can I feel the pain of another? How can I know the depths of another? Only as I open to God and pray for God to make me vulnerable can I develop some understanding.

Life becomes meaningful for those who can sense the surroundings, the neighborhood, and the needs of others. And the inexplicable beauty of God is hidden there.

Loving God, teach me to follow you in word and deed and to give you the glory! Amen.

Pastor, Christ United Methodist Church; Snyder, New York

Moses has an incredible encounter with God on Mount Horeb and is awestruck when he sees a bush burning and yet not consumed. Then a voice from the bush tells Moses, "Can you go and free my people, the Israelites? Can you deliver them from the bondage of Egypt?" (AP). Moses believes that he is talking to God, yet he wants more clarity. He prolongs the conversation: "Suppose Pharaoh happens to ask me who gave me this authority. What do I say?" And God replies in a profound way: "I am who I am. I was. And I shall be. And I cause to be what is" (AP). The strength of I AM empowers Moses to bring release to the captives and lead them to God's Promised Land.

The hymn writer Brian Wren raises similar questions in "How Can We Name a Love." Wren reminds us that we meet God each day "in a hundred names . . . at work, at home, or in the street." In the strength of God's name, we find ourselves delivered from captivity and brought to a promised land.

What power rests in a name? We have named God in many ways: father, mother, friend, liberator, creator, and redeemer. What name do you use when you desperately need God's presence? Every name has a significant story behind it. When my parents named me Theophilus, which is the biblical translation of the word Thevanesan, they dedicated me to God's service. My mother told me this story often during my childhood. Whenever I wavered and slipped in life, I remembered why my parents gave me such a name. That knowledge and the power of the name changed my outlook on life and helped me fulfill my parents' dream as well as my own aspirations. I remember also that I belong to the One who said, "I AM WHO I AM."

Lord God, help me do your will in all circumstances. Amen.

WEDNESDAY, AUGUST 24 ~ *Read Psalm 105:1-6, 23-26, 45c*

To gain a deeper understanding of this psalm, I referred to *The Message*, Eugene H. Peterson's translation. The psalm begins, "Tell every one you meet what [the LORD] has done." The excitement of God's story comes in the telling itself. By sharing with others how God has worked in the twists and turns of our lives, we practice God's grace. Proclaiming our story to the world is our mission as well as our calling.

Psalm 105 closes with the words, "Praise the LORD." I sobbed as I read them because that is the one thing I often neglect to do in my life. I take the praise of God for granted, assuming that someone else will do that for me.

These verses recount part of Israel's history, recalling her time in Egypt and reminding us of God's sending of Moses and Aaron. Perhaps looking back over my history will generate praise. What burning bushes do I see? As I note the evidence of God in my life and speak of God's marvelous work, praise rises to my lips.

How and when do you praise God? How can praise, thanksgiving, and giving glory to God become part and parcel of daily living with all its uncertainty, strain, and stress?

Some people say that their inability to deal with life's pain mutes their praise of God. However, when we recognize our own worth and our likeableness, we also see the loving nature of God in other persons. As I love myself, I love others. As I affirm myself, I affirm others. As I consider God's work in my own history, I acknowledge God's work in every person's life, and I join in the praise of our Creator's majesty. Perhaps you can do that as well.

Gracious God, through my speech and actions help me always to praise you! Amen.

The Psalms provide spiritual satisfaction. When I sit alone with the Psalms, I join thousands of others who have found nourishment and direction for their spiritual journeys over several generations. Today's psalm invites us to sing praises to God, to give thanks, to tell the world of God's gracious acts, and to call on God's name. I often wonder how people can give thanks to God in the midst of warfare, killing, genocide, homicide, hunger, and other horrors. I take comfort in knowing that the psalmists lived in times not unlike our own and they gave voice to feelings similar to my own—and perhaps to yours. The psalmists plead, weep, call for vengeance. They explode in desperation and curse enemies. The psalmists praise God and keep silence. They remember the past and live in hope. In all these circumstances they give thanks.

Psalm 105 calls to mind Israel's history during the time of slavery in Egypt. As the psalm relates Israel's past, I see in it my own biography. Perhaps you see your own story of captivity and deliverance. Psalm 105 helps me move with courage into the future with an attitude of gratitude to God.

The psalm writers did not use sophisticated words to express their devotion and loyalty to God; they reveal to us the feelings and longings of individuals, the yearnings of a community and a nation, the frustration of a nation's endless waiting for a day of justice and for the fullness of God's reign. They plainly assure us that God is real, God is with us, and God understands our pain. "Sing praises to [God]; tell of all his wonderful works." Amen!

Holy God, may I always live for you, despite all of life's distractions. Amen.

I often wrestle with one question: What does it mean to be a Christian these days? Whenever I travel across the United States of America, I see Christian churches and schools and colleges, Christian bookshops and counseling centers, Christian real estate businesses and Christian athletic clubs, and practically everything else Christian. I wonder if these buildings and institutions are Christian in name only. What difference does the name of Christ make? In other words, by adding the word *Christian* to everything around us, do we give lip service to Christ or do we live as Christ lived?

Romans 12:9-21 offers a prescription for Christian ethical living. Paul writes basic instructions that are hard to set aside and hard to do: "If your enemies are hungry, feed them; if they are thirsty, give them something to drink. . . . Do not be overcome by evil, but overcome evil with good." These words are not original to Paul; they come from Jesus in the Sermon on the Mount: Love your enemies, bless those who curse you, do good to those who hate you, and pray for those who mistreat you. These are hard words to practice in our daily lives. Living like Jesus requires a lot of heart work.

Paul describes heart work to the church in Corinth: Love is patient. Love is kind. It is not envious or boastful, arrogant or rude. Love does not insist on its own way. Love is not irritable or resentful. Love does not rejoice in the wrong but rejoices in the truth.

In heart work we practice the presence of Christ in our lives on a moment-by-moment basis. No revolution in this world will transform us to be more like Jesus unless we begin to live selflessly. When our actions reflect the actions of Jesus, then we act as Christians.

Compassionate God, lead me always in the path of justice and truth, and guide me to listen to you and to follow you. Amen.

SATURDAY, AUGUST 27 ~ *Read Romans 12:9-21*

Of all Paul's epistles, Romans is especially complex. Remember that Paul belonged to the tribe of Benjamin. He was an ardent Pharisee and an upright and blameless man by Jewish and legal standards. He learned from Gamaliel, a great rabbi.

Despite being steeped in such tradition, Paul broke with that tradition. He realized his calling through the grace and love of Jesus the Christ. When Paul began to follow the footsteps of his master, he was transformed. It is an understatement to say that his life changed. He became Christ-centered, and his life's mission was to show Christ to the world.

"Marks of a True Christian" is the guiding caption for Romans 12:9-21. When Paul invites us to live out a meaningful Christian life, it sounds simple. How can we genuinely live a life of love? The reading suggests that we bless those who persecute us, rejoice with those who rejoice, and weep with those who weep. Let our love be genuine. Hold fast to what is good and hate evil.

The human race belongs to the Spirit of God. Our life is a reality only through the love of God. If we understand this basic truth, then we have found a remedy for prejudice and broken relationships and warfare. Recognize that injustice anywhere on earth destroys justice everywhere; fear anywhere frustrates hope everywhere; hate anywhere kills beauty and love. Be love! Speak love! Live love—as Christ loved!

How will someone describe your life as a life of love? Add dimensions of love to your attitude. Face your concerns and make your choices with a sound mind and a compassionate heart. I can imagine Paul's concluding this passage with the same words he wrote to the Philippians: "Let the same mind be in you that was in Christ Jesus."

Living God, teach me to be faithful to you in good times and bad, in sunshine and shadow. Amen.

Jesus foretells his impending death and speaks of his last days on this earth. Along with his farewell discourse, he invites people to a deeper dedication of their lives for his cause. Jesus summons us here: "If any want to become my followers, let them deny themselves and take up their crosses and follow me."

Isaac Watts, reflecting on the sacrifice of Christ, wrote: "Were the whole realm of nature mine / That were an offering far too small / Love so amazing, so divine, / Demands my soul, my life, my all!" What a delightful experience it is to live life with Jesus—except when I am called to make some sacrifices for love's sake! Then I may put on the spiritual brakes or bargain, "Wait a minute. You want me to do what? That wasn't what I expected. Could you change your mind?"

God answers our bargaining: "I am that I am." Jesus points us to the way of the cross.

Mullah Nasrudin was a holy fool in ancient Persian stories who may have lived in the twelfth or thirteenth century. One day Mullah Nasrudin decided to learn to play violin, so he found a teacher. When Nasrudin asked the cost for lessons, the teacher replied, "Ten gold pieces for the first month and then one gold piece for each following month." "Excellent," exclaimed Nasrudin. "I will begin with the second month."

Are we waiting to become disciples of Jesus the Christ when the cost is less and the burden is light? Rabbi Hillel, teacher of Gamaliel and thus Paul, famously asked, "If I am not for myself, who will be for me? And when I am for myself, what am I? And if not now, when?" Jesus said, "If you want to follow me, take up your cross" (AP); now is the time.

Lord Jesus, quench my thirst with your living water, and feed me with your living bread. Amen.

Called to the Table

AUGUST 29–SEPTEMBER 4, 2011 • DEBORAH APPLER

MONDAY, AUGUST 29 ～ *Read Exodus 12:1-14*

Tables and relationships go together. Think about it. So many events take place around tables—tables of many shapes and sizes and stationed in various settings. Whether they have four legs with chairs underneath or lie flat on the floor of a Bedouin tent, tables are sites that reflect relationship.

At home, my mother escaped every morning to the kitchen table with her 5:00 cup of coffee for alone time with God. As my children grew up, our dining room table became the place not only to share meals but also to tell stories and work out the problems that needed our attention. The supplies and scattered papers tossed haphazardly on the coffee table reflected collaborative creative energy. These sacred eating and working spaces reflected the joy and hard work of being in community.

We sit at many tables—at home, in the workplace, at worship, and in the larger society. Some tables we look forward to joining with great excitement; others we dread, often because we are denied an invitation to them. This week we will explore some literal and metaphorical tables to which we are called—sometimes kicking and screaming! We go because we know that God asks us. Exodus 12 recounts God's salvific activities for Israel that call Israel to a sacred Passover meal. Psalm 149 and Matthew 18:15-20 call us to the table to work together on the difficult tasks of reconciliation and justice. Romans 13:8-14 clears the table of drunkenness and debauchery to make room for radical love and hospitality.

God, may I come to the table prepared to meet you in the laughter, love, confrontation, and reminiscing. Amen.

Associate professor of Old Testament, Moravian Theological Seminary; Bethlehem, Pennsylvania

The Hebrew people have experienced lack of food and power under Egyptian rule. They are at the mercy of their taskmasters until God hears and acts in response to their painful cries. This response takes shape in a table ritual, the enactment of the Passover meal. It involves sacrificing a lamb and sprinkling its blood on the doorposts to spare the lives of the Hebrew firstborn. A meal follows that includes sharing lamb, unleavened bread, and bitter herbs. While they were hurrying to find safety from an angry Pharaoh, God calls the people to sit at the table to share a meal—a meal of all things!

Nevertheless, God has a reason for calling the people to pause, eat quickly, and reflect. God offers specifics about the meal's preparation and the sharing of the meal. None in the community will be excluded from the table. Moreover, those who have access to a lamb too large for their own household are to share with another family. Hoarding resources is disallowed; all food must be eaten that very night or be burned. This ancient system of economics left no room for the unfair distribution of God's resources. God calls the Hebrew people then and us today to live in this promise with hearts set toward creating just communities where all have equal access to resources.

The annual Passover meal models justice and continues to remind participants that, while evil and injustice exist in the world, God has liberated, presently liberates, and will do the same in the future. Today is Eid-al-Fitr. Today those of the Muslim tradition break fast and celebrate the end of Ramadan, a month of fasting and prayer that calls them to experience the pangs of hunger and poverty that plague many all year and also calls them to action. We too, as Christians, are called to pause and to ask ourselves how we respond to today's oppressed.

God, you set a table of justice for all of your people. Your providence creates more than enough for everyone. Amen.

Ilove comfort food—the food you turn to when you need to feel good. My grandmother made the best homemade soup and fried chicken in the world. When the aromas filled my senses and the dishes hit the table, all of my worries and struggles would vanish. Food and conversation would flow as our family shared this time together. As much as I would have liked to stay at that table longer, I knew I had to face the day's work.

The Israelites share a meal of comfort food, knowing that the process of eating together in community will sustain them. The sprinkled blood of the lamb on their doorposts will spare them the painful loss of their firstborn. The people, once fed and reassured, now are called to leave the comfort of the table for the difficult task of becoming free and building the land of promise. They know the track they need to take, and they have to move fast.

Both Exodus 12 and Romans 13 emphasize the importance of actively working to create a new and just world. This mixed multitude of Hebrews were instructed to eat quickly, fully dressed and donned with shoes ready for a speedy departure. Likewise, Paul, anxious for the day when God's world will be renewed in Christ, calls for Christians to wake up and move! A struggling Augustine, leading a fairly licentious life, is led by Paul's words to embrace a God-filled life. Neither the Hebrews nor Augustine were perfect as people, but their journeys moved their communities closer to the world God wants—a world where peace and justice flourish for all creation.

What path is God calling you to walk? What keeps you from girding your loins, putting on sandals, and leaving the comfort of your table to help to create the land of promise?

God of liberation, I am only one person and the needs of the world are overwhelming. Help me take the risks that you want me to take. Amen.

THURSDAY, SEPTEMBER 1 ~ *Read Psalm 149*

Arthur, oblivious to his royal pedigree until he pulled a sword out of the stone, was crowned king over Camelot. One of his first symbols of rule involved the table he built to seat himself and his knights as they discussed the kingdom's needs. The table was round. All who sat there sat in equal positions of privilege because the table purposely had no head or foot. The modeling Arthur gave, though imperfect, empowered Sirs Gawain and Lancelot to ride off and seek justice for the realm.

I disliked the fact that sometimes the knights used violence to bring about this justice. I have the same negative reaction when I read psalms like 149 that begin by painting the picture of a Camelot existence in a land where people will sing new songs and live freely, only to shift to words of vengeance and violence. Does God call me to brandish a two-edged sword and fight the enemy? Or should I read about this violence metaphorically? Isn't vengeance God's and not mine?

This psalm was written most likely during the Exile after King Jehoiachin and his courtiers have been banished to Babylon; there are no more kings in Judah. Clinton McCann suggests that this psalm transfers the power and responsibilities of the Davidic monarchy, which involve keeping God's laws and serving as God's conduits for justice, onto the people—onto you and me! The mission proclaimed in Psalm 149 is clear: to establish justice among the nations. So how can we take on this royal responsibility? We all have gifts and opportunities to make changes in our community. We need to continue sitting at those community round tables like the PTA or the county or city council and find our niche.

Lord, help me to sing a new song in the community where you have planted me. May I cocreate that round table where all can sit and share together in love and mutual respect. Amen.

Most of us do not like to gather at tables where the tension cuts so deep that it causes pain, especially when we have an issue with someone sitting with us. It makes sense that we want to spend our limited time with friends, family, church members and colleagues in a conflict-free and low-stress setting. We find it difficult to share a hard truth with someone, especially someone we care about or love. We might not want to hurt his or her feelings, or we fear losing the relationship.

Yet Jesus calls for direct honesty in all our relationships, including members of our faith community. In today's passage, Jesus gives specific directions for dealing with difficult relational situations that can potentially damage the community as a whole if behaviors fail to change.

First we are to sit at the table with those with whom we struggle and throw down all the cards. We name and clarify the harmful actions, how these hurt us, and what we hope will enable healing. Confrontation is not easy. I often wish that we could just skip to the second and third steps, so that we could bring along a few friends or the pastor to help make confrontation more palatable. John Wesley states clearly that skipping the first step is problematic: "Our Lord gives no liberty to omit this, or to exchange it for either of the following steps." What makes us feel better might be unfair to our friend or fellow congregant who might be oblivious to the problem. A direct private conversation could alleviate the problem while protecting the dignity of both the relationship and the church.

The way we deal with conflict as Christians has a direct impact on how people of the world view our religion. They will know we are Christians by our love—and sometimes it is tough!

God, give me the strength to be honest and direct with my friends and family even when it is uncomfortable. Strengthen me to hear tough but loving things said to me. Amen.

SATURDAY, SEPTEMBER 3 ~ *Read Romans 13:8-10*

I have lived in my new house for over four months and am ashamed to admit that I do not know the names of my next-door neighbors or anything about them. From an unofficial survey that I have taken, I know that I am not alone. Many of us are transient because of jobs and life situations. Our busyness leaves little energy at day's end to expend on getting to know someone new. We covet our time and our space. Yet Romans echoes Leviticus 19:18 and calls us to love our neighbors as ourselves.

I often console myself by focusing on the broader notion of who a neighbor is. A neighbor does not necessarily live next door to me. In the global world, my neighbor can be the woman living in Mbeya, Tanzania, who struggles to find clean water for her family or the Muslim who lives in the next city who is being scapegoated by the community. When I work for justice for all God's people so that they can live life as well or better than me, then I am, in effect, loving my neighbor as myself. Nor am I to forget my neighbors who live close to me. My neighbor lives next to me, down the road from me, and in the global community.

To love our neighbors fulfills the law, which makes love our most important action. But how do we do this? The phrase "think globally and act locally," or "glocally," is important and implies our responsibility as Christians. But how do we love our neighbors if we do not know them? Perhaps this weekend we might take some time to touch base with someone who lives beside us or near us whom we would like to get to know better. Perhaps we can start by inviting them to the table—a good first step.

Dear God, give us the energy to open our hearts to new people in our lives. May we get to know our neighbors near and far. Amen.

SUNDAY, SEPTEMBER 4 ~ *Read Matthew 18:18-20*

One of my many weaknesses when I spent my sabbatical teaching at the Moravian seminary in Mbeya, Tanzania, was my lack of proficiency with ki-Swahili. One day a woman from the local Moravian church came to see me. She was a strong, spiritual woman whose husband left her with six children to support. She worked several jobs but still involved herself with the congregation. She possessed a wisdom and groundedness that I longed to experience, but our inability to understand each other initially brought us to an impasse. I served cookies and tea, and we sat together, speaking broken English and Swahili. That day we made a profound connection and were no longer strangers. We experienced firsthand that when two or three gather in Christ's name, Christ is with us.

Today is the first Sunday of the month, and many churches will participate in one of the most important rituals of faith: Holy Communion. We will gather at the table in Christ's name and remember Jesus Christ's saving acts in the past, celebrate what Christ is doing today, and look forward in hope to Christ's saving works yet to come. Like the Passover, Holy Communion is a justice meal and provides a foretaste of the reign of God and the messianic time when all pain, suffering, and oppression will be defeated by the risen Christ.

The Communion meal is also about the grace that is available to all who come to the table and open themselves to God's love. It is a table where all can recharge and share in the presence of both Christ and the community of saints. We do not know a fraction of the people gathered at the many tables, and we cannot speak all of their languages. Yet the act of communing together in prayer overcomes our differences and opens the door for Christ to enter.

Come, Lord Jesus. May your mysterious presence empower us to know one another more intimately in Christian love. Amen.

God of Surprises

SEPTEMBER 5–11, 2011 • RAY HOWE

MONDAY, SEPTEMBER 5 ~ *Read Exodus 15:1b-11, 20-21*

Often referred to as the "Song of the Sea," this passage triumphantly expresses in song and dance Israel's first great affirmation of faith in the mighty power of God. The Lord's strong arm delivers God's beloved children from slavery in Egypt by destroying Pharaoh's army at the Red Sea. The Exodus event becomes the definitive act of God in their midst throughout the Old Testament. It highly influences their worship and liturgy as well as their trust that God will act on their behalf in the future.

Most scholars consider Exodus 15:21 to be one of the oldest texts in scripture and the most ancient in the chapter. "And Miriam sang to them: 'Sing to the LORD, for he has triumphed gloriously; horse and rider he has thrown into the sea.'" Miriam, the first woman in the Bible to be called a prophet, took a tambourine in her hand and led the women (and there is reason to believe the men as well) in song and dance in celebration of God's great victory.

What a spirit of gratitude and thanksgiving filled the hearts and souls of the people of Israel on that day! Their saving God was in their midst.

When have you experienced the awesome sense of God's presence in your faith community? How did it manifest itself? How often do you find the joy of thanksgiving in your private devotions?

O God, awaken us to the joy we can experience in you. Amen.

Retired Episcopal priest who served parishes in Massachusetts and Pennsylvania for forty-four years; now living in Cary, North Carolina

TUESDAY, SEPTEMBER 6 ~ *Read Psalm 114*

Hebrew people still sing this hymn of praise glorifying the massive power and faithfulness of Almighty God as seen and experienced by the people of Israel through the Exodus event in preparation for the annual Passover meal.

The psalm is short and to the point. If God is for us, who can be against us? Surely not Pharaoh or his fearsome soldiers on horseback or even the great sea itself or the Jordan River that changes its course at God's command. God delivers the people of Israel from slavery in Egypt with a mighty hand and an outstretched arm.

As followers of the risen Christ, we view this awesome event as an important part of our heritage and our experience of God. We acknowledge and celebrate God's power and goodness in what God did for Israel, and indeed for us, in the Exodus. In much the same way, as Christians, we acknowledge another saving act by the same God who opened the gates of heaven through the suffering, crucifixion, death, and resurrection of Jesus Christ. We witness to how Christ conquered death; offers salvation to all; and calls his followers to love, service, fellowship, and dedication.

In both the Exodus event and the Resurrection, God acts in entirely unexpected ways. Ours is a God of surprises, over and over again. Perhaps we take this revelation for granted when we read it in the Bible but forget that this same God of awesome and unexpected dealings plays an active role in our everyday lives. God is forever at work in the lives of God's children—and full of surprises. God remains faithful but never predictable.

How do you open yourself to God's surprises?

WEDNESDAY, SEPTEMBER 7 ~ *Read Exodus 14:19-31*

A boy and his dad might throw a ball back and forth. A child might toss sand or pebbles into the ocean. We don't usually distinguish between throwing and tossing. But I found the use of the word *tossed* in today's passage chilling. It sounds so cavalier: "The Lord tossed the Egyptians into the sea."

I remember being much more chilled almost exactly ten years ago when a small group of us were reading Morning Prayer together on a weekday at the Church of the Atonement in Westfield, Massachusetts. Only a few days prior, terrorists had commandeered two American airplanes and slammed them into the twin towers in New York City, killing thousands of innocent people. The three of us reading Morning Prayer were still in shock—sad and angry, in part because we had seen fellow human beings on our television screens literally dancing in the streets and cheering this murderous act.

As one of the respondents reading the even-numbered verses of the appointed Psalm 58 from The Book of Common Prayer, I heard myself saying,

> "The righteous will be glad when they see the
>   vengeance
> they will bathe their feet in the blood of the wicked."

The words chilled me to the bone. Reading the Bible can be a chilling experience. We do find murder, adultery, torture, unspeakable treachery, brutality and genocide. Scripture unabashedly shows the seamy side of life. Yet I'll take the chills. I'll take the bones along with the chicken, because I believe scripture is the revealed word of God, inspired by the Holy Spirit, and a most powerful and wondrous gift from the Almighty. Thanks be to God!

Thank you, Lord, for your gift of the Bible. Amen.

THURSDAY, SEPTEMBER 8 ~ *Read Matthew 18:21-22*

I am a numbers person. I was blessed (or cursed) with a love of numbers—not any special ability with numbers, but I find them intriguing. I enjoy Sudoku, but calculus would have buried me. I remember being disappointed upon learning that Jesus' response to Peter's question of how often to forgive was more likely seventy-seven times than that of an earlier translation that indicated "seventy times seven" (or 490) times.

My curiosity is piqued by how many denaria there are in ten thousand talents (80,000,000+ according to some commentators) and how a slave or servant could possibly owe so much, especially if a denarius was a normal day's pay for a worker. I also know that Jesus uses numbers in this instance to stretch the spirit and mind of his listeners.

At a certain level I miss (or nearly miss) that Jesus does not call us to forgive seventy-seven times or 490 times but rather an infinite number. I *don't* miss the fact that the specific focus of forgiveness is "another member of the church." Nor do I miss that the Lukan version (Luke 17:3-4) explicitly makes repentance an integral part of the sin-and-forgiveness cycle. Nor do I miss the scare tactic in the unveiled threat of torture until the servant pays the entire debt when he does not offer forgiveness. Perhaps Jesus simply states the situation exactly as it is; but for my sake, I hope not.

I am very clear about one thing: God wants me to forgive. And when I am not ready, God wants me to want to forgive. And when I am not even there, God wants me to want to want to forgive. And if I am not there, my eternal soul is endangered.

Whom do you want or need to forgive? It is not too late. You could do it now.

Peter comes to Jesus and asks, "Lord, if another member of the church sins against me, how often should I forgive? As many as seven times?" Jesus replies, "Not seven times, but, I tell you, seventy-seven times."

Jesus then tells a parable about a slave who owes the king a large debt. Not long after the king mercifully cancels the entire debt, the slave imprisons a fellow slave who owes him a much smaller amount. When the king learns of this, he summons the first man and says, "You wicked slave! . . . Should you not have had mercy on your fellow slave, as I had mercy on you?"

Mercy and forgiveness are fundamental to Christian community and parish ministry. Their absence greatly limits healthy growth. We live under God's forgiveness and acknowledge the debt that we owe God because of our sin. Through grace we respond by offering mercy and forgiveness to others who also do not deserve it. This process is by no means easy or simple. Even with much prayer and the support of the sacraments of baptism and Holy Communion, it may not be completed in a lifetime.

Parishioners who live with joy, thanksgiving, and merciful forgiveness make the job of parish ministry so much easier. Members in the faith community (including the pastor) see how such people have "got it right" with God and others.

Nancy has been such a person for me. She's been through a great deal personally. She grew up in a family of twelve siblings. Her alcoholic father drank away his living and abused his wife and children on a regular basis. Yet Nancy will quickly tell you how she came to forgive her father through her understanding of a merciful, loving Savior who has forgiven *her*. Her gratitude, joy, and thanksgiving—as well as the grace to forgive—shine through Nancy, and that gives them hope.

Who offers hope to you?

I remember, as a young adult, discussing the Last Judgment with my mother. She suggested that when someone dies, that person meets Jesus and together they watch something like a movie of the person's entire life. She believed that each person gets to look back at both the good things and the not-so-good things he or she has done or failed to do during life on earth. She anticipated this to be a relatively short time of judgment that would be followed by an eternity of blessedness and mercy with the Lord. Experiencing the "movie" would be both very painful and very joyous but always bearable because of Jesus' presence.

The community in Rome was struggling with the issues of right belief or right observance. Paul moves beyond both issues to raise this question: Who are you to pass judgment on servants of another? Relationship to God through Christ takes precedence over all. It is God who judges, not human beings. Paul writes, "We will all stand before the judgment seat of God."

At the time I conversed with my mother, the concept of the Last Judgment troubled me. I believed that Christ would come in glory and judge the living and the dead, but I didn't like my chances in this arrangement one bit. At some level I feared that the demands of justice and judgment would limit God's mercy. My mother's way of thinking seemed rather simplistic and unsophisticated to me. In retrospect I realize that her words and her witness seeped into my being.

We are accountable to God. We are subject to God's judgment. However, our limited understanding of judgment in no way limits God's mercy. God loves us more than we can imagine and forgives us in Christ. We are all guilty before God. We all rely on the mercy of God in Christ. "Mercy triumphs over judgment" (James 2:13). What great news!

Reflect on a situation in which you have shown mercy and in doing so have drawn closer to God.

The main heading in my Bible for Romans 14:1-12 is "Do not judge another." Paul writes, "Why do you pass judgment on your brother or sister?" The apostle is in good company with Jesus, who states in the Sermon on the Mount, "'Do not judge, so that you may not be judged. For with the judgment you make you will be judged'" (Matt. 7:1-2).

A part of me is very drawn to these words. I like the idea of leaving all judgment to God. Who would want to make a harsh judgment and thus be harshly judged by God? Wouldn't it be wiser to mind my own business and leave well enough alone? Who am I to judge?

Yet when I am honest with myself, I realize that my willingness to leave judgment to God often has a close tie to my need to make other people happy and to avoid conflict. My knee-jerk temptation has often been to avoid making judgments that my roles require of me. This might be in my role as pastor of a congregation, father of my children, or simply as a human being. I want to avoid the hassle that comes with standing tall and making a firm judgment. However, when I make those difficult judgments, it seems to be with God's blessing.

Surely God calls the Christian community to make judgments. In 1 Corinthians 5:12 Paul writes, "For what have I to do with judging those outside [the church]. Is it not those who are inside that you are to judge?" Jesus tells the disciples that they will sit on twelve thrones, judging the twelve tribes of Israel (Matt. 19:28).

What a difficult task it is to discern when and how to make a judgment and when to avoid it like the plague!

Lord, give us the wisdom and discretion to avoid making unnecessary judgments, and the humility and courage to make those that we need to make. Amen.

God the Generous Giver

SEPTEMBER 12–18, 2011 • DAVID R. NICHOLAS

MONDAY, SEPTEMBER 12 ～ *Read Exodus 16:2-8*

My eight-year-old son, Andrew, sat in school crying because he'd lost his pet gerbil. Meanwhile, I'd searched and found the little critter, which had managed to find its way down three flights of stairs to our basement. It gave me joy to pick up the phone, call the school, and ask the receptionist to tell our son I'd found the gerbil. Andrew learned to trust me a little more.

Throughout the dealings of God with the people, there's always been the unseen miracle of managed events. All the while, God teaches the people to trust: "I will test them and see whether they will follow my instructions" (NIV). The people seem unaware of God's concern or the divine willingness to teach them to trust God more. The Holy One supplies food for stomachs as an attempt to convey God's care. Verse 6 clearly reveals that the reason for the provision of manna was to show that God is in control. "You will know it was the LORD who brought you out of the land of Egypt."

The Hebrews would discover that this same God has always been with them, caring for them at the Passover, keeping the promise made to Moses at the burning bush, and remaining with the people. Times have changed, but God hasn't. God's promises are sure and although the lessons may be tough, God seeks to draw us closer to God's self. The Israelites slowly learn. How quickly do we perceive God's hand at work in our lives?

Lord help us to learn the lessons you would teach us through your Word. Amen

---

Baptist minister and writer, currently serving a church in Tasmania

In my early days of ministry, I visited a woman who had been ill. I said," I believe you've been sick."

She glared at me and snapped, "Sick? How do you mean? Physically, mentally, or spiritually?"

I responded, "That's for you to tell me." While my answer won the day, she was one of the best grumblers I've ever known.

Grumblers United fittingly describes the Israelites as they approach Moses and Aaron full of complaints. The book of Exodus recounts not only a story of the Israelites' exodus from Egypt and their wanderings through the desert but also records the constant grumbling against God.

The crisis around food becomes a crisis around leadership. The Israelites come straight to the point when they confront Moses and Aaron. Interestingly enough, the scripture confirms that God has *heard* their grumbling. As a result of the grumbling and complaining, the people will *know* that Yahweh saves. And finally, the arena of knowing will be the barren desert, seemingly bereft of all life. The Lord God hears the complaint directed at Moses and chooses to answer the complaint directly and reveal God's glory in this wilderness wasteland.

Quail comes at twilight. Manna arrives in the morning. God supplies the people's needs. The result? "Then you shall know that I am the LORD your God."

Perhaps it's always been hard to trust God in difficult times. For the Israelites Egypt had been hard, but little did they realize that after the Red Sea came the desert. God's testing place. The lessons of God are easy to miss. This passage affirms that God hears us and responds. And when we "draw near to the LORD," we will see God's glory.

Gracious God, may I draw near and see your glory and acknowledge your provision. Amen.

WEDNESDAY, SEPTEMBER 14 ~ *Read Psalm 105:1-6*

Praise is the focus of this psalm. The psalmist calls for thanks to God, to sing and tell of God's wonderful works, and give glory to God's name. This passage of blessing encourages us to be thankful in all circumstances.

But some people never seem happy or satisfied. In one of his New Testament studies, William Barclay tells of a man who saved a young boy from drowning. When he returned the boy to his mother, she asked, "Where's his cap?" Often we see the glass half empty rather than half full.

The media pounds our minds with "works" that give little or no credit to God. We see scenes of devastation and violence; the media managers seemingly have no recollection of a wonderful God as they deliver media meals of doom and gloom. And sometimes neither do we. We can fall prey to the worldview of darkness and "bad things" and fear. We can ignore God and the wonderful creation. Because people crave the sensational, the media seldom announces joyful things on a regular basis. Good news does not sell papers or advertising time.

The psalmist has no television news to boggle his eyes. No newspapers block his mind to the things of God, and radio waves do not fill his ears with a zillion trifles of the hour. The psalmist sets his mind on God's faithfulness.

Like the people of Israel, we can suffer from spiritual amnesia for many reasons. Dissatisfaction with current reality can skew our recollection of a gracious past. And faith communities that cannot tell of God's wonderful works in the past can easily misconstrue the present. So, the psalmist's call to remember becomes the remembering.

O Lord, help me focus on all you have done. May I ever praise you and tell of your wonderful works. Amen.

Our verses today recall God's provision in the wilderness. The wilderness, a place of desolation, thirst, and famine becomes redefined as a place of care and respite through God's provision:

• The Israelites leave Egypt with some resources (silver and gold)
• Guidance through cloud and fire
• Food of quail and manna
• Water in the desert
• The Promised Land as their own

In case we're experiencing spiritual amnesia or hunkering down in fear, the psalmist reminds us of God's ongoing work in the background. The Israelites grumble, God supplies—not all the delicacies of Egypt but food and drink for the day. This passage confirms the wonderful bounty of God who "brought Israel," "spread," and "gave." These verses speak of a giving God who remains true to the divine covenant with "Abraham, his servant."

God chooses a people, displays wonderful works, and then asks for obedience. While the people of God forgot the covenant, God did not. As we follow the journeys of the Israelites, two items are worthy of note: the waywardness of God's people and the protecting hand and wonderful works of God. As we face times of spiritual hunger and thirst, isolation and the absence of God, let us remember God's wonderful works. Let us recall water in the desert and manna for provision. God makes the desert habitable and leads the way with cloud and fire.

Heavenly Father, help us this day to be more trusting about the way you deal with us, your children. Amen.

FRIDAY, SEPTEMBER 16 ~ *Read Philippians 1:21-30*

Paul writes to his beloved congregation at Philippi. He is imprisoned and does not know the outcome. He writes to assure the Philippians of his physical safety and well-being and to stress that whether he lives or dies, the work of Christ will move forward. Paul notes that his death will culminate in his desire to be with Christ, but he acknowledges the boost that his physical presence affords the Philippians: "to remain in the flesh is more necessary for you." He goes on to speak of his future visit and focuses on their living whether he is there in the flesh or not: "Live your life in a manner worthy of the gospel of Christ."

One of my congregants, an older woman in her eighties, was "imprisoned" by poor health with no one to care for her. One day when I visited, she was trying to light her fire. With matches in hand, she said, "Come on fingers, you've got to go on a little longer." She warmed her feet on cold nights with a heated-up brick wrapped in a piece of cloth. One Sunday morning after church service she said to me, "Pastor, I can't see you and I can't hear you, but this is where the Lord wants me." She focused her living and dying on Christ.

It's easy to lose our focus and forget the Lord. Yet for Paul, everything focused on Christ. Christ was in Paul and Paul in Christ; that was the beginning and the end of the matter. Paul realized that life was passing by and that only what he did for Christ would last. Our passage reminds us of several things. God is in control. Because Christ rose from the dead, we have a joy that can never be taken away. When we focus on Christ, even our suffering has meaning.

Heavenly Father, there are so many distractions. This day keep my spiritual eyes focused on Jesus. Amen.

SATURDAY, SEPTEMBER 17 ~ *Read Matthew 20:1-16*

This passage describes unhappy people. Sometimes we can be far too exacting and present a whole list of complaints. Many years ago our church treasurer worried about water loss due to a leaky faucet in the parsonage garden. He calculated the water drops by the minute, hour, day, month, year and reported his findings to the church officers. He grumbled mightily about wasted water.

In today's passage the workers grumble. Living in our age of trade unions, we probably find it hard to understand the employment situation in Jesus' day. Workers were not protected by unions. But the landowner is most generous, a man with a big heart.

If we view this passage through Christless eyes, we identify with the complainers who say to this effect, "They got more than us." As our children might say, or even we ourselves: "It's not fair!" If, on the other hand, we see life through the eyes of Christ, we'll realize how wonderful God's grace is toward each and every one of us. We receive far more than we deserve.

Jesus speaks this parable to the disciples, the so-called "insiders," who believe they have a leg up on others. Who wouldn't have come late to following Christ or late to work, if everyone gets the same thing?

The work requires more laborers. The landowner offers the current rate of pay for a day. Those who work all day and receive the agreed-upon sum don't quibble about that; what galls them is that some work only an hour and get the same amount. Yet the landowner is within his rights to pay the workers as he did.

What situations in your life make you question God's fairness? How does this parable address your desire for your just recompense? What makes you more deserving?

To learn contentment is great gain.

More unhappy people, more Grumblers United. We can get pumped up with our own importance and our demands for what we consider "our rights." Our passage clearly shows the landowner has the final say. The fact is he had the right to pay whatever he felt like paying. He kept within the law and paid according to the contract. No matter how people grumble in the final countdown, God has the final say. We might hearken back to the words of Abraham, "Shall not the Judge of all the earth do what is just?" (Gen. 18:25). Truly, "the last will be first, and the first will be last" (Matt. 20:16). There is nothing fair about God's overwhelming grace, except that everyone gets "paid."

Sometimes we can be legalistic when it comes to serving Christ. Others receive undue recognition, and we feel slighted. God gives us opportunities to serve. Like the landowner, God rewards faithfulness according to the opportunities we accept. Like the muttering worker, we often are all "grab," and we cannot understand that God is all "give."

Divine grace levels the playing field, ripping away privilege. That's a hard fact to take when we've based our lives, both Christian and personal, on merit. We want the rewards that honest work and putting in the hours bring.

It takes us a while to realize that we have no rights before God. We may indeed envy God's generosity. We may believe that we deserve more than what we've been given. But our faith grows stronger as we learn the economics of God's grace.

Gracious God, thank you for your overwhelming grace. Amen.

Always the Last Place You Look

SEPTEMBER 19–25, 2011 • JAY MARSHALL GROAT

MONDAY, SEPTEMBER 19 ~ *Read Exodus 17:1-7*

I once scoured my house for an hour looking desperately for sunglasses perched the entire time on top of my head. I had them the whole time and found them the last place I looked. That describes *my* experience of God's Spirit. From time to time, we think we've lost it. Life fills us with fear, anger, or loneliness: any debilitating condition can do it. We never lose the Spirit, but sometimes we forget that the Spirit is always perched on our souls like sunglasses hiding on our heads. So today perhaps the holiest thing we can do is remember that the first place to look for God's Spirit is within our soul.

Exodus 17 describes the wandering people of Israel as forgetful. They've forgotten God's promise of faithfulness. They feel lost, forsaken, hungry, and thirsty. Their souls are more parched than their bodies; they're angry at God, Moses, and every other blessed thing.

Who would blame them for complaining? But instead of smiting the people, God tells Moses to strike the rock at Horeb with the staff that struck the Nile. And there was water. God doesn't want to smite us; God wants us to remember. God does not want our souls to thirst but to be filled.

Do you suppose God looked around for the driest piece of desert to be found, a rock, from which to deliver life-giving water? God can transform even our fear, anger, and loneliness into the water of new life.

Loving God, with your power, I know that anything in my life can be transformed for your use. Amen.

Senior pastor, First Congregation Church; Akron, Ohio

TUESDAY, SEPTEMBER 20 ~ *Read Exodus 17:1-7*

God tells Moses in Exodus 17 to find water by striking not just any rock but the rock at Horeb. How ironic: Horeb is where all this Exodus-business started between God and Moses. Horeb is where God spoke to Moses through the burning bush.

This means that Horeb is also the place where Moses resisted God's call. Remember? God says, "Go to Egypt," and Moses responds, "Send anyone but me." Tense dialogue ensues with the Almighty finally reaching the boiling point.

Again we discover a God who does not choose to smite the misbelieving Moses. Instead, God tells Moses to focus on their relationship rather than on the impossibility of the task, to focus on God's love of Moses and the people of Israel, to focus on the reality that no matter how impossible the task, "I am with you."

Even a little bit of God is more than enough, God tells Moses at Horeb. In fact, a little bit of God is *everything*.

Like Moses at the burning bush, the people of Israel in Exodus 17 are misbelieving people. In their moments of hunger and thirst, they believe only in their ability to be angry and complain. So God tells Moses to strike not just any rock with his staff—but the rock at Horeb.

Poor Moses! After all this time he's right back where he started, at the mount of Horeb. This time Moses must deal not only with his own fears and faithlessness; he must also deal with everyone else's.

The Horebs are the places in our lives where transformation and new life, with all its white-knuckled newness, happen: the AA meeting, the hospital waiting room, the family supper table. Horeb-rocks may litter many places, just waiting to be struck.

Loving God, help me remember today that Horeb is everywhere I go and that the first place to look for new life is exactly where I am. Amen.

There is a large, beautiful waterfall in the national forest near my home. Over the years, visiting the waterfall has become an important religious act for me. It only takes me twenty minutes to drive to the waterfall, and I visit it about once a month.

Years ago the park service built a sturdy wooden staircase to the bottom of the falls. The rangers built benches at the bottom too. When you sit and look at the falls, the sound of falling water is loud. I sit and meditate with eyes, ears, and soul wide open.

As the years fly by, I've found that while I enjoy the beauty of the waterfall, I am drawn to the place because of the sound of cascading water. The rushing sound envelops me like a security blanket. In those moments I feel God's embrace and "hear" the eternal voice of God in the falling water.

Psalm 78:1 reads: "Give ear, O my people, to my teaching; incline your ears to the words of my mouth." Today is a good day to *give ear* to the teachings of God found in loud waterfalls, the laughter of children, and the rush of leaves in the wind. Sometimes, or perhaps most of the time, we *hear* God before we *see* God.

Today is a good day to choose to listen for God instead of speaking of God. We will hear God in the sounds of our lives, all of them, when we choose to give ear to the teachings of God that envelop us everywhere we go.

Loving God, remind me that a large, beautiful waterfall of grace cascades within me. Today may I give ear to the sound of its voice. Amen.

One of the most stimulating days of my life was the day I rode a whitewater raft on the New River in West Virginia. What an exhilarating, and sometimes frightening, joyride!

My friends and I spent much of the ride rushing through white water surrounded by huge boulders. We also enjoyed stretches on the river that were calm, wide, and peaceful. In one of these calm moments our guide suggested we jump in for a swim—keeping our life jackets on, of course—so I did. The guide told us that in these stretches the river was more than one hundred feet deep.

I'll never forget the feeling of being pulled by the strength of the river. The mighty river ripped me along at breakneck speed, but the ride was also soft and peaceful. I just let go of all my anxiety and let the river take over. The life jacket was like the living Spirit of God holding me up and keeping me safe.

The psalmist recalls the mighty power of God through the Exodus experience. This God divides seas and leads with cloud and fire. This God makes streams come out of rocks and causes waters to flow down like rivers.

Life with God is like being pulled by a strong river while wearing a life jacket. When we remember that God's Spirit is often found in the last place we look, we open ourselves up to the possibility that no matter where the river of life takes us, God is there, buoying us up, guiding us to a land of promise.

How would you characterize your life today? Are you enjoying a smooth, safe ride down a peaceful river, or are you in the midst of a life-threatening ride through the white water? If your ride today is a smooth one, thank God. But if your ride today is scaring you to death, remember that the life jacket holding you up is the living Spirit of God.

Loving God, may your Spirit be my life jacket today in the waters of life. Amen.

FRIDAY, SEPTEMBER 23 ～ *Read Philippians 2:1-13*

This passage includes some great theological images and metaphors of our shared life in Christ. Here Paul invites us to seek the mind of Christ Jesus. We learn also about the self-emptying (*kenosis*) of Christ. That self-emptying action serves as a model for Christian followers throughout the centuries; however, when we look at the larger context of Philippians 2, we discover that Paul appeals to the church to grow in its unity.

Kenosis serves as an example of the unity of Jesus Christ with God the Creator. Paul urges his readers to seek a similar unity within the life of the congregation: be of the same mind, have the same love, be in full accord and of one mind.

When we consider the state of the church—whether worldwide or a denomination or a specific congregation—we often see signs of disunity. We argue over history. We engage in conflicts about goals for ministry or mission. We fight for "our side" in theological disputes. The church in Philippi manifests evidence of conflict. In the midst of discord within the church, Paul offers spiritual counsel: have the mind of Christ.

What might happen in church life if, in the midst of our disagreements, someone interrupted our arguments by quoting these words from Paul? Might we then began to seek the mind of Christ concerning our squabbles? Tonight take time to examine yourself, your actions, and your inner conversation throughout this day. Ask: What did I do to seek the mind of Christ? When did I empty myself and become servant? When did the mind of Christ become real in my interaction with others? How did I promote the unity of the Spirit in the church?

God of the heights and the depths, hold before us the example of Christ's self-emptying and encourage us to seek unity of purpose and mission for the church. Amen.

SATURDAY, SEPTEMBER 24 ~ *Read Philippians 2:1-13*

In verse 11 Paul writes that "every tongue should confess that Jesus Christ is Lord." Several times in the epistles Paul uses the formula of Jesus as Lord: Romans 10:9; 1 Corinthians 12:3; and here. Many scholars think he is reinforcing the contemporary confession converts made when receiving baptism. Imagine that; today, whenever given the opportunity, we can use our tongues in quoting, for all to hear, a portion of the liturgy used at our baptism.

These verses also point to what our "life in Christ" might look like. They daily remind us to honor our tongues as one of the sharpest arrows we carry in our Christian quiver: in this context a Pauline arrow that can be used for grace.

Ironically, I received a poignant lesson in the power of words years ago when I contracted a case of laryngitis. For the first time in my career as a pastor, I couldn't speak for three days. I had temporarily lost my ability to communicate with words.

Otherwise I felt fine; so those three days I tried to do my job as best I could. I discovered my body trying harder to connect with my spirit so that I could communicate with others nonverbally. I found myself focusing more on what Paul describes as "the mind of Christ." Instead of communicating primarily with words, I tried to connect with others through Christ's spirit.

We always find Christ the last place we look. Today we can find him at the very source of the words we speak, the spirit of Christ within.

Loving God, may my words today reflect Christ's spirit, which brings love, joy, compassion, and sympathy. Amen.

This reading of Matthew 21 is nothing short of a slap in the face to those who think they experience the kingdom of God only through righteous living. Jesus cuts no corners in saying to the chief priests and elders, "I tell you, the hated tax collectors and the immoral prostitutes will experience the kingdom of God before you do" (AP).

I believe Jesus rides the religious leaders so hard in order to shake them to the core of their spiritual being. Why? Because their very sense of religiosity may keep them from experiencing the kingdom of God as a present reality. Jesus and the religious leaders exchange questions and get no answers, but the parable of the two sons brings the matter home.

The son who actually goes to the vineyard is the one who the chief priests and elders must finally concede has done the will of the father. And so, the one who gives the *appearance* of obedience is not the one who is obedient. For Jesus, doing God's will and being part of kingdom reality require a consistency of words and deeds, religious activity and obedience.

If we pay attention, we can experience the kingdom of God through small glimpses of everyday life. The kingdom of God can come to us through the darting of the hummingbird through our garden or the soaring of the red-tailed hawk overhead. It can come to us through sharing a cup of coffee with a friend, or it can come to us through reconciliation with an enemy.

And yes, the kingdom of God can even come to us through religious obedience when we remember that Jesus never said, "Go forth and be religious" but rather, "Go forth and love one another as I have loved you."

Loving God, we often find Jesus in the last place we look. Help us remember that your kingdom is everywhere, particularly exemplified in our obedience to your will. Amen.

New Mercies Every Day

SEPTEMBER 26–OCTOBER 2, 2011 • LARRY MAUGH

MONDAY, SEPTEMBER 26 ~ *Read Matthew 21:33-46*

The rich landowner sets up a winery with an implied under-standing between the owner and the renter. The owner expects reimbursement for investment and use of the land. When harvest time comes, the owner sends emissaries to collect what is due. The tenants respond to the request for payment by beating, stoning, and killing the landowner's slaves.

The owner sends his son to ensure that the tenants know that the request is legitimate. The misguided tenants think that killing the owner's son will resolve the issue.

The chief priests and Pharisees, indicted by their own response, take offense at this story. To some extent, the parable functions as a mirror, allowing them to acknowledge their response regarding John the Baptist. (See Matthew 21:23-27.) The parable holds a mirror up to us too.

The religious leaders face indictment, as do we. The parable clearly reminds us that the land does not revert to a particular people who are members of the "right" community. No, as Jesus goes on to say, "The kingdom of God will be taken away from you and given to a people that produces the fruits of the kingdom." And in Matthew's Gospel, "good fruit" comes from a changed life of radical obedience.

What does the mirror of this parable reflect to you? What fruits of the kingdom does your life bear?

Jesus, you continue to tell me the stories I need in my life. Let me hear fresh and new the parable of the tenants. May I bear good fruit in grateful obedience. Amen.

Pastor who has served a number of charges in the Mississippi Annual Conference of the United Methodist Church

The movement of the earth, the smoke, and the fire accompany God's presence. As the Israelites witness events over which they have no control, they grow fearful. Moses intercedes for the people and brings the rules of God to them. These "rules," a self-test ensures an awe of God that inspires obedience and saves from sin.

Electricity is one of the things I fear. Having worked in the field of construction as a general contractor, I learned that electricians seem to be the most technically sophisticated of the trades. They deal with an invisible medium, which is potentially deadly. Rumors and statistics related to the misuse of electricity abound. Because of our awareness that electricity can be dangerous, we use licensed electricians to wire our homes and businesses. We want an expert to guide us in its proper use.

We all know the dangers associated with the misuse of electricity: do not use electric appliances while standing in water; do not allow a metal ladder to touch power lines that feed buildings; and do not touch bare wires if the power is not off. If we don't follow these rules, death may result. Our inherent fear of electricity makes us follow the rules that keep us safe.

God's rules handed down to the people through Moses promote that safety. We fear God, so we follow God's rules, which keeps our relationship with God on good footing.

Do you want to know how your relationship with God is progressing? Go over today's checklist, the self-test found in the passage. Those who love God, accept no idols, and live in a loving relationship with others have nothing to fear. Fear comes only of the unknown. If you know God, what is there to fear? You will pass the test every time.

Lord, I love you. As I review your Ten Commandments, I know that on a good day I cannot quite get it right. This day, walk with me and show me how to love and be loved. Amen.

WEDNESDAY, SEPTEMBER 28 ~ *Read Exodus 20:12-20*

With the thunder and lightning, trumpet sound and smoking mountain, we can see why the Israelites would think they are "goners for sure." In that moment I imagine that their lives flashed before their eyes, all questioning their faithfulness to the covenant with God. How many times had they entered daily activities with no awareness of God?

Now as the mountain smokes and the earth trembles, each of the Israelites thinks, *Why should God have mercy on me? I have gotten it all wrong.* When I find myself in this type of situation, I want to hide; I do not like confrontation. I can hear myself saying with the Israelites, "Yes, tell Moses to go and find out what God wants. We will do whatever is required. Just don't make us talk with God; we know we will die."

I can only imagine what Moses is thinking as he addresses the people: *Get a grip. God has given these rules to allow you to do a self-test, designed to remind you of God's plan for your lives. To that end a little fear will keep you on your toes.*

Today, each of us has the same self-test with ten points to consider. Number one: "You shall have only one God, no idols" (AP). Number two: "You will not misuse God's name" (AP). And so on. You get the idea. Being one of God's chosen ones brings some expectations. God expects that we will make God the most important relationship, and that relationship will make all other relationships different. God does not come to harm. God offers a self-test, so we can remain close to God by living out the life God created for us.

> *God of relationship, when I come to you, I come empty handed. I commit myself to you daily, asking that you use me as you will. Remove impediments to my use. May I come closer to you today than yesterday. Amen.*

THURSDAY, SEPTEMBER 29 ~ *Read Psalm 19:1-6*

Walking along the Tennessee-Tombigbee Waterway offers the soul a place to observe God's presence in nature while observing the marvel of human building prowess. Each day as I walk, I am eager to see what river traffic is moving through the locks. The ability to dam the water while allowing tugboats and barges to traverse the waterway is a technological wonder. This use of the waterway allows for a highway of commerce while creating pools of water for creatures large and small. As one who enjoys showing up for a daily walk, I always come with anticipation, not sure what I will see and knowing that I rarely see the same things.

In the summer months, I walk earlier than in the winter months. In the summer heat I walk at daybreak while the winter cold encourages me to come well after the sun rises and has had time to heat the earth. The owls still fly at the time I know as "tween." The nocturnal creatures begin a period of rest and yield the landscape to those who hunt and eat during the periods of light.

Taking in the rhythm of life consumes me with thoughts of praise and prayers. The sun sitting on the horizon, greeting all of us who are awake, reminds me once again that the order of creation is itself a gift. We can channel God's handiwork, but we cannot create it. Every time I show up, the created order around me bears evidence of God's love. Whether I am here on the banks of the river or standing on the streets of a large inner city, the "bridegroom" comes forth each day to speak, not with words but with a visual reminder of God's love.

Merciful God, new are your mercies every day. May this day be the day that I gain awareness of you in everything I see, hear, touch, smell, or taste. Thanks be to you. Amen.

FRIDAY, SEPTEMBER 30 ~ *Read Psalm 19:7-14*

Righteous indignation, standing with your pulse pounding, railing at how others got it wrong feels good sometimes. It is usually then, as the moment passes, that a small feeling mounts into a tidal wave that floods my soul and alerts me to the fact that I am wrong. *How can this be? I did nothing wrong. Yet the feeling says I did.* In those moments I confront my limited understanding of how life seems to work, as God's precept gently reminds me of the order created for relationships.

I do not fully understand God's precepts, but I think I have the general outline. Living into a relationship with God involves so many subtle nuances.

Memories of my Old Testament class still surface from time to time. I remember my professor chiding us on our attitudes toward the scripture. "Why do you pick from the scripture the things you want to follow and ignore the others?"

"For instance," he would say, "the scripture says, 'Do not eat that which is cooked in its mother's milk.' And you continue to eat one cheeseburger after another." These comments always provoked lively conversation with the students as we tried to justify not following the command. Invariably it opened my eyes to the fact that in my life I do not avail myself of the fullness of God's law; I pick and choose my precepts.

The psalmist wants cleansing of hidden faults, to be innocent of transgression, to be blameless. How can I ever be blameless? If I do not believe that some of God's precepts will work or do not follow some decrees through ignorance, how can I be blameless? I *can* voice the concept and belief that the "law of God is perfect." Apart from God I cannot stand.

O God, "may the words of my mouth and the meditations of my heart be acceptable to you." Amen.

Racial reconciliation is one of the stumbling stones over which we in Mississippi continue to trip. We struggle with how to be a Christian while harboring racist thoughts and actions. Mission Mississippi is one of the groups in our state encouraging Christians to begin a dialogue across racial divides.

In a recent gathering, the leader began the discussion by asking those assembled to introduce themselves by giving their name and telling "what they do." Everyone responded with his or her name and occupation. Then the convener asked persons to reintroduce themselves without using a name, occupation, what they do in life, who their families are, or any other "label of knowing."

It was with a sense of loss that I sat in silence, only able to mutter to myself, "I am a sinner." One of my sins is racism. Beyond my relationship with Jesus the Christ, I was unable to voice who I was, or how others might know me and trust me.

Paul begins by laying out his credentials: "a Hebrew born of Hebrews in the tribe of Benjamin . . . " Does that impress you?" It only tells me that Paul's audience in Philippi needs some persuasion that the one addressing them has some credibility, that he has experienced what is important to his audience. Once he has convinced them, Paul throws his credentials aside as having no worth, in order to set in place the person of ultimate importance, Jesus the Christ.

Paul's approach challenges our beliefs. He asks us to consider a greater truth than the one we accept: a path that leads to God. I hope others will choose with me to be like Paul, not leaning on our own abilities but allowing Christ to transform us.

Loving God, keep me in your presence. This day I need to know that I am yours. Do not let pride separate me from you or from other human beings. Make me mindful that separated from you, I am nothing. Amen.

The parable of the tenants fills me with guilt. The reading surfaces the many times I have exhibited an ungrateful attitude, choosing to assert my right to do things *my* way.

When I graduated from high school, my parents wanted me to get a college education, which was a financial struggle; but they willingly sacrificed for me. I moved onto the college campus and into the fraternity house of my choice. My tuition, housing, and living expenses were paid. The only expectation of me was to attend classes and do my best.

I chose to attend all the parties I could, sleep late, not go to class, and socialize in the campus meeting places. I responded to my parents' love and support by assuming I had no one to honor for my life and its consolations. Like the ungrateful tenant I wanted to write my own rules and ignore those of the owner.

This parable tells of a good God who fills the world with all that is needed for an abundant life. Once we feel empowered to make our own choices, we forget about the source of our gifts and act as if we have no responsibility to the giver. Historically God's response to humanity came through the prophets who reminded God's people of their covenantal obligations. When the people of God were unable to grasp the truths proclaimed by the prophets, God came as the son, Jesus.

God comes in Jesus the Christ offering us a gift of life. It is possible to miss the gift of life by not seeing the value of what is before us. I look at that period of my life as one marked by greed, conceit, and self-centeredness. I usurped God's role by making myself god. Today I give thanks to the God of second chances. Through God's grace and mercy I can stand with Jesus the Christ, giving thanks for the greatest of all gifts: God's presence with me.

Gracious God, forgive my sins. Let me always be quick to confess and eager to receive your mercy. Amen.

Obedience and Accountability

OCTOBER 3–9, 2011 • MARLU PRIMERO SCOTT

MONDAY, OCTOBER 3 ~ *Read Exodus 32:1-6*

Aaron listens and quickly gives directives. He fashions gold earrings into a golden calf, a visible god demanded by the Israelites. Aaron proclaims a festival to the Lord, which was to take place the next day. Everyone rises early, offers burnt sacrifices, and feasts.

Obedience requires loyalty while demanding accountability. A pastor in our Native American community prides himself on meeting in the Long House, the Native American place of worship. Often one can sense a tone of hubris under the guise of establishing an inclusive church on the reservation. While Natives feel hospitality and inclusivity overflowing, some remain confused by the mission. The directives to participate in the Long House under the guise of Christian practice leads to confusion.

Might it be a simple matter of misunderstood leadership? Recall a time when a leader persuaded or coerced you to do something under a false pretext. The issue of leadership that offers agendas cloaked in personal interest is a serious and pervasive one in faith communities. We cannot always see the glitter of a golden calf, but we sense a form of subtle idolatry. Whether we speak of Aaron in the wilderness or twenty-first century pastors, leadership cannot always be trusted to choose wisely. Followers need wisdom to discern truth.

All-knowing God, forgive us when we stray from your commands. Give us wisdom to perceive your ways, strength to resist false pretense, and courage to obey. Amen.

Founding Director of JRS Memorial Center, Healing and Spirituality, Union Theological Seminary, Dasmarinas, Cavite

The Israelites demand a visible god. Aaron listens and gives direction. Though the path he takes includes doxologies to the Lord, it also leads to disobedience to God's command.

Today's reading portrays serious intercession by Moses on behalf of the Israelites. His relationship with God allows him to run interference. God's wrath could have easily fallen on the wilderness sojourners. But it does not! Moses, propelled by the mission God called him to do, stays focused. He pleads for those God sent him to set free, reminding God of the divine promise made. Moses feels confident in his relationship with Yahweh.

These qualities frame Moses' relationship with God: God's fairness, God's powerful character, and God's name. He knows personal yearning for justice and emancipation for the Israelites has gotten him into trouble with the authorities, but God's fairness, power, and reputation redeem Moses' past. God calls him to lead the Israelites, to claim the promise of freedom in a land they would someday call their own. How confident do you feel about your relationship with God? Confident enough to intercede on behalf of folk who have wandered far from grace?

In my ministry, intervention continues daily. A young man realized he wandered too far; but reassured of God's love, he came to church repentant and desired baptism—not only for himself but for his three children. His wife, a born-again Christian, had longed for this moment. Transformation ensued. He started two narcotics anonymous groups and attended church regularly. Then he "fell off the wagon." Finally, he came again to see me. With a collaborative community effort to fight alcohol and drug abuse, this young man is now one of the leaders in our community struggling to combat underage drinking. What promises of God draw you to intercession? to tussle with God on behalf of another?

Gracious God, make me confident of my relationship with you. May I intercede for others and myself in that confidence. Amen.

Psalm 106 continues our week with praise of God's wonderful works. This psalm captures incidents in Israel's historical narrative that reflect God's ongoing presence and judgment: "Remember me, O Lord, when you show favor to your people; help me when you deliver them."

One can sense the joy of the psalmist as he sings, "Praise the Lord! O give thanks to the Lord, for he is good." The psalmist's praise hinges on a recollection of the "mighty doings of the Lord." These mighty doings lead to his ability to affirm God's steadfast love.

In verse 3 the psalmist sets the standard for living in the world with God: "Happy are those who observe justice, who do righteousness at all times." These are the "happy" and blessed people. So the psalmist sets the bar for what follows in the recollection of Israel's behavior in later verses. And then moving from the singular "I," he aligns himself with the community of Israel in confession of sin: "Both we and our ancestors have sinned."

In the context of God's mighty doings, the psalmist asks that God's faithfulness might override the consequence of sinful patterns of behavior. The way of blessedness stood at the ready, but Israel chose to commit iniquity.

We all face these options: to pursue justice and righteousness or to take a shortcut or compromise. Recall those times you have faced a difficult decision but chosen to observe justice and do righteousness. Thank God for God's steadfast love. Pause for a few minutes and bask in the glory of God who waits to bless you with favor.

God of righteousness and justice, give me grace to realize those times when you have enlightened my understanding and guided my judgment. Amen.

Yesterday's portion of the psalm commenced with thanksgiving. As today's verses unfold, the psalmist recalls his ancestors' violation of God's commandments. The visible god the wilderness sojourners clamored for became a reminder of their misdeeds. In no time they had forgotten the wonders in the land of Ham, the phenomenal acts by the Red Sea, and their miraculous release from the clutches of Pharaoh. Because of their infidelity to God, Moses intercedes for another chance. The psalmist marvels that the Israelites willingly "exchanged the glory of God for the image of an ox." Seeing no God in their midst, they celebrated their self-sufficiency by creating one.

On September 11, 2001, a tragedy brought about God's work in our midst. Churches were packed. People dropped to their knees in thanksgiving and grief. In light of life's fragility and God's care, we began to treat one another with more respect. Communities around the country modeled hospitality to strangers in need. Unfortunately, the wonderful aura of neighborliness did not last.

The desert dwellers had a life-giving relationship with God. But they did not remember and made a disastrous exchange. Even as Moses is on the mountain hammering out the covenant, the people below become self-indulgent.

We can easily judge the religious misdeeds of others. Yet we also allow a life-giving relationship with God to slip away, or to be bartered away for something in the moment, or to be compromised. When have you exchanged the glory of God for something less that promised more?

Praise God for second chances. Pray for strength to face challenges that demand sacrificial effort for the good of the community of faith.

Today's passage strikes a nerve. Paul could be writing this letter to any church today, and it would be applicable. Disagreements in congregations exist. In this situation, Paul longs for the dispute to cease. He encourages reconciliation.

Paul, writing from prison, first advises the believers at Philippi to "stand firm in the Lord." Keep on keeping on; remain faithful to the practices and beliefs Paul has conveyed. Paul then addresses the next concern quite specifically, his concern for unity in the body. Paul raises here the issues that he mentioned in Philippians 2, in which he counsels being of the same mind and taking one another's interests to heart.

As designated leaders, Euodia and Syntyche "have struggled beside [Paul] in the work of the gospel." Might Paul's failed attempt to reconcile the two women be due to the absence of understanding obedience and accountability? The cause of the misunderstanding in the story is unclear. However, we can surmise that the confusion comes as a result of bruised egos. Paul perhaps senses this.

How might Euodia and Syntyche implement Paul's suggestion to be of the same mind in the Lord? What wisdom might today's reading offer members of a congregation struggling with conflict? What means of grace can church leaders model when an extravagant dose of disobedience necessitates a resolve? Being of the same mind in the Lord implies that the whole body of believers look to one another's best interests.

Take a few seconds, close your eyes. Imagine some of the people in your church who tend to lock horns. Pray a prayer of reconciliation and healing. Continue this ritual for three days. Encourage others to join you in your prayer exercise for three more days. Watch for a shift in attitude. Praise God for reconciling healing!

Reconciling God, bestow on us obedience to serve you. Amen.

How can the congregation in Philippi rejoice amid its discord? Paul, like Moses, does not waver but focuses on the task on hand. He consistently encourages the community of believers to rejoice in whatever station they find themselves, whether in discord or in harmony. And Paul himself, now imprisoned, serves as a living witness to his own testimony.

"Do not worry about anything, but in everything by prayer and supplication with thanksgiving let your requests be made known to God." Is Paul in denial? in conflict avoidance? On the contrary, he is simply igniting the faith of the church in Philippi. Confidence in God's providence sets worry aside. Paul goes further to note that "the Lord is near," his first explicit reference to the end-time, the culmination of God's work. So with confidence in God and unity among themselves, the Philippians may indeed "rejoice in the Lord always." Even as Paul finds his own life threatened and considers a physical end to his relationship with the Philippians, he pours out joy over them and their future ministry together.

When have you allowed the peace of God, which surpasses all understanding, to color your perspective? How did that sense of peace about a situation release you from anxious thoughts and worry? Consider setting aside some time with God, to rest in that confident presence. Bring to the fore your worries and cares and place them before God. Pray that their hold over you might diminish. Rise in joy.

Compassionate God, help us to trust in you. Give us strength to stop worrying. Grant us gentleness of heart to rejoice always, no matter what comes our way. Amen.

Aking hosts a banquet, and no one comes. Rather than feel privileged, the invitees make excuses. The king then invites those on the street and fills the hall with guests—both good and bad. One man comes with no wedding robe. When confronted, the man is speechless. We, like Jesus' hearers, may draw back at the punishment of "outer darkness" when the poor guy has just wandered in off the street. Matthew's Gospel takes a different turn from the same story recounted in Luke 14:15-24. In Luke, lots of invitees make excuses, and others are invited from the street. But no guest is cast into outer darkness.

So what are we to make of this parable? Does Jesus tell this story to discourage followers or to ascertain that those who hear his commands will live out his instructions? Perhaps, like those on the initial guest list, the improperly attired guest does not realize that the invitation is a privilege that carries with it responsibility. Maybe once again, as with the "good fruit," obedient discipleship results in a tangible dimension: our lives display a trustworthiness. We live without pretense and take God's grace seriously.

Are we taking Jesus' invitation lightly? When have you made wimpy excuses for not keeping your daily appointment with God. What prevents you from faithfulness to your covenant discipleship? What bars you from faithful obedience to the king's invitation? Take a moment and mentally catalog your justifications for a complacent attitude. Ask God for mercy.

Patient and loving Lord, grant us an extravagant desire to obey you always, especially when we turn away from your invitation. Amen.

The Grateful Heart

OCTOBER 10–16, 2011 • STEPHEN P. WEST

MONDAY, OCTOBER 10 ~ *Read Luke 17:11-19*

Jesus clearly tells all ten lepers to go and show themselves to the priests. In Jewish practice, these are not unusual instructions for those hoping to get well. So they embark on the journey but, surprisingly, experience cleansing en route.

Yet one Samaritan, ironically a foreigner but one who would know about ritual washing practices, turns back as soon as his skin clears. Jesus finds him lying at his feet and commends him.

True gratitude involves more than simply following instructions and mustering up an obligatory thank you. It is being overwhelmed with joy. All ten experienced the same miracle of healing on the outside. Yet Jesus praises the one who is changed on the inside. "Your faith has made you well."

We have a difficult time with gratitude because we live in a world of doing and accomplishing. We solve a problem and move on. We get the job done, and we're on to the next task.

But the tenth leper reminds us that gratitude brings completeness to our healing. I love to worship because it deepens the thankfulness of my heart, bringing an extraordinary wholeness to the grace I have received.

In a world of functionalism, we are called not just to do our part and follow the basic requirements. We are called to be in relationship with the One who makes us well.

When have you been overwhelmed with joy? Get in touch with memories and moments that have drawn you back to the feet of Christ. Give praise in a way that makes your joy more complete.

Pastor of Grace United Methodist Church, Huntsville, Alabama; husband, father, minister, musician, and writer

I vividly remember anxieties welling up in me when I was sent as a denominational missionary to start a new church. "Where do I start? What if I fail?" Perhaps the most urgent question on my heart was, "Who can I find to help me?"

I suppose this gives me a partial glimpse of Moses' anxiety when charged with the daunting task of leading God's people into the Promised Land. No wonder he starts a friendly argument with God. His fear of "going it alone" is valid. God has called them stiff-necked, told them to go on into the Promised Land, and does not plan to accompany them. "Now take off your ornaments and I will decide what to do with you" (33:5, NIV).

Yet Moses faithfully visits the tent of meeting, approaching God like a friend. He becomes the hero of intercessors everywhere. Moses gently persists, "You have been telling me, 'Lead these people,' but you have not let me know whom you will send with me" (NIV). Like so many who are called to step out on faith, Moses has no idea how to make it happen without some help.

Maybe Moses is asking for a few assistants, but I am guessing he hoped God had something else in store for him. God seemingly has a change of mind, promising that God's very presence will go with him.

One secret to developing a heart of gratitude is that we don't wait for something to be happy about. We stretch ourselves and claim the blessings of God's presence in every situation, no matter how lonely we may feel. Eventually, we might hear the same voice speak to us as it did to Moses: "My Presence will go with you, and I will give you rest" (NIV).

Join me in my breath prayer, breathing this prayer many times during the course of the day: "Lord, fill my presence with your presence."

WEDNESDAY, OCTOBER 12 ~ *Read Exodus 33:18-23*

How strange that God shows Moses his back side! The verses prior to this week's readings state that they spoke "face to face, as one speaks to a friend" (33:11). Maybe Moses has grown accustomed to the tent of meeting. I can't imagine getting used to God's descending in a cloud and my being left with a shiny face.

But Moses desires more. He yearns for a sense of God's presence. In today's reading, he pushes the envelope a little farther and asks for a glimpse of God's glory. God reminds him that he cannot see God's face directly, then places him on a rock and passes by, removing a hand from Moses' eyes long enough for him to get a glance. It gives Moses the assurance he needs.

Grace is strange indeed—both passionately present and mysteriously distant. Experiencing this duality is the essence of knowing the glory of God in Christ.

The journey to a grateful heart begins with a willingness to look for God in mystical moments great and small. We cannot grasp God; God is revealed. We do not reach out and touch. God comes to us. Our part is to be attentive.

Many of us desperately search for God. We read books, attend worship, go to Bible study, and apply principles; yet we still experience a profound hunger. Perhaps goodness passes by us all the time. We miss it because we are wired to be consumers rather than people of gratitude. Thank God for those mystical moments that open our eyes!

When have you experienced God this week or caught a glimpse of God's back side? Ask God for more awareness.

THURSDAY, OCTOBER 13 ~ *Read Psalm 99*

Reading the psalms differs from reading other scripture. We step onto the ongoing prayer path of generations, hopping onto a bandwagon of continual worship that went on long before us and will keep going long after we are gone. Singing and praying psalms takes us beyond surface feelings and our verbal comfort levels into a whole new world.

If we are honest, we might note that Psalm 99 is one that we are prone to skim or skip over. It envisions God enthroned on high. The earth shakes and the nations tremble. An awesomeness accompanies the name of God. It's not that we don't believe this; it's just that we've heard it before. And some part of us would rather think of God as warm, fuzzy, and friendly.

But the more I pause to pray the psalm, the more it sensitizes my heart to the holy. It is curious that this week's readings remind us of God's presence hovering over a tent and appearing in brief glimpses. This psalm recalls that God spoke to Moses and Aaron in a pillar of cloud. An anonymous fourteenth-century writer of Christian mysticism described God's presence as the "cloud of unknowing."

The psalmist moves our spirits from the smaller picture of our needs, our hopes, and our wants to the larger picture of God's mysterious presence. We don't praise God because we feel like praising but because God is God.

Perhaps praise is not something we do at all; it is something we join. The psalms have a mysterious way of unlocking the secrets of true gratitude by ushering us into the ongoing praise of all creation.

Take time to read and reread this psalm. Let the words sink in. Chant or sing it if you can, letting it become the song of your heart. Let God expand your perspective beyond the blessings and challenges in front of you to a sense of the holy.

I was leading a Bible study in which participants discussed different forms of prayer. As we approached the subject of intercession, a woman exclaimed, "I don't get anything out of praying for other people. It doesn't do any good, so why bother? God knows what they need."

I mustered a response, reminding the class that many people find this way of prayer rewarding. But I admit that her comment caught me off guard—many of us miss out on the joys of intercessory prayer. I am also aware that her doubts resonate with where I have been many times along the way.

Paul helps my doubtful stance. Paul opens his letter with gratitude by telling the Thessalonians that he and his companions "continually remember before our God" (NIV) their faithfulness. This idea of persistent remembering captures the spirituality of intercession.

I recall the humorous experience of hearing someone pray for the sick, making sure to mention their hospital room numbers. What if we thought of prayer not as giving God information that God already knows but as "continually remember[ing] before God" those for whom we pray?

It is difficult in a culture fixated on functionalism to fathom such mystery. I find that it helps to move intercessory prayer beyond words. At times, I envision lifting those I am praying for into holy light to receive healing and blessing.

This week we have spent time with Moses, the greatest of intercessors. He boldly remembered before God all that God had promised! He interceded not to give God information but to embrace a profound truth. Prayer makes a difference for others; but in our praying, we are also changed. Lifting up others is an essential part of our journey toward gratitude.

Spend some time remembering before God persons you long to pray for. Imagine lifting them into God's healing light.

J esus said some strange things. At times his words project the radical values of the kingdom of God. At other times I wonder if he simply intended to stump his critics. When he says, "Give to Caesar what is Caesar's, and to God what is God's" (NIV) he is doing some of both. Jesus certainly knows the hypocritical attitude of those quizzing him about taxes. But he answers the question nevertheless.

It is hard to live from your center when people seem to be plotting against you! Yet Jesus does not couch his answer in a way that takes sides. Instead it has spurred imaginative thought for generations. For Jesus, the way of gratitude boils down to a core question. How much of who we are belongs to God?

Gratitude is not a matter of tipping God for services rendered or volunteering a portion of our time. Our giving reflects our living. My favorite phrase in the wedding liturgy is spoken at the exchange of rings: "With all that I am and all that I have, I honor you." We might best direct that phrase to the one who gives us life itself.

Many commitments occupy a role of importance in daily life, spanning everything from family to church, from community to career, from nation to denomination. Jesus' saying on taxes ironically holds both sides of a proverbial coin in tension. It is not that we can only serve *one or the other* commitment. The question is how we honor God in the midst of *all* our commitments.

Giving is a spiritual discipline that cultivates a grateful heart. Jesus said, "Where your treasure is, there your heart will be also" (Luke 12:34). We do not give only to change the world. Our giving also changes us.

Take time to meditate over your checkbook, credit card statement, or bank account. How might you live in a way that honors God more completely? Pray for renewal.

It seems a bit vain that Paul affirms the way people "became imitators of us and of the Lord." I am generally turned off by the idea of following along like a copycat and calling it faithful. And who am I to say to my congregation, "Imitate me"?

Maybe I am reading through eyes overly sensitive to our culture's worship of what I call the "new Trinity" (me, myself, and I). Perhaps Paul's words emphasize not that they "looked at me" but that they "looked at God by looking beyond what they saw in me."

We have noted Paul's remembrance of others before God in gratitude. Here we read more about why he was so appreciative of his friends, "Our message of the gospel came to you not in word only, but also in power and in the Holy Spirit." The Thessalonians absorb the word in more than pure intellectual assent; they become imitators of those who lived and preached among them. And their genuine enthusiasm generates interest so that the imitators have imitators!

Paul evidences joy, and he affirms the joy in them. In spite of their suffering, they "received the word with joy inspired by the Holy Spirit." Paul surely considered it a great compliment to know that friends who follow his lead do so with joy, despite the struggles of discipleship. Joy is of God.

Our culture's "prosperity spirituality" takes root in dissatisfaction and the idea that if I do more for God, God will do more for me. Yet God's greatest desire is to instill gratitude in us rather than reinforce our chronic anxiety for more. Perhaps contentment is a form of liberation.

Take some time to list your blessings. Try to focus less on what you have, including relationships and opportunities, and more on what God has brought you through and the joy it brings. Give praise.

Focus on Formation

OCTOBER 17–23, 2011 • JUANITA CAMPBELL RASMUS

MONDAY, OCTOBER 17 ~ *Read Deuteronomy 34:1-12*

I can see it now, Moses standing atop Mount Nebo one hundred and twenty years old, still bright-eyed and agile enough to make the climb. What a legacy the great leader standing before the majesty of the promise of God manifests after forty long years of managing a nation. Moses had accepted God's challenge to help God's people understand the spiritual formation needed for God's glory and their good.

As a pastor I often feel stretched as I try to hear God's word and then implement what I hear, knowing that God is forming me and our congregation for the ultimate: a life with God. I can see Moses standing with a panoramic view of the future home of God's people and hearing that he will not enter into that future. I wonder why he doesn't put up a fight or at least a "could you let this cup pass" because I'm still capable and fit for the job. The scripture records none of that. Moses, the servant of the Lord, dies and is buried in an unmarked spot. Today's scripture eulogizes Moses: "Never since has there arisen a prophet in Israel like Moses, whom the LORD knew face to face. He was unequaled."

Today's passage serves as a strong reminder that I am not being shaped only to face my future, however long or short that might be. I am being formed to face the Lord for all eternity. All my life experiences—my joys and sorrows, my sins and successes—are forming me to live in the presence of divine love forever. We are all being formed to live face to face with God and enjoy God forever.

God, make me aware of your fashioning me both for now and the future. Amen.

Contemplative, pastor, teacher; Houston, Texas

I found myself challenged when my most theatrical daughter experienced an emotional crisis. Something that day had gone terribly wrong, and she couldn't adequately express herself in words. Her countenance had totally changed. I asked out of desperation, "How much longer do you need to feel what you are feeling?" I asked her if fifteen minutes was enough time. That worked for her; at the moment she needed space and time to deal with her emotions. I didn't try to fix her but gave her permission to be with her feelings for a set period of time.

Depression has a track record for about three generations in our family. But my daughters and I are choosing to make different choices about how we manage our feelings; counseling has helped tremendously. I googled a "feelings" list on the internet. The list contains several hundred words to name and identify our feelings—life-giving fuel to move us on with our lives.

Our family members give one another permission to be formed by God in the most emotional of times. We are learning that we are being formed by our endings for our new beginnings just as the Israelites were. The ritual period of mourning was thirty days. They mourn for Moses in verse 8, and they move on in verse 9. Who's to say how much time it takes; spiritual formation is the work of a lifetime.

Gracious God, remind us that even our endings are forming us in your likeness. You have made us beings with emotions, and that too is a gift. Amen.

Last October I was experiencing some indigestion. By mid-week I was in my doctor's office. She immediately scheduled an ultrasound for the next day. I went from ultrasound to CT scan before I left. I was later diagnosed with renal cell carcinoma.

The next week I sat in the office of a specialist at a major cancer center who said hastily, "Let's get this thing out so you can move on with your life." He suggested a date for surgery three weeks later. I was stunned. Things were happening so rapidly. I knew I had to walk the labyrinth to get centered in prayer. One of the words I heard was *remember*.

Psalm 90 opens with the reminder that our only true home is God. And in light of my life-threatening situation, I heard in a new way God's command: "Turn back, you mortals"—turn back to dust, to nonbeing. All of life is willed by God; the grass renewed in the morning withers at night. And God's time is not ours; in the span of time, our days are "like a dream."

The decision is less to cling to life than to cling to the Lord of life. I remembered God as "dwelling place," my refuge and strength. Over my lifetime God has brought healing into my life and the lives of those I love. I remembered and gained peace. I remembered that God had been shaping me all along. I could trust the Lord of life. I did not know the specialist who would perform my surgery, but I knew the Healer who had been our family's dwelling place for many generations.

Lord, you have been our dwelling place in all generations. Help us remember that you have formed us and that you are with us, especially when we feel overwhelmed and bewildered. Amen.

Joe, a former Marine, personal trainer, and friend, runs a training gym. Under my breath I ask, "How long, Joe? Have a little compassion on me. Make tomorrow a little easier; you almost killed me today." I am a fitness dropout with no daily discipline. I run to Joe to get whipped into shape for vacation.

Joe is patient; he knows me. I forget that I need him because I can't do it alone. I want to get fit. I realize he knows what he's doing. I have seen his results in the past. But in the midst of the suffering weights, pushups, squats and such, I often lose focus and give in to the discomfort of my fitness regimen. Joe has a plan and the results come through my implementing that plan under his firm guidance.

The word *turn* uttered by the psalmist is the same word used by God in verse 3: "Turn back." The psalmist, aware of the transitory nature of life, expresses his own neediness and yearning as he petitions God to turn, have compassion, satisfy, show favor, prosper his work. The psalmist looks to God for more than a break-even life of meaning.

We all desire the benefits of a life lived fully with God, but the spiritual regimen can be trying. We typically want nothing to do with the suffering that accompanies all of life. "No pain, no gain" moves beyond the gym to describe the formation process of every believer's life. We express our wistful longings to God who uses our experiences to shape us. I choose God. I have seen the results. I like the look.

> *God, as you shape me, help me to focus on how you are making me your own. Help me sense your love and rejoice even in the discomfort of my formation, knowing that your best good for me is being manifested. Amen.*

As a child I always followed the rules. I remember thinking when classmates broke the rules, *Well, I won't get caught doing that because I want to be a good Christian.* I would distance myself from playmates who got in trouble because the rule says you're known by the company you keep. I based my relationship with God on rule-keeping because I wanted to be a "good" girl.

At St. John's, the church I serve, I have met all the people I didn't play with as a little girl. I have met drug dealers, addicts, prostitutes, bail jumpers, adulterers, liars, thieves, white collar criminals, you name it! The church is filled with people that I would have ruled out as a young girl, because the church is filled with rule breakers.

The mission at St. John's is to tear down the walls that get built when rules become more important than relationships, when law has superseded love. Behind every broken rule, I have found a wounded soul. I have confronted my own brokenness, which led me to take refuge in rules. My relationship with rule breakers has freed me to know God's love over my dependence on laws. Laws form judgment; love forms relationships.

All of us are being formed by our circumstances—childhoods, crises, conditions, and catastrophes—for which there are many societal rules. Jesus shows us a better way: the way of love. It has been an incredible journey to discover that God is more concerned with relationships than with rules, with love than with law. As a child I had no way of knowing that rules boxed people in and often boxed God out. Now God's love is forming me. I am learning to love God, to love others, and to love myself.

Gracious God, you look beyond my faults and see my needs. Help me to remember that you are shaping me to fully love you, my neighbor, and myself. Amen.

Jesus asks the Pharisees a question that silences them. The Pharisees, students of the scripture, have no reply to Jesus' question as how the Messiah can be both son and lord of King David: "The LORD [God] says to my lord [Messiah] . . ." Jesus stumps the professors. The official educators have not encountered the ultimate teacher. While the Pharisees may have known the law, David has known the maker of the law. David's relationship with God has given him insight by the Holy Spirit. At the core of spiritual formation resides the intimate relationship we establish with God. *The Life with God Bible* says that Jesus uses the passage referencing David to help his audience "understand the nature of life with God and to provide insight and discernment that [would] enrich our own spiritual life."

The Pharisees know the literal law but are seemingly void of insight related to the revelation that God offers those who seek God's heart. Jesus' question confronts the Pharisees with a true understanding of messiahship—a messiah not of military might but of love and suffering. The Spirit illumines our understanding as we are being formed.

This story is not simply about the silence of the Pharisees. I wonder how many times you and I have fallen silent because of a Bible passage. We may read Jesus' instructions to forgive seventy times seven and remember the grudge we've carried too long. We may read Matthew 25 and experience silence in response to Jesus' words about visiting him in prison because we realize that the local jail is a mile away and we've never visited there. We may catch the latest news and then read the prophet's word concerning justice and experience a loss of words because justice seems absent. Moments like these jolt us first with silence and then the Holy Spirit prods us to act.

God, may I allow your Holy Spirit to open my understanding so that I too can be formed in faith to a life with you. Amen.

SUNDAY, OCTOBER 23 ~ *Read 1 Thessalonians 2:1-8*

Friends of my family have recently become parents. They have suffered numerous miscarriages and the heartache that goes with the disappointment and grief. They have experienced rough times attempting to do what happens naturally for many—become parents. They have spent thousands of dollars on numerous options. Finally, they quit mentioning tests and results.

Many of us wondered why they didn't simply adopt. But mutual friends took it one step further. They are adoptive parents and basically helped this couple over time—and during one particular meal—to consider adoption. Our family friends called a local agency, arranged an appointment, and within thirty days they were approved and became parents. Their son is a delight; I find myself making regular baby visits. This couple glows now. Everyone in their midst knows that they have one agenda: their new baby. Lovingly, gently, and tenderly they attend to that agenda. This beloved couple has been formed and transformed.

Spiritual formation and transformation work the same way. The apostle Paul and his friends have worked diligently among the Thessalonians. They came to share the gospel with courage and integrity. Within community, the character of relationship changed. Those who brought the word of God find that they are vulnerable. And their care for the people among whom they minister is that of gentleness, as a nurse cares tenderly for her own children; as parents care for a child.

Spiritual formation is a tender process that includes disappointments, losses, grief—and includes joys and delights. We share with others not only our good news of Christ but our hearts as well. In the process of intentionally helping to form others we too are being formed. We learn to be gentle, tender, caring, and to give of ourselves more fully.

O God, remind me that you are forming me not just for my own good but for the people to whom you have called me. Amen.

Living Authentically

OCTOBER 24–30, 2011 • JIM MELCHIORRE

MONDAY, OCTOBER 24 ~ *Read Joshua 3:7-17*

Joshua is struggling to establish his legitimacy. God aids him with a promise and a sign. The promise is the assurance of success in claiming the land beyond; the sign is the miraculous halting of the river.

We all struggle, if not for legitimacy at least for authenticity. We like to think our lives reflect our beliefs. So what message can we learn from the story of Joshua at the Jordan?

God, "the Lord of all the earth," is ultimately in charge, then as now, and accompanies us on the journey. We live in a world where not everybody believes that, and those persons can also live authentically. But if we believe in a loving and caring God who actively participates in the world, then let's live as though we believe it.

To a nomadic nation thirty-five hundred years ago, God's faithfulness meant a homeland. We follow a carpenter/rabbi who taught a prayer about God's kingdom coming on earth as well as in heaven. So complacency about war, capital punishment, and widespread malnutrition caused by poverty becomes a challenging reminder of how radically different the life of discipleship is. The path of authentic living is a journey toward a destination. Let's take up the invitation to be partners with God in the work of love, so that all of God's creation may receive more abundant life, authentic life.

God of all journeys, remind us that you always travel with us, even when the road is rough, loving us, caring for us, and convicting us to make the difficult choices of discipleship. Amen.

Journalist, video producer, and English as a Second Language teacher; New York, New York

Paul's first epistle to the emerging church at Thessalonica is generally considered to date from about 50 AD, making it the oldest of his letters. And Paul spends a lot of words defending himself, making a case for his integrity.

Describing his team as "holy, righteous, and blameless" (NIV), Paul writes that they worked day and night and never became a burden to the community by looking for handouts or imposing on anybody. Modeling through word and deed, Paul now asks the community members to consider how they are measuring up. As recipients of the gospel, how are they living out the call? It's not a bad question for all of us to ask. The path of Jesus, when walked authentically, is counterintuitive and revolutionary.

Love your enemies. Whoever wishes to be great among you will be your servant. The meek will inherit the earth. Are we committed to a gospel that "comforts the afflicted, and afflicts the comfortable," even when we ourselves are the "comfortable"?

Later, in verse 13, Paul offers thanks for the people of Thessalonica and for the way they accepted "the word of God, which is at work in you who believe." How have we permitted the word of God to be "at work" in us? How is that revolutionary and counterintuitive way of life visible to those who observe us?

Do we find ourselves at the side of the elderly, the immigrant, the homeless? Does our busyness include both works of charity and works of justice?

Paul says to the Thessalonians: Look at me and my colleagues. How are you continuing in the gospel life? Let's ask ourselves the same question, and be willing to answer it truthfully.

Almighty God, from whom nothing is hidden, give us the courage to accept the sometimes uncomfortable truth about ourselves, knowing that you always offer the invitation to start anew, to choose a better way. Amen.

A couple of years ago, while walking around in my New York City neighborhood, I noticed a campaign poster from a lesser-known political organization, what we might call a "fringe party." The words on the poster proclaimed the platform: "Putting poor and working people first."

Not a terribly realistic notion. Successful political campaigns usually preach unity among their various supporters with no single group placed in a privileged position. Besides, winning campaigns require "clout"—money, prestige, access—and "poor and working people" have none of those. Who in the world could truly put "poor and working people *first*" as a matter of principle?

Then it occurred to me that Jesus is the guy who says "the greatest among you will be your servant." That must have sounded positively ludicrous in a hierarchical society like Roman-ruled, first-century Palestine. And it still makes us pretty uncomfortable in much of our contemporary society.

A few years ago, Jim Wallis of the Sojourners Movement and some seminary students went through the Bible to chronicle every reference to the poor. In the Hebrew scriptures, the subject of poverty is second only to idolatry in terms of frequency. In the Christian scriptures, one of every sixteen verses deals with the poor. In the Gospels, the ratio is one in ten. In the Gospel of Luke, it's one in seven and in the epistle of James, one in five.

I'm not a political strategist and I'm not sure that putting poor and working people first would guarantee a successful political campaign. But as a phrase to live by, for those who aspire to authentic discipleship with the carpenter's son from Nazareth, we could do no better.

Creator God, you are the parent of all. Surely such knowledge will change the way we treat one another. Amen.

In an interview, I asked Dr. Rowan Williams, the 104th Archbishop of Canterbury and leader of the Anglican Communion, about the role that greed had played in causing and complicating the 2008 financial crisis. Dr. Williams did not blame greed but rather pride: "the view that, somehow, my concerns, simply because they're mine, take precedence over everyone else's. I ought to be capable of running my own world. I don't want to be dependent on anyone."

Jesus lowers the boom on "the teachers of the law and the Pharisees." He chides them for wearing large phylacteries—boxes carrying parchments on which verses from Torah were written—and long tassels, as outward signs of inner righteousness. Pride also seems to be the culprit here, self-satisfaction that privileged status confers legitimacy and importance.

I grew up Roman Catholic. In the Baltimore Catechism, pride always topped the list of the seven deadly sins. I think pride is just as dangerous as ever. So let me tell you an experiment I tried a few years back. I banished the words *pride* and *proud* from my vocabulary. Instead of saying "I'm proud of my children," I'd say, "I'm blessed by my children." In place of "I'm proud of the work our team did," I'd substitute, "I am honored to be working with you."

The experiment forces a fundamental shift from portraying ourselves as "possessing" something (pride) to "receiving" something (blessing and honor). Try the experiment long enough and your attitude changes to seeing life as "gift."

Creator God, you know well that this problem of pride has plagued us since our beginning. Make us aware that our lives are all gift, to which the only responses are gratitude in receiving and generosity in giving away. Amen.

FRIDAY, OCTOBER 28 ~ *Read Matthew 23:8-12*

Years ago, I heard someone draw a distinction between the words *humbled* and *humiliated*. The speaker noted that being humiliated is always a hurtful experience to which we should never be subjected. Being humbled, though uncomfortable, is an experience that can be good for us.

I live in New York City. One chilly winter day on the Upper West Side near 102nd Street and Amsterdam Avenue, I passed a man who asked me for money for food. We New Yorkers often encounter people on the street who are homeless or otherwise marginalized and who ask for assistance. I try to carry snacks in my backpack to offer to those who ask.

But that day I was in a hurry to get to my son's basketball game and simply wasn't in the mood. When I was fifteen feet past him, the man shouted, "You could at least look at me!" What a moment of truth-telling. I had truly exalted myself, proclaiming through my actions that my schedule was so important that I could pretend I didn't see or hear him, as though he didn't exist. I stopped, apologized, and gave him a couple of dollars. The incident humbled me, made me quite uncomfortable, and may have been the most important blessing of that day.

With only the slightest jogging of my memory, I could recall a half-dozen other times in recent months when my actions fell short of the standard of authentic Christian discipleship I claim, instances when I exalted my own needs or simply my convenience above all other considerations of that moment. Perhaps you would acknowledge the same.

Truth-telling can set us free but not before sometimes humbling us, forcing us to examine the authenticity of our discipleship and recommit to the path of following Jesus.

Creator God, help us to be honest in our self-evaluations and in our confessions, not for your sake but for ours. Then lead us on the road called repentance. Amen.

This episode from Matthew's Gospel includes such a ferocious blast at the scribes and Pharisees that we might miss Jesus' instruction to his listeners to "do whatever they teach you and follow it." By not practicing what they teach, Jesus' critics have ceded their legitimacy. But Torah, the law given by God to Moses, survives with its authority intact, even when enforced by corrupt leadership.

Rules and regulations have always had great appeal. At their best, they can define our unique identity by describing what we believe is important. At worst, they become fences, an easy way to show who's in and, always more important to us imperfect creatures, who's out. That's why I've been intrigued by a book I've read recently, written by Episcopal priest Robert Farrar Capon back in 1974. Capon writes that the church should never be in the morals business, manufacturing elaborate codes, rules, and laws for living. Instead, he writes, the church's business is forgiveness.

The world has no shortage of rules, laws, or moral codes. The problem comes in our repeatedly falling short of the ideal they set. Hence, the necessity for forgiveness and its succeeding stage: reconciliation.

Forgiveness is rarely easy and often counterintuitive. True reconciliation takes even more time. Jesus goes on to say, "Do not do as they do, for they do not practice what they teach." If the goal is wielding authority and passing judgment, then rules, regulations, and codes are hard to beat. But when it comes to authentic discipleship, reconciliation is worth the investment.

Loving and merciful God, remind us that the work of judgment is yours, not ours and that in the work of forgiveness, we follow your example and the example of Jesus. Amen.

SUNDAY, OCTOBER 30 ~ *Read Psalm 107:1-7, 33-37*

I annually observe an intentional period of reflection during this week. October 30 is the birthday of my late mother; October 31 is the eve of All Saints Day, which falls on November 1; and November 2 is All Souls Day. I wouldn't call it a preoccupation with death but an acknowledgment and celebration of eternity.

Psalm 107 refers to the perils of life: desert wastes, prisoners in misery and in irons, ships vulnerable to the perils of deep oceans, and the sickness caused by personal and societal sin. But notice the theme of enduring trust throughout the verses and the numerous explicit uses of the term *steadfast love*. My dictionary defines *steadfast* as "not subject to change."

Here in New York City a controversy brews about subway ads that promote atheism. One woman complained that she tries to teach her children about God and that the ads will make them think she is lying to them. While I sympathize with the mother, I suspect that she needs to emphasize to her children that faith is not a measurable fact; it is gift and also a choice.

It is a gift and a choice to believe in the God whose "steadfast love" threads through Psalm 107. The psalmist invites "the redeemed of the Lord" to bear witness to God's beneficence: "a desert into pools of water, a parched land into springs of water." Physical and spiritual benefits abound. Faith in that steadfast love connects us to what the writer of the Book of Hebrews describes as "so great a cloud of witnesses," the communion of saints who travel with us, right now, through eternity. Our ancestors, both blood relatives and others, chose to accept this gift. Faith gave their lives authenticity and does the same for us.

Omnipotent God, time does not exist for you. Help us to understand that your love and care are steadfast and unchanging. They unite past, present, and future into that great mystery of your eternity, forever and ever. Amen.

God's Whisper of Love

OCTOBER 31–NOVEMBER 6, 2011 • BEN F. PADGETT

MONDAY, OCTOBER 31 ~ *Read Matthew 25:1-13*

The parable of the ten virgins lends itself to a division between the good and bad, the prepared and unprepared, or the believer and nonbeliever. Such dichotomies fit comfortably and seem right on with American cultural expectations. Saints, however, have realized that both wise and foolish virgins live within each individual and each community, representing the internal struggle of those committed to serving God.

The foolish virgins within lead us to pass right by God who stands on the corner begging for food. Our internal foolish virgins blind us to seeing the holy in those who differ from us and, thus, dull our compassion. The wise virgins within seek God's way. John Wesley often spoke of our being on a journey of prevenient grace, justification, and sanctification—all the work of the Spirit within us. The saints grasp what God is about and join in. The saints have eyes that see and ears that hear.

Our faith story is not about "us" and "them" but about God. Ours is a story of God's loving us, in our foolishness as well as our wisdom, without our earning or deserving such love. As we become formed and transformed by God's love, we will gather at the Lord's wedding feast to celebrate and sing praises.

Our foolishness of listening to the calls from culture rather than to the whispers of God will keep us outside the wonders of God's present kingdom until God's redemptive transformation becomes stronger than "self."

Meditate on your personal foolish and wise virgins and how God's love transforms "self."

Ministerial Assessment Coordinator, North Alabama Conference, the United Methodist Church; Lookout Mountain, Tennessee

TUESDAY, NOVEMBER 1 ~ *Read Matthew 5:1-3*

ALL SAINTS DAY

Recall a time when you were at your rope's end or what Matthew identifies as being "poor in spirit." Poor in spirit can take many forms, including relational situations of loss, anger, violence, or watching a loved one's gradual self-destruction. Poor in spirit can be a time when the struggle to live seems greater than the struggle to die. It is a crisis or a dangerous opportunity. How do we continue on?

Some saints standing around God's throne came to the end of their ropes—hidden, frightened, facing conditions beyond their control—and there came to know Jesus. When we are at our rope's end and are spiritually poor, we can move from knowing *about* Jesus to *knowing* Jesus. Years of questioning and misunderstanding give way to a new beginning of living as Jesus lived. The end of our rope becomes the starting point of depending on the Jesus Way. Through our spiritual poverty, the end of our rope, we meet the grace of God in Jesus; and we have an opportunity to venture in a new direction.

The end of my rope came when I lost sight of any purpose in living. At the very bottom of personal deterioration, I heard God's whisper calling me to live. In the least expected place, during the least expected moment, the end of my rope became the beginning of a new life.

I hope to stand in that great crowd described in Revelation. I will stand there not on my own merit but because salvation belongs to God. I look forward to meeting others in that crowd who discovered new life at the end of their ropes and became spiritually rich from spiritual poverty.

Meditate on those things in your life that you have not been able to resolve. Look at them through the lens of God's love. Stand with the saints surrounding God's throne.

For many of those surrounding the throne singing praises to God, the great tribulation resided in the tension between knowing who they were and whose they were. They, like many of us, feared that others would discover their inadequacy and turn away. They felt certain that anyone seeing them as they really were would dislike them.

Adam and Eve hid from God, fearing God's reaction to their action. Moses backed away from God, claiming his speech inadequate. Isaiah cried out, "Woe is me! . . . For I am a man of unclean lips" (6:5). Jeremiah shied away from God's call by proclaiming his youthfulness. Peter felt so inadequate that he fell on his face and begged Jesus to get away from him. Personal inadequacies are real and troubling for those called by God. How do we move beyond these barriers to response?

Self-esteem, knowing who we are, has become a modern idol. When we worship "Who I Am" we separate ourselves from God and others. Instead of asking, "Who am I?" we are led to ask, *"Whose* am I?" Whose we are directs who we are and what we are about each moment of our lives. We can best learn who we are by being true to whose we are.

Jesus reminds us that as long as we feel certain we have the world by the tail, we deceive ourselves. Jesus leads his listeners, then and now, in a new way of considering self. If we truly want to know who we are, we have to begin with whose we are. The foundation of meekness rests on knowing our creation by God for the purposes of working with God for the salvation of all. To inherit the earth is to become unified with the visible and invisible through God's Spirit. To be meek means knowing God's salvation plan includes everyone.

How does "whose you are" help you know "who you are"?

A friend said, "Ben, once you have food, clothes, and shelter, everything else is for keeping score." My friend could see the power of our consumer culture and what it offers those who have the most toys and titles.

During my early years in ministry, I dreamed of being pastor of the largest church in the conference. I felt a surge of energy, fantasizing my voice proclaiming the good news there. Serving that church would make me important. When moving from pastoral ministry to hospital ministry blocked that path, my goal became to direct a hospital pastoral care department. When I fulfilled that career goal, I experienced what many people experience: the achievement of status did not diminish my sense of inadequacy. My life story had become about "who I was." I focused on merely surviving.

Ultimately, the struggle to live became greater than the struggle to die, and I made plans to end it all. At the darkest moment of my life, God called me to become who God had created me to be—a person to care for others. As my focus turned toward others, a transformation began that has continued for more than twenty years. When I became merciful, I received mercy. Life has not always been easy. However, God has filled me with a presence beyond my understanding.

Turn your life toward the needs of others and watch what happens. Life becomes a venture of experiencing God's love for everyone through our delivery of that love. God's transforming work is going on constantly within us and others. Our call is to join all the saints, past and present, in listening to the whispers of God and in partnering with God in personal and community transformation.

Meditate on God's transforming work around and in you.

Simplifying comes in learning that I can more easily get rid of others' things than my own. Pureness of heart works in much the same way. We more easily see others' faith flaws than our own. We point a finger at persons who don't attend church rather than ask ourselves why we haven't invited them to join us for worship. We look critically at non-Christian traditions rather than consider that the shape of Christianity now resembles our culture.

No doubt many saints surrounding the throne of God with singing and praise came through the finger-pointing process: men and women who knew how easy it was to see "them" and "those people." Their sainthood originated through looking first at the impurities of their own hearts and seeking God's transforming Spirit.

Jesus preached that when we dig deeply into whose we are, we see God within ourselves and then in others. By seeking within our very soul for the One who created us, we see the One who created "them" and "those people."

Notice the awe in Revelation's description (7:13-17) of the scene that includes multitudes of people from all nations, all tribes, and all languages. The author tells us that these people have "come out of the great ordeal." Having been washed in the blood of the One who saves, they will no longer hunger or thirst or experience abuse of any kind.

By looking in our heart, we find that God alone is doing the saving. God alone makes us worthy. That simplifies life! A pure heart declares whose we are and also to whom "they" and "those people" belong. Rather than pointing fingers, we join in singing God's praises.

Meditate quietly; listen to the saints singing praises to the One to whom salvation belongs. Listen until you hear your voice joining with the voices of the other saints.

SATURDAY, NOVEMBER 5 ~ *Read 1 John 3:1-3*

Worse than feeling inadequate are our endeavors to overcome our sense of inadequacy by ourselves. While self-help books and psychotherapy led to some important positive changes in my daily life and relationships, the gnawing sense of inadequacy still plagued me.

Trying to rid ourselves of feelings of inadequacy reflects our desire to manage our own lives. The first step in Alcoholics Anonymous acknowledges persons' inability to manage their own lives. To experience sobriety, we must depend upon a Power greater than ourselves. The writer of First John reminds us that God, a power greater than ourselves, has called us children of God. And what is the distinctive characteristic of God's children? It is the love given to them by God and out of which the children of God relate to all believers.

Our patient and loving Lord takes the initiative. We respond remarkably well to this love at times, while falling short at other times. God's love is not a one-time gift to hoard. God's love, as demonstrated by Jesus, is the faith-environment in which we live and have our being, an unmerited gift that nurtures our growth in faith and leads us to serve others.

Even the disciples, who left everything to follow Jesus, did not learn God's way at once, nor will we. Accounts of their struggles assure us that God is with us even when we are confused and falter. The love God gives us as God's children continues to whisper to us as our guide through life.

Meditate on God's love whispered to you.

SUNDAY, NOVEMBER 6 ~ *Read Revelation 7:9-17*

We moderns have come to depend so much on the intellectual and scientific perspectives of life that we miss the messages and gifts of suffering. When a malady develops, our first thought is to find a physician to alleviate our symptoms and cure the illness. Seldom do we seek God's guidance or listen for the life message that the malady may deliver. Many in the world live without health care insurance or access to medical care. I suppose that some of those gathered around the throne singing praises to God fell into this group. Many may have been children of God who suffered while living next door to those of us more fortunate than they.

We can readily imagine God wiping away tears of sorrow, suffering, and pain. We can imagine God spoon-feeding those who have slowly starved to death. We think of God doing what is necessary to balance the scales of justice for those who experienced very little justice in this life. What about those of us who tip the scales? Where does God figure into the picture for us?

The writer of Revelation invites us to sing God's praises with these saints. He invites us to allow our maladies to open our eyes to ways we can balance the scales as God would desire. We can join God in wiping away the tears of suffering, and we can help feed the hungry.

We wait for the end of time out there somewhere by joining with God's way in the present. As we wipe away the tears of others, God wipes away our tears. As we feed others, God satisfies our real hunger, the hunger beyond earthly bread. All eternity is right now. Gathering eternity into a present moment by joining God's final promise today places us with the saints around the throne.

Meditate on your eternity in the present moment.

The Unexpected

NOVEMBER 7–13, 2011 • PAUL L. ESCAMILLA

MONDAY, NOVEMBER 7 ~ *Read Judges 4:1-7*

God writes straight with crooked lines." So goes an old Portuguese saying. Our lives and the Bible are good examples of this axiom. Scripture is filled with interruptions, detours, and unexpected turns in the road upon which the people of God travel. The Song of Deborah in Judges 5 puts it well: "He asked water and she gave him milk" (5:25). God continually surprises or confounds both friend and enemy, faithful and faithless. Perhaps this is God's way of countering our efforts to bolt everything down in certainties and control. When we're expecting water, we get milk.

Today's story presents a predicament of national proportions for the people of Israel. In a cycle of disobedience and repentance all too recognizably human, they have done well; then they have done evil; stability followed by stupidity. What we know about evil, or self-conceit of any sort, is that it narrows the sphere of vision, leaving us vulnerable to those who would prey upon us. Soon the errant Israelites are struggling under the oppressive governance of neighboring Canaan.

When the people cry to God for help, Deborah is in a unique position both to understand and execute God's response. She leads her people in the successful overthrow of their oppressor. Sisera, Canaan's general, meets an unexpected end. (It is he to whom the Song of Deborah refers when milk is substituted for water.) God has once again written straight with crooked lines, and, beyond belief, Israel is free again.

Merciful God, if you are to lead us in unsought ways and give us milk when we ask for water, then nourish us more deeply than we could ever have expected. Amen.

Elder of the United Methodist Church, appointed to Perkins School of Theology, Southern Methodist University; Dallas, Texas

TUESDAY, NOVEMBER 8 ~ *Read Judges 4:1-7*

Before we leave the story of Deborah, let me mention another unexpected feature or two. Deborah, a leader of Israel, is both attuned to God and authorized by God and the people of Israel for leadership. The people look to her to hear from God.

The unexpected aspect about this portrait is a detail easily overlooked: Deborah functions as a female leader in a highly patriarchal society. This society regarded women as property, objects of others' decisions rather than free to determine their own life choices. Women certainly did not merit regard as national or spiritual leaders—not normally. In such an environment, Deborah's presence as the definitive leader and divine representative of Israel moves beyond unexpected to unorthodox.

This leads to the other unexpected feature of this brief historical account: the narrator makes nothing of this extreme role subversion. Rather, in the most matter-of-fact way, the writer presents Deborah as Israel's judge and national leader for that point in time—no questions asked. Furthermore, her virtues include the following: capable, self-assured, divinely appointed, and trusted implicitly by the people.

What does all of this relay to us? Perhaps the Bible and its Israel are less patriarchal than we had imagined. Perhaps God can thwart expectations in ways that subvert even deeply entrenched structures for the cause of mercy and redemption. Perhaps you have another theory. Centuries later, the apostle Peter will declare that "God shows no partiality" (Acts 10:34); God can and will use the unlikely and the unsanctioned to accomplish God's purposes. Deborah proves that Peter's pronouncement is not new information but a truth that sacred history has repeated for centuries.

Holy God, is there a song of Deborah in me? Am I the unlikely one chosen for your holy purposes? Help me to trust that regardless of my status or social limitations, I too am called and claimed by you. Amen.

WEDNESDAY, NOVEMBER 9 ~ *Read Psalm 123*

Known collectively as songs of ascent, Psalms 120–134 provided musical accompaniment for groups on their journey from remote villages to the Temple in Jerusalem. In this song of ascents, the psalmist equates the posture of one who waits for God's merciful action to that of one who waits as a servant or maid for the good graces of the one in whose charge they find themselves. The servant knows not when or how the master will be generous; nor does the maid know in what season or by what means the mistress will bestow favor upon her. In such relationships, lives are shaped around the uncertainty of another's mercy and generosity. Will we have the holiday free? Will there be a special Christmas gift? Will the master retire early and leave me an evening to myself? Will the mistress travel and, taking me along, introduce me to new worlds?

Identification of the person of faith with a servant or maid is not uncommon in scripture. One familiar reference is Mary's song in Luke 1, in which Mary speaks of herself as God's "handmaiden" (KJV) or "servant." Such allusions may sound strange to our ears, particularly if we or our ancestry have no known history of being maids, servants, or slaves. But all, whether rich or poor, servant or free, can identify with this much: in life we wait for everything that is really worth having, and most especially for mercy. At the sacred altars to which we go when we are in need of this divine gift, the most powerful king is a peasant in want, the most celebrated queen a beggar to God. Some things, mercy among them, cannot be purchased or commanded; they must be received by all on the same humble terms: with upward-turned eyes.

When we gather as your people, O God, turn our eyes to you as those who can find mercy only from your hand. Amen.

As they move toward the holy city of Jerusalem and its Temple for worship and prayer, travelers from an outlying village will have many things on their minds, some practical, others spiritual. Travelers would certainly be mindful of keeping their group together, fed, and free from harm. They would be thinking ahead to the matter of finding accommodations upon arriving in Jerusalem. Have they brought along sufficient provisions? Will their money be safe from robbers?

Their litany of preoccupations are ours too any time we step from the safety and certainty of home. Any journey undertaken, even around the block, calls for some consideration of what to bring along, as well as an awareness of the possibility of the unexpected happening somewhere between our departure and our return.

And then the spiritual considerations come to the fore. The psalm situates the traveling community somewhere between need and hopefulness. They are scorned for their faith, ridiculed for their beliefs, perhaps even persecuted and discriminated against. In their particular circumstance, "mercy" translates to "deliverance." The word can, in other contexts, mean other things: forgiveness, assurance, healing, hope. What we find so compelling in the witness of this traveling band is that its members go up to Jerusalem expectant but uncertain. We hope for mercy, but what form will it take? We feel confident in God's promise to deliver us, but what will that mean? "Ascending" to worship with God's people, whether in Sunday gatherings, on retreat, or in some other context, is a practice of both heightened expectation and surrender of expectation. For two things, above all, are true when God's people gather in devotion: God will grant mercy, and we know not how.

Open me, O God, and open us, to meeting your open hand in whatever form mercy takes. Amen.

If Mark 13 is known as the "little apocalypse" for its brevity in speaking of the mystery of the end times, then we might consider this text the "littler apocalypse." As in Mark, here all the expansiveness and strangeness of meanings surrounding "the day of the Lord" are vividly compacted into a handful of image-laden verses. We have thieves, antepartum labor pains, light, darkness, wakefulness, sleep, sobriety, drunkenness, breastplates, and helmets, all in the span of fewer than a dozen verses. If Paul has in mind creating a sense of kaleidoscopic unpredictability in portraying the fulfillment of history, he succeeds beyond our wildest dreams.

Three things come without warning according to the ancient Talmudic wisdom: the Messiah, a found article, and a scorpion. With a sting of irony this saying reminds us that with the things of God, the expected is tightly braided with the unexpected. We have reason to hope but also to be unsettled. We have cause for acute alertness ("the day of the Lord will come like a thief in the night") but also for deep assurance ("whether we are awake or asleep we may live with him").

The faithful posture of those who wait and work for the fulfillment of God's reign is one not of closed certainty but of open trust. The difference between these two dispositions makes all the difference in the lives of those who claim the Messiah as their own. The declaration that "there is peace and security" is, except in the most qualified sense, a presumption not afforded the people of God. For there is not peace and security—not for all, not everywhere. Smugness in the mysteries of God's ways and purposes will precede destruction; by contrast, reliance on God to provide will surely sustain us through unknown times and seasons.

Come, Lord Jesus, in expected and unexpected ways, as you will; but come in mercy, we pray. And may we be ready. Amen.

Parables, like life itself, often lead us by unsought ways. And just as in life we resist unexpected turns in the road and unwelcome surprises along the journey, so we are tepid in our enthusiasm when a parable doesn't go the way we think it should.

Today, the unexpected turn comes with the presentation of a hard-hearted man as the parable's protagonist. Unlike the generous householder giving proportionally greater pay to laborers who worked fewer hours (Matthew 20:1-15), the hard-hearted master takes away from those who have put forth earnest but misguided effort and gives more to those who have proven themselves industrious. Whereas in the earlier parable rewards extend in all directions, here they are reserved for the brightest and boldest, and withheld—severely—from the cautious and timid.

The parable falls in the middle of a three-parable set—the wise and foolish virgins and the separation of the sheep from the goats being the other two—dealing with the theme of eschatology, that is, the "last things." Virtually every biblical discourse on this subject includes the exhortation to "be ready" or "stay alert." This parable is no exception. Readiness in this instance, however, means something rather different than simply being alert to the return of the master. We could acknowledge that the third, cautious servant is entirely alert to that eventuality and he still fails to please his master. Readiness, in this instance, means something more counterintuitive; it means the willingness to take chances with one's holdings during the waiting period. Being prepared for the coming of God and God's reign is not a matter of battening down the hatches and safeguarding possessions and provisions but the very opposite. In the context of this parable, readiness involves risk-taking.

Eternal God, teach us to risk what we treasure as a practice of devotion to you, trusting you with what you have entrusted to us. Amen.

Ostensibly, this parable tells the story of financial investment and yield. Two servants invest the money entrusted to them by the master at his departure, realizing a 100% increase by the time of his return. The third servant hides his portion of the endowment, realizing no earnings. The two high-yield producers receive praise; the producer of zero yield is berated and punished. The parable can leave the reader with one of three reactions: offense at the hard-hearted master, appreciation for a realistic portrait of market forces, or some combination of the two.

Imagine for a moment that the talents involved are a currency other than silver or gold. Perhaps they represent the gospel itself, either broadcast widely or kept to oneself. Earlier in Matthew's Gospel, Jesus says "Let your light shine before others, so that they may see your good works and give glory to your Father in heaven" (5:16). What if the talents are an inconvenient truth, more easily hidden away than voiced before an unwelcoming audience? In that same sermon from Matthew 5, Jesus encourages those who risk doing or saying what is right when their action may result in persecution, "for theirs is the kingdom of heaven" (5:10). In both cases, the risks are great, but the yield greater still.

Another parable follows, which narrates the labors of love extended by the faithful toward the stranger, the sick, the hungry, the prisoner. Let us not presume that these acts of mercy are any less risk laden than positioning talents to double in worth over a few years' time. The marketplace is not the only setting that calls for courage and a gambler's grit. Every arena of discipleship entails risk and promises great rewards.

Teach me, Lord, to speak boldly, love generously, and live transparently, so scattering treasure that, regardless of risk to myself, others may glorify you. Amen.

The Reign of Christ in the World

NOVEMBER 14–20, 2011 • TOM CAMPBELL

MONDAY, NOVEMBER 14 ~ *Read Ephesians 1:15-19*

The threads in this week's scripture passages weave together the theme that leads up to Christ the King or Reign of Christ Sunday. A frequent thread involves shepherds and sheep, their respective roles and the ends to which God will go to make sure sheep receive proper care. We see ourselves as both sheep and shepherds of God's flock. We receive instruction about how to approach and worship God and garner special insights into right relationship with God; and we read of God's judgment.

The church at Ephesus was pivotal to the spread of the gospel in Asia; these verses provide a good start for our week. We come to them with thanksgiving for a God so powerful as to create the entire universe, yet so loving as to desire relationship with us. We also give thanks for other believers with whom we form community and from whom we gain strength.

Christians believe Christ reigns at the right hand of God in heaven. But what do we believe about Christ's reign on earth? Do we find it only in certain faith communities or geographic areas? What would it be like to live in a world without strife, a place where people treated each other with respect and kindness, where no one went without food or shelter and all had opportunity for education, health care, and meaningful work?

Let us pray for wisdom and revelation this week. May the eyes of our hearts, our inner emotions, and convictions help us turn faith into action that manifests the reign of Christ on earth.

Dear God, may we be shepherds leading others to Christ while, like sheep, willing to faithfully follow that lead. Amen.

Layperson, publisher of the Efird Bible Study Series, Sunday school teacher; Raleigh, North Carolina

TUESDAY, NOVEMBER 15 ~ *Read Psalm 100*

A retirement service for two beloved Salvation Army officers became a genuine celebration when the Timbrel Brigade of young boys and girls marched into the banquet hall striking their tambourines while singing the song taken from Psalm 100, "He Has Made Me Glad." Without prompting, those in the crowd rose to their feet, clapped their hands, and sang the familiar tune about how entering God's gates with thanksgiving and God's courts with praise will indeed make us glad.

On the way home, my wife and I discussed the fact that those young people, without knowing it, had immediately changed the mood of the event with their loud, enthusiastic singing and playing. Their witness inspired us and raised the level of worship.

John and Charles Wesley, founders of the Methodist movement, knew the importance of music in worship. They, along with William Booth, the Methodist pastor who founded the Salvation Army, often employed music to attract large crowds for their open-air services. Charles Wesley has been credited with writing words for hundreds of hymns and brother John implored followers to sing lustily in praise to God.

Too often our participation in worship confirms us as the "frozen chosen" instead of as passionate Christians entering God's presence with praise and thanksgiving. What would happen if you (and perhaps others you enlisted) did sing lustily in worship? No doubt a few heads would turn; some might even consider you disrespectful to sing so loudly in church. But some might respond like those who gathered that day when the Timbrel Brigade brought us up to their excited level of praise. Surely God delights in our joyful, glad praise. Just as importantly, our joyful noise lifts our spirits and inspires others to join in.

O God, we give thanks for your steadfast love and faithfulness, and we rejoice in worshiping you. Amen.

The Hebrews believed prophets had contact with the Holy and acted as intermediaries to speak a message or convey a vision from God. My wife and I know a prophet. Billy Wise showed up unannounced one morning at 6:00 wanting to clean our gutters. Short, with several teeth missing, Billy was dressed in dirty work clothes, talking a mile a minute. After cleaning our gutters he came inside and had a cup of coffee, asking if he could pray with us before he left. Can you imagine our amazement?

Weeks later, when the doorbell again rang at that early hour, Billy asked for a cup of coffee and told us God had sent him because a family issue was causing unrest in our home. God told him to tell us to have faith and to do what we thought was right, and everything would work out well. *How could Billy Wise have known such truth?* we wondered. Now we know when the doorbell rings early in the morning that it is Billy. Sometimes he just wants to clean our gutters, get a cup of coffee, a hug, and have prayer; sometimes he has a message for us.

Ezekiel begins with a prophetic message of hope for the Israelites exiled in Babylon. He speaks to them words from God. God as shepherd will search and gather the sheep, bringing them to good pasture. God will collect the lost and the strayed, binding up the wounds of those with injuries.

What if the person working next to you, in line at the grocery ahead of you, or coming to clean your gutters is a prophet? You may not recognize that person as a prophet but listen to the words of hope and challenge. When you're receptive, someone might have a message for you.

God, make me open to your messenger and your message. Amen.

THURSDAY, NOVEMBER 17 ~ *Read Matthew 25:31-46*

Today's lesson describes Jesus on the throne of glory. He sits in the judgment chair and separates the righteous, those in right relationship with God, from those who are not. Scriptures tell us to expect a judgment day, and we want to sit on the right hand, among those who are favored.

Imagine yourself in that wondrous kingdom serving Christ and rejoicing with the saints. But Jesus turns things upside down for us. Instead of serving earthly kings, seeking great wealth or prominence, giving great sums to charity, or even being pious in our worship, Jesus says we will be judged on how we treat the least among us.

Our lives are so full of busyness that we willingly give money rather than personally serve others. We justify ourselves by saying that with our taxes the government hires others to help the poor and heal the sick. Our contributions to church will pay pastors and staff or mission teams to provide needed help.

But Jesus doesn't say inasmuch as you paid taxes or inasmuch as you gave money you did it to the least of my people. Jesus says inasmuch as *you* serve the poor, care for the sick, spend time with strangers and those in whatever prison they might occupy, you do the same for me. His words don't allow for surrogates.

Christians have been waiting more than two thousand years for Jesus' return. Maybe we have gotten this all wrong. What if Jesus is waiting on us? Might Christ be patiently waiting for us to become true shepherds who tend God's flock, thereby bringing to reality God's kingdom on earth as it is in heaven?

Shepherding God, help me establish my priorities so as to be among those in right relationship with you and my brothers and sisters. Amen.

FRIDAY, NOVEMBER 18 ~ *Read Psalm 100*

I grew up in a time and geographical locale that permitted public schools to begin the day with a Bible reading and prayer. Whenever I hear the words of this psalm, I remember my fifth-grade teacher, Miss Purvis, who taught us to recite Psalms 23; 24; and 100. At the time I, like others, thought this repetition of scripture was a waste of time and didn't have much relevance to our lives. Much later I came to understand that my obedience to this memorization process signified a small step in learning a larger obedience to God.

Do you hear the two primary themes of this psalm? The first reminds us that God is God, and we are not. It's pretty obvious that even the ancients believed they were "self-made." Times haven't changed much since Adam and Eve ate the forbidden fruit so as to have as much knowledge as God. Look in any bookstore and you will discover that self-help books are among the perennial best-sellers. We want to play God.

We are God's sheep, placed in God's pasture. The shepherd and sheep imagery we can understand. God's unconditional love and mercy remain timeless truths for all generations.

In appreciation of a God who loves us even as we sin, we give thanks and praise, worshiping with raised voices. These words call us to action, not just passive obedience. Serving with gladness and joy is both our duty and our privilege.

In these words of beautiful prose we derive both an understanding of God and our response to God. Just as we give thanks for a teacher who understands the importance of learning scripture, we offer praise and thanks to a creator God who loves us unconditionally.

Set your love in our hearts, O God, and help us always to remember to make a joyful noise in our worship of you. Amen.

SATURDAY, NOVEMBER 19 ~ *Read Ezekiel 34:20-24*

When I was young, I spent many a Saturday afternoon watching black-and-white Western movies. A quarter would buy admission to the theater, a box of popcorn, a drink, and a piece of penny candy. My friends and I couldn't wait for Roy Rogers, Hopalong Cassidy, Lash LaRue, Gene Autry, Johnny Mack Brown, and others to beat the bad guys each week. The lessons were obvious: people who did what was right and obeyed the law prevailed. Those who didn't were run out of town or worse.

We still want to believe that those who do right and follow the rules win, while those who don't obey get what's coming to them. Perhaps that's why we take so much comfort from today's scripture. God instructs the prophet Ezekiel to deliver a message to the leaders of the Hebrew people: they have become fat, greedy, and corrupt. They will be judged and will receive sure and certain punishment.

Christians are called to discern the difference between "right" belief and action and that which does not coincide with our faith. All too frequently we start down the slippery slope from evaluating ourselves to judging others, deciding who is good and who is evil. Some even judge who will or won't get to heaven. Our piety becomes ugly, exclusionary, and takes our focus off the joy and fullness of life in Christ.

Most every translation of verse 20 records God's words, "I myself will judge. . . . " Read those words again. God alone is the judge. God will hold people accountable. This good news removes the responsibility from us, while mandating that we stop judging others. That's God's job, and we are not God. We may take assurance from reading that God is on the job, and good will prevail.

God, help me to stop being judgmental and let you do the judging. Amen.

SUNDAY, NOVEMBER 20 ~ *Read Ephesians 1:20-23*

REIGN OF CHRIST

The apse of Christ United Methodist Church in New York City has a beautiful mosaic of Jesus sitting on a majestic throne. In his left hand are the scriptures, while his right hand gestures a sign of peace. In 1925, Pope Pius XI established this last Sunday before Advent as "Christ the King" Sunday out of concern over what he saw as a frightening increase in secularism and nationalism in the world. Obviously the pope saw growing numbers of people who did not acknowledge Christ as the supreme authority in their lives, instead worshiping their possessions, their positions, their professions, and even their preferences for how and where they spent their time.

What does it mean to recognize the reign of Christ? We are to put ourselves in Jesus' hands, and those hands in the mosaic in Christ United Methodist Church give us the answer. On the one hand Jesus holds the scriptures that tell us how to live in right relationship with God and one another. This week's scriptures tell us to deal honestly; love others; and serve by feeding the hungry, clothing the naked, tending the sick, even visiting those in prison. We are to be faithful in worship and prayer. On the other hand, Jesus signals peace, which is more than an absence of war. Peace is a posture of life, a way of relating that we seek in every contact with every person.

This week's readings depict Jesus as judge, separating sheep from goats—but also God as shepherd who seeks the lost and returns them to the flock. In these portraits we recognize the supreme authority of Christ while also giving thanks that this Sovereign wants us to be part of the flock. What a King!

Lord, as we prepare for Advent, may we pause to remember your supreme authority in our lives and to place ourselves under your reign. Amen.

Forward to What?

NOVEMBER 21–27, 2011 • GEORGE HOVANESS DONIGIAN

MONDAY, NOVEMBER 21 ~ *Read Psalm 80:1-7*

In Psalm 80 the psalmist or leader addresses God, and then the gathered people beseech, "Restore us, O God; let your face shine, that we may be saved." Those words appeal to many of us. We know brokenness, the pressures of life that cause disruption. We long for restoration. As we enter the first week of Advent, the lectionary texts confirm our hope for salvation.

The first two verses of the psalm invite God, somewhat politely, to give ear to the people's complaints. They pay homage to God's saving acts through history and refer specifically to Ephraim, Benjamin, and Manasseh. We begin to see an appeal to the history of Israel. Benjamin, Ephraim, and Manasseh carry in their tribal history the history of God's actions on behalf of the people.

The next stanza dives deeper emotionally. "How long will you be angry with your people's prayers?" A deeply troubled spirit unexpectedly voices these words. The respectful salutation of the first three verses does not offer any hint of the psalmist's distress. Nor is there any reason at the first to suspect the anguish of the people. Both the psalmist and the people fear that God, in anger, is ignoring their prayers. Hence, the plea for restoration.

Sometimes, despite our intellectual understanding of God's love, we, like the psalmist, fear that God is not listening or caring for us. In the midst of our fears, Advent offers us the grand truth of God's loving restoration and reconciliation.

In the midst of doubt and disruption, Holy God, restore us; let your face shine, that we may be saved. Amen.

Armenian activist; former editor, Discipleship Resources; Greenwood, South Carolina

TUESDAY, NOVEMBER 22 ~ *Read Mark 13:24-37*

Verses 24-37 come from the lengthy thirteenth chapter in which Jesus foretells the destruction of the Temple, the coming of much persecution, the desolating sacrilege, and the coming of the Son of Man at the end of the age. At the conclusion of the chapter, we read of Jesus' reference to signs in nature that tell of the changing seasons and the need to watch for similarly relevant signs of the end of the age.

If an itinerant today preaches or teaches about the signs of the end, we might brush off those words as insincere or hypocritical. Or we might, as we approach the end of the calendar year, begin to think of the various "predictions"—whether from the Mayan civilization or Nostradamus—concerning the end of the world in 2012. Many people seem to consider quite seriously such "predictions" that come from ancient and now gone civilizations. Some others of us, having lived through earlier predictions of the end, may scoff or laugh at various predictions of the end of the age.

Our text, however, comes from Jesus. How will we take seriously his words about the signs of the end and the need for watchfulness? This question is critically important for disciples, and we dare not ignore or avoid Jesus' words. Jesus offers a basic truth in the final words of verse 37: "Keep awake!" That message is a key understanding, not merely for Advent but for all life. How easily we allow ordinary routines and demands of life to dull our awareness!

Jesus invites us to live in the present moment. Do not waste your days remembering the wonders of past experience or projecting a new and glorious personal future. Live in the now! Pay attention in this moment, and do not let false teachers—whether religious teachers or the larger culture—seduce or mislead you.

What causes us to wander from our discipleship in the present moment?

The lament of Isaiah 64 recalls, as did Psalm 80, the time in Egypt. These verses express a longing for God's decisive action that makes known the utter holiness of the Lord.

But the longing goes beyond simple remembrance of the past. Written shortly after the Babylonian conquest, the words of this lament are strong, forceful, and decisive in their grief. Incomprehension rules the people who recall that once they were God's holy nation and now foreigners who do not worship the God of Abraham and Sarah and Moses herd them away from the holy land of home. They say that they have become unclean and their "righteous deeds are like a filthy cloth." Continuing in this psychospiritual turmoil and terror, the people, through the prophet, cry out that no one calls on the name of God and that God is now absent from the people.

Perhaps we understand this disorientation far more deeply than we realize. We know people who have had to leave their homelands, not because of choice but because of persecution. These foreigners began anew, often in places not particularly friendly to the aliens. They may have escaped genocidal efforts in Rwanda. They may have escaped drug lords who controlled their city or nation. They may have experienced persecution because of religious beliefs.

Still closer to many of us are the people who experience this disorientation because of unemployment or the end of a marriage. We know them. We see them in the mirror.

To all of us, the prophet ends the lament with the grace of a tender reminder: "O Lord, you are our Father; we are the clay, and you are our potter." We pray that God will shape our unformed and rough edges as we await the Christ.

What response to your lament do you seek?

THURSDAY, NOVEMBER 24 ~ *Read Psalm 65*

Thanksgiving Day, USA

Today many of us in the United States will join in Thanksgiving celebrations with family and friends. Long before such feasts in the United States, the Bible witnesses to celebrations of thanks to God for deliverance and for bounteous harvests. Psalm 65 offers such a thanksgiving for bounteous crops, but the psalmist does not limit such thanksgiving to the yield of a region or a nation; the psalmist extends that thanksgiving to the whole earth. You may wish to read aloud Psalm 65 as part of the prayer before the meal. Whether you read it aloud before the meal or simply reflect on the psalm during some quiet time, consider actions that the psalm celebrates. God

- answers prayers;
- forgives transgressions;
- answers with deliverance;
- makes the gateways of the day shout for joy;
- enriches the earth;
- crowns the year with bounty.

In response to God, the psalmist writes that the meadows clothe themselves, the valleys deck themselves, and together these shout and sing for joy. These actions grow from God, whose first attributes in the psalm are to answer prayers and to forgive.

After reading Psalm 65, take time to answer these Thanksgiving Day questions:

- How did God answer my prayers during this year?
- What seeds, physical or spiritual, have I planted in the earth or in the human soul?
- What growth have I seen from these seeds?
- Who has nurtured growth in me?
- How will I praise God today?

O God, I thank you heartily for all your good gifts. Amen.

FRIDAY, NOVEMBER 25 ～ *Read Psalm 80:1-7, 17-19*

Thanksgiving Day is over, and the news outlets in the United States declare today as "Black Friday," a day in which consumers shop heavily, promoting businesses' success and profit for the year. Advertising pressures many of us to find and buy the perfect gifts. Consumer attitudes range from adrenaline-fueled excitement to weary cynicism. That emotional range differs from a biblical sense of life in thanksgiving and expectation. Perhaps the frenzy of pre-Christmas consumerism is actually an unvoiced plea for restoration from a state of spiritual dislocation.

Restore us, O God of hosts; let your face shine, that we may be saved.

While the psalmist addresses his words primarily to Judah's disorientation following the destruction and captivity of the Northern Kingdom of Israel, Psalm 80 speaks to our own dislocation and disorientation. So many people want to celebrate a peaceful Christmas, a Christmas without expressions of greed and anger, and yet, these same people feel driven by forces beyond them to seek and find treasures "as seen on television." To rephrase a prayer of Augustine of Hippo: "Give us simplicity, but not right now."

Restore us, O God of hosts; let your face shine, that we may be saved.

Here also is a note of witness and history: When Moses returned from Mount Sinai, his face glowed "because he had been talking with God" (Exod. 34:29). Moses' shining face created fear in Aaron and the rest of the Israelites. Moses then veiled his face whenever he went among the people; but when he went to God, he removed the veil. The Israelites would again see that the face of Moses was shining. May our faces reflect the shining love of God to those whom we meet today and throughout Advent.

Restore us, O God of hosts; let your face shine, that we may be saved. Amen.

Forward to What? seems an odd theme for a week's meditations, especially as we begin the season of Advent. Advent and Lent point us forward to new ways of God's interaction with humanity. We cannot remain stuck in the past. We need to move forward to the territory marked only by God's gracious invitation.

In Mark 13, Jesus refers to signs of the coming of the Son of Man. He speaks in a nondramatic way about himself, and he speaks about false messiahs and false prophets who will "produce signs and omens, to lead astray, if possible, the elect." Yet even when he speaks of the sacrilege of the Temple (Mark 13:14-23), Jesus remains calm and reminds his listeners to be alert. Jesus does not try to establish himself as a fearmonger.

As we move through Advent toward the great celebration of Incarnation, those who see signs of the end of the world will accost us. They will seek ways to prove that the apocalypse is near, and they apparently plan to profit by the sale of emergency food supplies and gold. Such attitudes fly in the face of Jesus' words; however, many followers of Jesus go astray because of these appeals to fear. These followers move forward to the same old stuff, the same old attitudes, and the same old fears that seduced Jesus' first followers.

To go forward into the new requires that we be alert, keep awake, and live without fear because God incarnate is our guide and our defender. Jesus did not come into the world to scare people into the reign of God; he came to love people into God's grace. This love of Jesus moves us gently and firmly into the new life of God's love—a life without fear.

God of the ages, throughout history people have lived in fear of the end. Help us to live freely in your love, to love without fear, and to let others know of this love in Christ Jesus. Amen.

SUNDAY, NOVEMBER 27 ~ *Read 1 Corinthians 1:3-9*

FIRST SUNDAY OF ADVENT

Grace to you and peace as we move forward. Context is everything. When we move further into First Corinthians, we meet a church so divided that it cannot share the same loaf of bread or jug of wine during the Lord's Supper. The members of this community fail to get along because some disciples boast of special powers and gifts and look with condescension on those who seem to have "lesser" or different gifts. Despite these multiple divisions, Paul offers thanks to God for this church and the witness it offers in the midst of a cosmopolitan and multicultural seaport, awash with the influences of Rome and of Rome's trading partners.

In his thanksgiving, Paul offers a model for the church's understanding of mission and ministry: "I give thanks . . . in every way you have been enriched in [Christ], in speech and knowledge of every kind . . . so that you are not lacking in any spiritual gift as you await the revealing of our Lord Jesus Christ." Everything that follows this letter's introduction grows from Paul's very specific thanksgiving model. To paraphrase later words in this letter: "Of course, you have different gifts, but they are all of equal value to God. Do not look down on any brother or sister who does not have what you have." Everything, Paul notes, comes from Christ.

Today global Christianity seems as divided as the Corinthian church; however, Paul reminds us that our gifts come from the Christ. Our use of those gifts bears witness to the world in response to the love of God that we know in Christ. Whether we see signs of the end or signs of congregational diversity and division, Christ strengthens us and invites us to move forward into the gracious future of God's reign.

What divisions do I see in my congregation? What gifts do I see? How may I become a means of reconciliation?

God Comes with Comfort & Challenge

NOVEMBER 28–DECEMBER 4, 2011 • M. THOMAS THANGARAJ

MONDAY, NOVEMBER 28 ~ *Read Isaiah 40:1-5*

A couplet written by a poet in the first century CE says that choosing a bad and hurtful word in place of a good and comforting word is like choosing an unripe, sour fruit when one could have a ripe, sweet fruit. God chooses comforting words to speak "tenderly" to Jerusalem and to us.

God does speak to us tenderly, assuring us of God's forgiveness and God's mercy. Especially in and through the life, death, and resurrection of Christ, God has spoken tenderly to us and offered us new life.

While God speaks a comforting word, God speaks a challenging word too. Isaiah reminds us of God's call to prepare the way of the Lord—to lift up the valleys, to make low the mountains, and to level the uneven ground. As we examine our lives, we do find valleys that need a lift: moments of despair that require God's assurance. We discover mountains that must be made low: situations of self-assertion and pride. And we uncover occasions of hesitant and uneven discipleship that demand a leveling. God calls us to prepare the way through deep introspection and humble obedience.

Then, as Isaiah says, the glory of the Lord will be revealed, and those around us will definitely see it. God has spoken, and it will surely come to fruition in our lives. Hear the echo of Jesus' words: "Let your light shine before others, so that they see your good works and give glory to your Father in heaven" (Matt. 5:16).

O God, may your assurance of grace strengthen me so that my life reveals your glory. Amen.

Presbyter of the Church of South India and Emeritus Professor of World Christianity, Candler School of Theology, Emory University; Atlanta, Georgia

TUESDAY, NOVEMBER 29 ~ *Read Isaiah 40:6-11*

I have a hibiscus tree in my yard that opens out stunningly bright red flowers every morning. These flowers dazzle in the light of the morning sun. But by evening they wither and fall to the ground! Such is the character of our life on this earth. Isaiah reminds us of the impermanence of human life using the metaphors of grass and the flower of the field: "All people are grass, their constancy is like the flower of the field."

The transience and impermanence of our lives become real to us when we experience the loss of a loved one. When my mother died at the age of fifty-eight, death became more real to me than ever before. We become even more aware of our finitude when sudden and tragic death happens due to an accident or sudden illness, either in our family or in our community. We are gripped by the disturbing power of death.

In those moments of experiencing the impermanence of our lives, God's word comes to us. We become aware that God comes with power and might coupled with loving care and concern. Even in this passage that compares God to a powerful ruler and an awesome judge, it also describes God as a gentle and caring shepherd. God comes as one who rules and rewards while gathering and carrying us.

We have nothing to fear in the arms of a gentle and loving God. But we cannot just rest there; we need to get up and announce to the whole world, "Here is your God!" God carries us so that we can carry the good news of God's grace-filled presence into our lives, our neighborhoods, and our world.

Loving God, help me remember at all times that you carry me, so that I can carry your love to all around me. Amen.

WEDNESDAY, NOVEMBER 30 ~ *Read Psalm 85:1-2*

When I read the newspaper or watch the news on television, I will be apprised of murders, burglaries, violence, wars, shortage of food or health care, accidents on the road, and so on. Yet, if I close my eyes and remember my childhood days in the small villages of South India, memories of good times, sumptuous food, loving friends, caring church community, and so on would pop up in my mind.

The psalmist begins this psalm with the memories of good and pleasant times. He proclaims God's favor on the land and the restoration of the people's fortunes. As he revels in that pleasant memory, he looks to find a different world around him. It looks as though God in anger has abandoned God's people forever. Therefore, he pleads with God to restore the world to its original splendor. He prays, "Show us your steadfast love, O LORD, and grant us your salvation" (v. 7). The memory of a glorious past gives the psalmist the confidence to pray for a restoration of all things to beauty and goodness.

We too pray for a new earth and a new heaven. Where does our confidence come from? Does it not come from the glimpses of heaven we have had in our own lives? Is it not based on our past experiences of God's redeeming activity in the world and in own lives? God says, "I am the LORD your God, who brought you out of the land of Egypt" (Exod. 20:2).

Perhaps we might now return to the newspaper and television, looking for such glimpses of hope and signs of good news in the various events of the world. God is restoring the world.

Loving God, may the memories of the joy of salvation embolden me to pray and act for the restoration of the whole world to justice and peace. Amen.

THURSDAY, DECEMBER 1 ~ *Read Psalm 85:8-13*

People in our churches, neighborhoods, and nations probably approach issues of peace and justice from different vantage points. Some focus so intently on the issue of peace that they often overlook injustice and inequality in the world. The peace that is brought about may become a cover-up for the existing situations of injustice. Others are so caught up with the question of justice that they may unfairly label people as good folks and bad folks, victors and victims. The world gets fragmented, and peace among peoples becomes a dim and distant reality.

The psalmist reminds us that when God speaks peace it is not a peace that glosses over the world's injustices. He sings that justice and peace will kiss each other when God comes in all God's glory with the offer of a flourishing life for the world.

If we consider the places of conflict and war in the world, we will note that in most cases there are breaches in both justice and peace. Lack of justice leads to lack of peace and vice versa. So in every situation we need to raise two questions: What is going on? and Why is it going on? The what question uncovers the divisions and the why question exposes the underlying injustices. The what question and the why question need to kiss each other in every missionary activity of the church and in every act of kindness of an individual Christian.

How? is the next question. Our faith that looks up to God, together with the gracious justification of God that comes down to us in Jesus the Christ, can bring peace with justice in the world. The meeting of our faith and God's grace can transform the world into a community of peace and justice.

God of justice, God of peace, pour your spirit on me that I may be your harbinger of justice and peace. Amen.

Waiting is not always fun. When my wife and I travel from India to the United States, we find the times of waiting in airports more stressful than the actual flying time. One time my colleague and I had to wait twelve hours at Gatwick airport in London to get our connecting flight to Harare, Zimbabwe. I find such a long wait difficult and tiring. So imagine the early Christians' wait for Christ's coming during a time of persecution.

The time of the writing of this epistle was a time of persecution and suffering for Christians. Christians were hunted for torture and death. The early Christians grow impatient with the delay of Christ's second coming. They want Christ to come and free them from the awful situation of persecution and take them to glory. Some even think that God is slow and tardy in delivering on God's promise!

The author dispels the doubts and worries of these believers by appealing to two things. First, the time we measure by the clock is not the same as God's time. Our clock-bound minds need not attempt to imprison God in our networks of time.

Second and more important, the slow coming of God's promise would be better met with thanksgiving. God's patience gives us the time to repent and set right our lives. The author reminds us that when God comes, "the earth and everything that is done on it will be disclosed." So God is offering some lead time, challenging us to a life of faithful living in the present.

The Advent season gives us a time for waiting and patience, a time for repentance. God's divine mercy puts judgment at bay. When God discloses our lives, may we find ourselves ready.

Thank you, God, for your patience with me. Open my heart that I may bring forth fruits of repentance. Amen.

SATURDAY, DECEMBER 3 ~ *Read 2 Peter 3:11-15a*

In a song made popular by Doris Day, three people pose the same question with regard to the future: a child and mother, the grown-up child and her significant other, and then the child of the child. The response is quite deterministic; seemingly no one or entity is in control. In terms of what the future might hold, "Whatever will be, will be." Such a view can lead us to throw up our hands, dispense with lives of holiness, and say, "Whatever."

Today's passage offers a different view. It begins by mentioning the sudden and unexpected coming of the day of the Lord. It will come like a thief—and it will come with the usual fanfare that we associate with the Second Coming: loud noise and fire! Being ready for that day requires less emphasis on timetables and more emphasis on living with an air of expectancy. Since we cannot predict the future, especially the coming of our Lord, we do not say, "Whatever will be, will be." But rather we "strive to be found by [God] at peace, without spot or blemish." Moreover, we consider "the patience of our Lord as salvation." We believe that a loving and caring God shapes and determines the future; therefore we will never wait passively, saying, "Whatever."

A new and refreshing confidence about the future comes out of trust in God. We acknowledge God's control even if we do not see signs of God's coming in glory. God holds our tomorrow, so we live in active expectancy of the new heaven and new earth. We lead lives of holiness and godliness as we await the new world where "righteousness is at home."

O God, may we actively wait for your coming and celebrate your righteousness today. Amen.

SUNDAY, DECEMBER 4 ~ *Read Mark 1:1-8*

SECOND SUNDAY OF ADVENT

We all know that it is not easy to accept criticism, especially when we are fully convinced that all is well with us. I turn in my best-written paper to my professor, and when I get it back, it pains me to read through all the critical remarks in the margin in red ink! We learn in the course of time to accept that a spouse's criticism actually signifies his or her love for us. True friendship *does* involve a willingness to point out the errors in the other and call for change.

We have such a friend in John the Baptizer. Every year on the second Sunday of Advent, we remember the ministry of John the Baptizer as he prepares the way for Jesus' ministry. As we make ready to receive Christ who comes to us in every moment of our lives, John calls us to turn around and make a new beginning in our lives every day. That is why his is a baptism "of repentance for the forgiveness of sins."

The repentance that John proclaims involves a shift from an attachment to penultimate things to a commitment to the Ultimate. He carefully points out to his followers that he is *not* the one they should look for. He is simply a preacher pointing to the ultimate source of life in all its fullness. He points to Jesus and says, "Here is the Lamb of God who takes away the sin of the world" (John 1:29).

In this season of Advent we take stock of the penultimate things and persons that demand our attention and loyalty and turn around to a commitment to Christ, the ultimate source of joy and peace.

O God, grant me the wisdom to recognize the lesser things and turn around to adore you as my ultimate source of life. Amen.

What's a Prophet to Do?

DECEMBER 5–11, 2011 • HARRIETT JANE OLSON

MONDAY, DECEMBER 5 ～ *Read John 1:6-8*

In a recent visit to the Museum of Art, I had no trouble identifying statues of John the Baptist, even though they were created hundreds of years after his death and with no photographic evidence. Maybe we, like the sculptors, work from received ideas or stereotypes when we think about prophets in general, and John the Baptist in particular. In the *New Interpreter's Bible* commentary, Dr. David Peterson notes that prophets are "boundary figures, representing God to humans and humans to God." Perhaps this role extends beyond prophets in ancient Israel to include Christians today who seek to be authentic in life and witness.

If this supposition is on target, then we are multitasking. First, we attend to the things of God. We see God's imprint; we hear God's harmony; we see God's hand at work. We perceive a spiritual dimension to life that enriches and centers it, that gives it meaning and purpose. We hear and see differently, which gives us something to speak (or testify) about!

Second, we listen for God's voice. We hear it in the occurrences of our daily lives; and while we may test it, we do not wonder that God may speak to us directly. After all, we follow in the line of Israel's prophets.

Finally, we speak. We remark on having seen God's signature in a rainbow or a storm or an exchange between people or in someone who spoke up for justice or . . . ? We see God at work in our world, and we must name it. God, the Light, has appeared and is appearing in the world as we know it . . . and nothing will ever be the same.

O God, help us to see your work and hear your voice today. Amen.

Deputy General Secretary, Women's Division, General Board of Global Ministries of the United Methodist Church

Why does Israel's history contain prophets, priests, and kings? In a theocracy, it would seem that only one "branch" of government would be needed to represent God to the people and to represent the people to God. However, the activity of the prophets seems to stand in a sort of "checks and balances" relationship to the leadership. In some eras, prophets speak for God. In other eras, we get a clear picture of the fallibility of the prophets—or at least their reluctance to challenge current reality.

First Samuel notes "the word of the LORD was rare in those days" (3:1). What must it have been like to keep the flame alive when God was not often heard? How does that resonate with your experience? Perhaps you have more in common with the prophets of Israel than you knew! What is it like to feel called to speak for a God who seems to be silent? Some of us relate very strongly to this question! Others wonder if it comes from a position of heresy or unbelief.

Perhaps the prophets serve as a "counterbalance" in the authority structure of Israel, spokespersons more open to God's influence and less subject to regional or family loyalties than the king or political party might be. What might that say to how we fulfill the role of prophets in our time and place, in our faith community or denomination, or in our local community or nation?

We are to be alert not only to our own biases and presumptions when we speak but also to our own assumptions when we are inclined *not* to speak. Scriptures tell us that the "spirits of prophets are subject to the prophets" (1 Cor. 14:32). We are warned that an element of judgment accompanies our task. The prophet bears responsibility to see that each impulse (toward speech or silence) is "of God" and not captive to human loyalties or to our own needs for affirmation.

Let us be quiet enough for long enough to hear God's voice through the clamoring of interests around us.

It is hard to do something "always" or "without ceasing." Some days we feel everything is possible, and some days nothing seems right. Of course, persistence and the willingness to try again are important to the faith-filled life.

Different times in our lives seem to call for different patterns of prayer. Sometimes we come to God with torrents of questions or hurts or thanksgivings. Sometimes all we can say is "help" or "thank you." What we know is that we must keep praying, keep seeking the alignment of our spirits with the Holy Spirit that results in forming lives of holiness and faithfulness.

One way to get help in developing a consistent spiritual practice is to participate in a group in which you can share your thoughts and prayers and receive both encouragement and correction. I vividly remember a Bible study group in which each member would draw a slip of paper out of a pile that listed requests from each group member each week. I confessed one week that I felt a little guilty taking time over my prayers and study each day when I had so much to do. One of my friends looked at me archly and said, "If you get my prayer request, I hope you'll take the time."

Our need to pray is not just for ourselves but for others. A good friend or two may encourage us to build a practice that can sustain our spirit as nothing else can.

We might also heed the language of this passage: rejoice, pray, give thanks. We're twice instructed to praise and only once directed to pray (in general). Does this suggest that our prayers might be more weighted toward praise than toward petition? These practices position us to receive the blessing of wholeness: an integration of spirit, soul, and body. Thus we become complete, sound, and holy.

May it be so! "The one who calls you is faithful, and [God] will do this."

Today's passage instructs the reader (including you and me) to pay attention to the words of the prophets. It seems as if the letter refers to contemporary prophets and prophecies, rather than the prophets of Israel whose words were already collected in the Septuagint. However, the writer is well-acquainted with apocalyptic thought and prophets or prophecies that did not align with the biblical text. So he instructs us to "test everything."

It is difficult to test everything. Current academic debates insist that all arguments have a starting position. We have propositions that we find convincing; we make connections with other propositions because we believe them to be true; that constitutes our worldview. When it comes to "testing" prophets or prophecies, the question is this: How do we hold our own worldview lightly enough to hear something of God's worldview? The prophets who point us to the ways of God or the heart of God are the ones we want to hear.

This list of instructions has some interesting pairings—do not quench the Spirit, do not despise the prophets. How might we rephrase this affirmatively? Fan the flames of the Spirit. Honor the words of the prophets. Perhaps these two find connection when the unquenched Spirit witnesses to our spirits about the truth of a prophet's words and the honor accorded.

Again we bring our own judgment to bear, judgment that requires attentive listening to the speakers (prophets) around us and to our own points of comfort or discomfort with what they say. Why does this speaker's comment resonate or rankle? Why am I prepared to "re-tweet" or "share" or comment on one set of observations rather than another? Am I listening for the voice of God or reinforcing my own point of view or position?

Unquenched Spirit, keep us honest in the delicate work of listening. Tune our hearts to resonate to your voice in any prophet or prophecy within our hearing. Amen.

What's a Prophet to Do?

FRIDAY, DECEMBER 9 ~ *Read 1 Thessalonians 5:23-24*

S *anctify you entirely.* In the relatively recent history of the Wesleyan movement in the United States, these might have been read as "fighting words." How often we have turned something meant for blessing into a way to distinguish ourselves from others! Even the word *sanctify,* which carried such power for John Wesley, the founder of the Methodist movement in England, may sound more sanctimonious than faith-filled.

What if we looked at the energy flowing through this blessing to the church? First, we might see that sanctification is something to be sought. We are in a process of sanctification that involves God's action, the commitment of heart and mind and the action of the believer in a dynamic process that engages all of who we are.

Second, we might notice that the writer asks that God sanctify the Thessalonians. Sanctification is not the result of pure living, pure thinking, or pure intent of human beings; those are the results (or fruits) of sanctification. Obviously, a state of sanctification may not be entire, only partial.

How appropriate that this blessing continues with a prayer that the believers' souls and bodies be kept "sound" and blameless until Jesus' return. The Bible often uses the concepts of sound, whole, complete, and perfect interchangeably. I connect them with a eucharistic prayer that confesses that we have not acted as God intended. How often do we need to pray to become "whole persons through Jesus Christ"?

This blessing follows a list of instructions that includes "pray without ceasing." How else would we continue being transformed?

Think of the missionary letter writer praying for this congregation and for us that we might be kept in the posture intended for us at the beginning—and claiming God's faithfulness to fulfill it. How great a cloud of witnesses!

John, as described in this passage, clearly understands his role: he testifies or "points" to the light. Of course, if your father received a vision at the announcement of your birth and was speechless for nine months, your mother conceived after her time and received the mother of Jesus in her home, all before your birth, you might also have better clarity about your role. This presents a strong contrast to the religious leaders whom the text depicts as "blind guides."

Humans get confused about this sort of assignment. We get a glimpse something true and profound and become convicted about it. We start telling the story—maybe even elaborating upon what we grasped so fleetingly in that transformative moment. We may easily start feeling that it is our truth, that we own it in some way, rather than knowing that this is God's truth and that as powerful as our glimpse may have been for us, it is still partial. In one quick step we can move from that misplaced certainty to begin pointing not to God but to ourselves.

John has this virtue to a fault. The leaders ask him, "Who are you?" He replies, "I am not the Messiah." The text describes him as answering the question he supposes they have, rather than the question that they actually put forward. John is not Messiah, not Elijah—merely one who points to the light.

How hard it is not to claim to know more than we do or to imply that we have more authority than has actually been conferred on us! How difficult it is to have our authority or maturity or wisdom challenged without defending ourselves! We only need to do our part; others in the community will also point to Jesus and help to carry the burden. Everything we do, even when challenged, points to Jesus.

How will my speech and action today point others to the light of Jesus?

SUNDAY, DECEMBER 11 ~ *Read Psalm 126*

THIRD SUNDAY OF ADVENT

The region that we refer to as the Middle East ("east" being relative, of course) has long been a crossroads of culture. Traders from everywhere, headed to somewhere. Empires seeking control of ports and access routes and burgeoning industrial powerhouses seeking slave labor all traversed this region. This land is criss-crossed by "wadis" or riverbeds that remain dry until the rainy season and then they run wild with a rush of water in a dry land. Pity the traveler who stops in one of these riverbeds unsuspectingly! As happens in a parking lot or roadway surface, the water from a downpour sheets across the surface pushing all sorts of things that are in its path.

No wonder the harvest depicted in this psalm comes with "shouts of joy." This is a tumultuous, riotous "whoosh" of joy across a surface that is already prepared for it. Indeed, the planting is done, albeit with tears. What an image of keeping on! Perhaps the sower trudges or drags forward, putting one foot in front of the other. Then we all wait for the seed to germinate and grow and "put forth fruit in due season." But this is not the way we return! Even though the sheaves are heavy, bulky, and dusty, we come home "shouting."

Indeed, God restores the fortunes of Zion. After the long dream, waiting for the fulfillment of God's promises, we rejoice!

What a gift to us from the poet—mouths filled with laughter and tongues with shouts of joy! The physicality of the rejoicing is exuberant and unexpected, like the belly laugh that catches the family by surprise after a funeral. We find ourselves in the period of waiting this Advent season, anticipating the coming celebration of Jesus' birth. May it be as vibrant and tactile as the rush of water through the desert wadis.

Rejoice! The Lord has done great things for us!

Signs and Mystery

DECEMBER 12–18, 2011 • HEATHER MURRAY ELKINS

MONDAY, DECEMBER 12 ~ *Read 2 Samuel 7:1-11, 16*

An I-beam is the weight-bearing beam that holds a structure together and keeps it level. This girder is essential for a firm foundation. The first sentence of chapter 7 is the weight-bearing girder for the story of God's house and the history of a people and their hero David. "Now when the king was settled in his house, and the LORD had given him rest from all his enemies around him, the king said to the prophet Nathan, 'See now, I am living in a house of cedar, but the ark of God stays in a tent.'"

This first sentence holds the weight and the tension of Deuteronomistic history: the journeys of the ark of the covenant, David's call and conquests, the unification of the tribes, and the founding of a kingdom of the poet king. This sentence/structure links the royal house of David to the captives' quarters in Babylon to the household of an obscure carpenter known as Joseph who was engaged to a young girl named Mary. The passage then extends its strength into our lives in the season of Advent 2010; but it doesn't end here. It promises to provide steadfast weight-bearing work for generations to come.

Weight-bearing, indeed. The unnamed writer reconstructs the history of a royal house in the backstreets of Babylon. His handiwork offers consolation as well as revelation. We might wonder what good were stories of a king or structures of a kingdom that had been brutally destroyed. What shelter does this story offer to those who need it?

Lay this text next to the old news of foreclosures and the new class of homeless. Lean hard on this story of a God who refuses a house but promises to be home to us now and forever.

Professor of Worship, Preaching, and the Arts, Drew University

I is the ninth letter of the alphabet. A speaker or writer uses it to refer to himself or herself. It often signifies a sense of self-actualization. It can also signal the shockingly real presence of an overwhelming power. This scripture passage begins with an "I" statement. "I am living in a house of cedar," says David. The intention of his "I" statement is clear. David, the hero king, wants to build a permanent home for the wandering God who has blessed him. David, the poet politician, wants to bring a nation together under one roof by reconstructing the metaphor of a traveling Tent into a permanent Temple. He never actually says, "I will build . . . ," but Nathan gets the point and blesses David's "I" agenda.

In the end, the I's have it but not David's. God's "I" is the only one that matters. The shockingly real presence of an over-whelming power named I AM invades Nathan's dreams. The sound of a divine voice saying, "I, I, I" shakes the prophet awake. Count the number of times the Holy One refers to God's self. "I took you. . . . , I have been with you. . . . , I . . . " This is the voice of I AM, the One whose word creates worlds. Here is the I-beam of eternity, the weight-bearing means to hold it all together and level.

God's "I" changes everything; it rearranges all the building plans of king and prophet and nation. God's "I" can construct and deconstruct a king, raise up or tear down a prophet. This is the Holy One who upsets human expectations, especially of those who believe they know God best. Role reversals are the order of God's day: a shepherd boy becomes a king; a young country girl will mother the Prince of Peace. A house not made with hands will be God's Temple. Such is the wonder of Advent.

Awake or asleep, in dreams or in daylight, God will surprise us.
May we dwell in the house of the Holy One forever.

If this is the time of Time itself, it's a mean and lean season.

Reason and hope find little to say in the jingle jangle news of the day.
Patience with unanswered prayer runs out.
Maybe even God prefers a little peace and quiet.
But before it's too dark, too sad, or too late,
teach us to pray.

A haze of holiday habit conceals the bottom line.
Holy absence makes a heart grow hard,
then harder, without a purpose or design.
Teach us to pray, lest we who know the story best
become accustomed to this restless season.
Teach us to pray for a sign.

Scatter proud powers that refuse to imagine.
Shatter the loud towers of Hate, the high walls of Forget.
Lift the homeless whisper, the sigh that says, "Alone?"
Fill the hungry emptiness that echoes
in the marrow of our bones.

When times are tough,
a rumor of angels is never enough.
We need holy terror to startle expectation,
and altar us with outrageous grace.
Wreck our rational designs with celestial encounters.
Let us hear the rustle of wings as we take out the trash.

Teach us to pray.
Gift us with a presence so potent
that life is conceived in mere hearing.
> If we fail at first to believe, instruct us in sign.
> But let us be the bearers of such mystery
> that even our gestures give us away.
> Teach us to pray . . .
> God is with us in ways we can't fathom or imagine.

Signs and Mystery   361

How do we see what we see? For all the intimate details of an eye that medical science provides, vision is still a mystery. What is the source of our sight? What forms our insight and why do we "see" some things and not others? These questions take on an existential energy as I hear my ophthalmologist explain to me again about the importance of patience when recovering from cataract surgery. I find the ancient Greeks' notion of the soul's generating an "eye beam" of light strangely appealing as I make a list of what I want to truly see as I recover my sight. The Greeks understand this "eye beam" to be generated from within and directed through the eyes into the physical world. The images didn't randomly invade; the soul selected what it wished to encounter and then connected to that reality. The object to be perceived was touched, embraced even, by this energized beam of pure spirit. That formed an imprint that was then carried back through the eyes into the soul. Since what you chose to "see" resulted from an intimate connection, seeing was a matter of soul as well as sight formation. The eye was essential to the I; seeing is a process of becoming who we are and who we will be.

So, how do we learn to see the holy in the ordinary? How do we learn to embrace the mystery of holy time in the commonplace corners of our busy day? Mary's song reminds us of God's eye/I work. "My soul magnifies the Lord, and my spirit rejoices in God my Savior, for he has looked with favor on the lowliness of his servant."

This biblical text is God's eye/I chart that leads to transformation in human life and vision. With Mary, we learn to see as we are seen; we learn to see ourselves through the eyes of the Savior. We're touched, embraced, surrounded by the seeing eye of God; we recognize what that vision will mean when we can say with Mary, "Let it be."

Holy One, heal our heart's shortsightedness. Amen.

FRIDAY, DECEMBER 16 ~ *Read Luke 1:26-38*

In the first year of my ministry, a statue came to live in the corner of my office. Her advent in my life wasn't a simple matter or an easy delivery. One Saturday morning, my husband, Bill, and I set off on a rescue mission of "catholic art," in response to a friend's plea. He'd been hired to clear the grounds of a former monastery purchased by an oil corporation. He'd gotten nervous about bulldozing "religious stuff" and offered it to anyone who wanted it. I had to smile at our ignorance as Bill and I walked the overgrown lawns and looked at figures of two-thousand-pound saints sentenced to rubble. Whom can we possibly rescue with our bare hands or drive to safety in an old VW Beetle?

We walk almost a mile when we stumble on our mission. Beside the hermit's cabin, the figure of a young woman lies face down in the leaves. We turn her over, brush off her face and recognize Mary, grave and full of grace. Her face is serene; curled around at her bare feet is a subdued serpent still clutching the eternal apple in its jaws. Mary's hands are missing. We search for them without success until the light begins to fade; it grows darker as we debate the possibility of our mission. We'll have to carry her through the woods for almost a mile, and she easily weighs over a hundred pounds. There's no convenient way to carry her. What good is a broken Madonna anyway? The last rays of the sun reach her face, and its earthy glow dissolves our doubt. "Hail, Mary, full of grace."

It's not an easy journey. More than once she slips from our hands in the dark; more than once we have to grit our teeth, get a grip on our temper and our trust by reciting, "Nothing will be impossible with God." She's made herself at home in each place I've served. Every new location prompts the same question from those who are surprised by her unexpected presence. "Aren't you a Protestant?" "Oh, yes," I say. "She's in my Bible."

Incarnate One, fill us with your grace. Amen.

I'm a list-making addict, as well as being a hard-to-motivate housekeeper. I keep a list of must-do jobs on sticky notes in several places so that I'm never guilt-free. On the bottom of every list, in the lowest-of-the-low place is "scrub the tub/toilet." I'm not spiritually advanced enough to view this task with any kind of favor, so it startled me to see an earthy version of the Magnificat positioned exactly in that lowest place. One of the clay sculptures depicts Mary scrubbing a bathroom floor on her knees. As she works her way from the tub to the toilet, she pauses to look up toward a small window. It is a barred window, but the light and perhaps a bird song creates a moment of grace. Charles McCollough, a poet, theologian, and sculptor, created this relief sculpture as part of a series on the Magnificat for the halls of Drew University, his alma mater. His art captures the heart of Mary's song; it transforms the drudgery of housekeeping into an unforgettable proclamation of God's promise to the "house of David."

The bubbling sense of joy that rises from the song is captured in another clay tablet, "God lifts the lowly." Mary has gotten off her knees and has opened the barred window. Her scrubbing brushes are set aside. She now happily soaks in a tubful of bubbles, lifting a glass in toast to the Holy One who has done great things not just for her but for all the least, the lost, the lonely. This God who resists human lists and upends all expectations has altered the status of the lowest of the low forever.

Will this vision change my perspective on scrubbing? It intrudes at unexpected moments. I find myself smiling at the memory of Mary's bubbles of soap and joy. I remember I'm not alone.

A scholarly word for this experience of visual transformation is **theoria.** *It occurs when what you see is so startling, so insightful, that your perspective is changed. Then it moves from the realm of theory to* **theoria,** *which changes everything.*

SUNDAY, DECEMBER 18 ~ *Read Romans 16:25-27*

FOURTH SUNDAY OF ADVENT

The final text of the fourth week in Advent may seem anticlimactic when compared to the dramatic songs, stories, and prophecies of this week's readings. Just as the momentum for Christmas reaches its peak, we read a text that summarizes the complexity of the season in a single sentence, an act of the liturgy, a benediction for the people of the household of Christ in Rome.

The letter to the Romans contains Paul's most important theological writing, and its impact on the history of Christian thought and life was and is foundational. As a liturgical act, this benediction reminds us, as Gentiles, that we all have been adopted into the family of God though the work of Jesus the Christ and the mercy of God. The early church referred to sacraments as the "mysteries," and this text echoes those mysteries in its summary of the gospel of Jesus the Christ.

Hearing Martin Luther's preface to the epistle of Romans read aloud in 1738 transformed John Wesley's understanding of the doctrine of justification by faith and fired his call to a radical discipleship, "the obedience of faith." Among the many gifted leaders whom he equipped for ministry was a woman named Jane Clark. The account of his visit with her as she lay dying contains a poignant expression of this obedience in Christian life. He asks her if she has faith that is free from fear. "Sir," she replies, "I never had any faith but by love, nor any love but through faith." In this season where the name and the nature of God is clearly revealed as Love, here is the Gloria, the blessing that will bring all things on earth and in heaven to a peaceful end. "To the only wise God, through Jesus Christ, to whom be the glory forever! Amen."

As we ready our houses and our hearts for the celebration of the birth of Christ, what better way to prepare than through the celebration of the sacramental mysteries of the Table. Christ is born. Christ has died. Christ is risen. Christ will come again.

The Wonder of It All

DECEMBER 19–25, 2011 • SUSAN PENDLETON JONES

MONDAY, DECEMBER 19 ～ *Read Psalm 98*

The psalm for this last week of Advent invites us to consider the beauty and wonder of God's steadfast love as well as God's role as judge of all the earth. Psalm 98 opens with an invitation to the congregation to sing praises to the Lord in gratitude for God's love. Instruments of praise, the lyre and the trumpet, join the voices of the congregation. Soon, creation itself joins in praise.

Everyone is singing and praising God. Why? because God is coming to judge the world. There is no fear or dread at the coming judgment. The psalmist believes that God will come with righteousness and equity, with a "judgment of grace."

Advent is a season of repentance. But we must remember that repentance is not the first word; God's mercy and steadfast love come first. Once we experience the gift of God's deep love for us, it elicits in us a desire to repent and makes us long to live as children of God—to live in a way that pleases God.

Most parents understand this. If we tell our children to change their behavior, they will probably rebel. But if we love them in a way that they feel deeply, if we tell them how proud we are of them, then often they will change their behavior because they want to live into the good that we see in them and the love they feel from us. When we first experience love, often we desire to live into that love. Once we know ourselves loved by God, we begin to live under a "judgment of grace" that invites repentance because we know what it feels like to be loved and forgiven.

Loving God, may we open our hearts to you this Advent season, not because we must but because we may. Amen.

Director of Field Education, Duke Divinity School; Durham, North Carolina

TUESDAY, DECEMBER 20 ~ *Read Hebrews 1:1-12*

A missionary who lived years ago served as a teacher in Africa and became good friends with his students. The missionary had been talking to his students about the significance of Christmas. The next Advent, one of the students presented the missionary with a seashell of extraordinary beauty. The missionary, recognizing that such seashells could only be found miles up the coast from their village, said to the student, "What a beautiful shell. Thank you for traveling so far to get me such a lovely gift." The African man replied, "The long walk is part of the gift."

The Advent season reminds us of God's long walk to us in Jesus Christ, who was first foretold through the prophets and now in these latter days has come to us as God incarnate, as the very son of God. But this is no ordinary son. This is a son of extraordinary beauty, the very reflection of God's glory, and even grander, bearing "the exact imprint of God's very being."

These verses in Hebrews tell us that when we come to know Jesus, we come to know God! God has given God's self to us in this one named Jesus, born in a humble stable in Bethlehem. Yet this same Jesus is superior in being to all the angels, the writer of Hebrews tells us. He lives on high at the right hand of God!

During this season, we marvel at the mystery that the Infinite God becomes one with us, in human form, in the person called Jesus of Nazareth. How much God must love us to make that long walk to give us this extraordinary gift of the Son!

In this holy season, we give you thanks, O God, for the gift of your son, Jesus Christ, who has shown us the power of your love and has shared with us the very nature of your being. May we, in turn, live as your beloved children. Amen.

WEDNESDAY, DECEMBER 21 ~ *Read John 1:1-5; Hebrews 1:1-4*

In our fast-paced, twenty-first century world, words bombard us: news and weather channels run 24/7; email inboxes overflow; land lines, cell phones, pagers, text messaging, iPods, You Tube videos, never-ending streams of messages and commercials, much of it meaningless and redundant. We are saturated with words!

Even though many of the words we hear each day amount to background noise and have little impact on us, we acknowledge that words have power. They can persuade, berate, or congratulate; they can harm deeply or provide soothing comfort. According to scripture, words brought all things into being: "And God said." Hundreds of years later, these first chapters of John's Gospel and Hebrews remind us that God spoke—and the world was created.

During this season of Advent, Jesus becomes the "Word made flesh." What was once spoken about through the prophets is now revealed in the flesh. Because Jesus is God incarnate, we know that when we hear his words, when we study his teachings, we hear the voice of God. Through the parables that he spoke, through the enacted parables that he lived, and through the death that he died for our salvation, we come to know what God is like.

We see in the Word-who-is-Jesus *our* words' intention: to communicate truthfully, lovingly, gracefully our relationship with God and with others. We do not need more words so much as we long for redeeming words appropriate to the Word.

We thank you, Jesus, that you are God's Word made flesh, for you are both eternal and true. May we live each day knowing that you are the same yesterday, today, and forever. Thanks be to God! Amen.

THURSDAY, DECEMBER 22 ~ *Read Isaiah 52:7-10*

From the delivery room, the new father texts all his friends with the good news: "It's twins: a boy and a girl!" The director of admissions calls: "We'd like to offer you a full-tuition scholarship." The nurse returns your call and says to you, "You can rest easy now; the test results came back, and they are negative." In the recovery waiting room the doctor greets the family: "Your husband made it through the surgery with flying colors!" With each message of good news that is delivered, we give thanks, and we are grateful for the messenger.

These verses express in poetic form this kind of gratitude at receiving good news from a messenger. More than a generation earlier, the city of Jerusalem (referred to in our text as Zion) has been overthrown by the Babylonians. The city and the Temple lay in ruins; the Jewish inhabitants have been scattered, most of them being deported to Babylon and held in captivity there. The psalmist tells us that they sat by the rivers of Babylon and wept.

Now many years later, the people have renewed hope that their God will triumph. They begin to hope that God is redeeming Jerusalem. A messenger arrives. Has he run from Babylon to Jerusalem? He announces peace, brings good news, and proclaims to the remnant left in Jerusalem: "Your God reigns."

These verses relay a message of hope that awaits the return of the people from Babylon. But more importantly, this message foreshadows the hope that beginning in Jerusalem, the Messiah will come to restore Israel. God will redeem God's people, and all the ends of the earth shall see the salvation of their God. What better news than this to share during this season of Advent?

Thank you for the hope we have in you, Loving God, the One who redeems, restores, and makes all things new. Amen.

When our older son, Nate, was a little boy, his favorite professional soccer player got engaged. The fact that I was performing the wedding ceremony and that he was invited excited Nate to no end. He got up at 7:00 the Saturday morning of the wedding, put on his best suit, tie, and dress shoes, and went downstairs and sat on the sofa. My husband and I feared that a ten-year-old boy can exhibit only a limited amount of "good behavior" time, so we asked him to put on play clothes. He refused. He wanted to be ready for the 2:00 wedding. All during the wedding he behaved like a prince. At the reception he displayed good manners and even danced with elderly ladies. What had happened to our normally rambunctious, mischievous little boy?

Nate wanted to make the groom proud, not because we told him he had to, not because the groom required it but because the groom had earlier befriended him. He had taught Nate soccer moves; he invited Nate to be on the field with him for the national anthem during a professional soccer game. In response to the gift of friendship that Nate had received, he wanted to live a different way, even if for one day.

The book of Titus reminds us that in Jesus Christ "the grace of God has appeared, bringing salvation to all." What a gift of friendship! God has befriended us in Jesus Christ, offering us salvation and grace in the flesh. Jesus is God's grace appearing, Titus tells us, so that we might live into that grace and put away all "impiety and worldly passions." In gratitude for God's befriending us, we, in turn, seek to live a new life even while waiting in hope for God's full glory to be revealed.

Thank you, loving God, for befriending us in Jesus Christ, for offering us salvation through him, and inviting us to live more godly lives in you. Amen.

CHRISTMAS EVE

Luke's description of the circumstances surrounding Jesus' birth is stark and spare. He dates Jesus' birth during the reign of Emperor Augustus. Jesus' mother, Mary, travels from Nazareth to Bethlehem in the last stages of pregnancy; and, because there is no room in the inn, Jesus ends up being born in a stable. Luke also tells us that the baby Jesus is wrapped in bands of cloth and that his mother lays him in a manger. *How silently, how silently, the wondrous gift is given.*

Yet out in the fields, angels herald the good news of the birth, causing fear in the shepherds who watch their sheep nearby. The angel's message is exactly what Luke has described earlier: a child has been born and wrapped in bands of cloth and placed in a manger. Yet now we hear that this is no ordinary child: this baby, born in such humble conditions, is the Savior of the world—the Messiah. So the shepherds go quickly to see for themselves, and they find the baby with Mary and Joseph just as they had been told. When they see with their own eyes, their fear turns to amazement, and they begin praising God. *The hopes and fears of all the years are met in thee tonight.*

We can hear this familiar story over and over, and it can remain just that—an old, familiar story. We think of it and become sentimental. But the true gift of this story resides in the promise that God really is "with us," that we are not alone in our sin and self-concern. This day we celebrate the best "good news" ever: that God came to live among us—and to die among us and live again—so that we might come to know God. *Cast out our sin, and enter in, be born in us today.*

On this Christmas Eve, we pray, O God, that you will come to us and abide with us, our Lord Emmanuel. Amen.

SUNDAY, DECEMBER 25 ~ *Read John 1:1-14*

CHRISTMAS DAY

For many years, I have been interested in iconography, the art of depicting or "writing" sacred images, usually upon wood, that are used for the adoration and worship of God. One of the rules of iconography entails not depicting God the Father in image form, since this could be construed as creating a graven image. God the Father is Spirit and Truth, the Invisible, Immutable One. Therefore most icons are of Mary with the child Jesus; or of Jesus as the Teacher, Miracle-worker, or with the Twelve. Icons also often portray any of hundreds of saints who have lived and died. But an icon is not to depict God the Father.

How, then, do iconographers portray the story of Creation? If we understand God the Father as Creator, then how are icons of creation "written"? Usually we would see blue sky and green grass with many creatures teeming in each. Off to the side stands Jesus, the one who was with God from the beginning, from the time of creation.

This reading reminds us that from the very beginning Jesus was the Word, the voice of God, bringing all things into being. This same Word through whom the world came into being chose to take on human flesh and blood in the person of Jesus. Through the miracle we call Christmas, God has chosen to enter into our time, our social location, our flesh. To paraphrase one of the early Church Fathers, "Only what God has assumed can God redeem." God became human in the one called Christ to redeem all humanity. The first chapter of John gives us a glimpse into this mystery, and we are filled with wonder.

We praise you, O God, that you are the Word made flesh in Jesus Christ, who has come to live among us, forgive us, and redeem us. May we find true life and light in you, the One who is full of grace and truth. Amen.

After the Birth

DECEMBER 26–31, 2011 • NATALIE A. HANSON

MONDAY, DECEMBER 26 ~ *Read Isaiah 61:10–62:3*

This section of Isaiah places us in the midst of songs sung to and by a people living in exile. Because themes of exile remain central to our human experience—distance, strangeness, loss, dependence, imbalance, yearning for home—we don't have to live in Babylon to feel them resonate in our hearts. They may have resonated for Joseph and Mary, plain folks caught up in God's huge vision, embarking with this birth on a journey into exile and strangeness, into loss and distance. The birth of Jesus turns them upside down.

Birth does that, though—many kinds of birth but especially the birth of a child. At that moment, our lives are no longer certain with self-focus; the world is suddenly fraught with care and danger. Parents are as new a creation as the child, exiled in an instant from the creatures they were just moments before.

So we have from Isaiah this "little magnificat" that sings we are never truly abandoned, never wholly on strange ground, because God is with us. Anticipation trumps angst. Hope trumps practicality. Trust in God's direction allows us to stand and take the first few steps. Wobbly as we feel, we are mercifully told we are becoming whole and lovely in God's hands.

After the birth of one of our daughters, I was alone and suddenly paralyzed with fear of my own inadequacies. A wise nurse walked in and, seeing my face, said, "Oh, honey, don't cry. It's going to be all right." I burst into tears; not tears of sadness, but tears of relief and hope. I hope, the morning after Jesus' birth, Joseph and Mary had Isaiah's words to sing softly to each other.

Holy One, you turn my cries into song. Amen.

District superintendent, Niagara Frontier District, the United Methodist Church; Buffalo, New York

TUESDAY, DECEMBER 27 ~ *Read Psalm 148*

Psalm 148 appears to be a song of praise that parallels and recalls the Creation story in Genesis. Praise for the Creator rises from every strata and corner, heavenly hosts and creeping things, dark deeps, and (my personal favorite) sea monsters!

It is tempting to see only a hymn of the natural world. Often when our culture offers up "inspiration," it does so through images of breathtaking sunsets, fern-banked waterfalls, and baby wild things. What's wrong with this picture? Reality. The real natural world is clawed and red-toothed. The greenest leaves are bug-eaten. The clouds I love to watch can drown a city. Our anthropomorphizing of young wild things can end in cruelty, and we habitually make sea monsters extinct.

A turn toward the end of the psalm brings two new thoughts. Verse 13 notes that we do not praise creation itself but the One whose life-giving Spirit inhabits creation, a power and potential always greater, wilder, and more mind-boggling than the sum of all our current parts. Verse 14 returns us from the timeless to the human and reminds us that God actively participates in history's changing circumstances, raising up a horn (of saving leadership) in response to the people's emerging need.

In one sense it is enough and more than enough of a grace and a miracle that Jesus was born of Mary those many years ago, wedding heaven to earth and earth to heaven. But I also hear the suggestion that Christmas is not a one-time event, that the God who has been giving God's self away all this time in a thousand different ways for our sake and for the sake of creation will not stop; there will be Christmas after Christmas . . . Christ born again and again among us and God over and over wowing us into adoring silence. Praise the Lord, indeed!

Creating God, don't stop remaking us but renew us again and again in your image. Amen.

I don't remember being scared often as a child, but I twice remember feeling desperate. One memory is a comedy of errors: I had walked to one location to meet my family. As I took a shortcut through the fields, they returned home to look for me. By the time I trudged back home they had left again, still looking. We finally connected, but I can still taste the bitter fear that I might never be found. Another day the older kids sent some younger ones of us off to play hide-and-seek and never came seeking. We waited long before we caught on, and our sense of betrayal and unimportance was acute. What a hollow and horrible thing, to be lost with no one looking to find.

Boaz, future husband of Ruth, root of the house and lineage of David, served as a redeemer for his clan. He was one chosen to seek family who had been distanced or sold into slavery and to buy or bring them back, healing person and clan. Naomi, living in a foreign country and seeing her son marry outside the people, was one of the lost ones. The line of David—and of Jesus—is founded on Boaz's act of bringing Naomi home by marrying and "bringing in" her son's widow.

Galatians says that we are not lost with no one searching. God-in-Jesus names us all as family and comes looking, intending that all might be brought into community and the human community healed. The emphasis is not sin but reconciling relationships. "You are no longer a slave, but a child, and . . . also an heir," Galatians says. Too precious to be forgotten, too important to the health of the whole to be ignored.

We call God "Abba" not in sentimentality but to own our identity and responsibilities as redeemed ones in the family. For the other lost ones out there, who fear no one will come looking, then we will be called to be redeemers too.

Redeeming Lord, help us honor our adoption by reaching out to expand the family. Amen.

Astory that I first heard years ago has grown deep roots in my heart and mind. I don't know if the story itself is fact or legend, but I know it speaks a truth.

A retired couple lived in a Miami neighborhood that was in transition from middle-class Anglo to blue-collar Hispanic. One by one those who had raised their families in the community made arrangements to move, some further out into the suburbs and some into senior developments. After church, some longtime neighbors approached the couple to say, "We've sold our house, and we're moving in a month. What are your plans?" The older couple looked at each other and replied, "We're going to learn Spanish!"

I am struck, in Luke's story, by Simeon and Anna's courage and graciousness. Jesus is small enough to be held by an old man and much too young to have proved himself or revealed his character in any significant way. Simeon sees the potential and embraces what is coming, even though he knows all will not be smooth. He puts his own claims to preference or honor aside in favor of God's future. Simeon says, in effect, "My time is done and I rejoice in that because I can see your new world coming." Anna offers her praise in the same spirit, rejoicing in a redemption that will not take shape until long after she is gone.

As I move farther and farther into my fifties, these stories offer a sharper challenge. Can I bracket my way of doing things in order to welcome and nurture new generations of leadership? Can I place the meaning of my life more in God than in my own creations and be freed to let go and to change? Can I learn the language of my immigrant neighbor or of my young adult daughter?

Lord, may I rejoice to give up my place at the table if that makes room for the new thing you are bringing to birth. Amen.

We begin by imagining the mind of John of Patmos, imprisoned on an island, powerless to shape the fate of his beloved churches on the mainland, raging in bitter grief over the destruction of Jerusalem, desperately afraid that the community of Jesus-followers might be lost. Yet in the midst of threat and uncertainty, John explores a vision that the gap between the divine and the human is veil-thin. In his final chapters, the veil disappears altogether as God bridges every distance.

Historic Jerusalem may be lost, its walls leveled and its fields salted; but here is a New Jerusalem, accessible forever because it resides in God's heart. The Temple is destroyed beyond hope of rebuilding, but we hear a voice crying, "All is not lost! God will make the people themselves a temple, and dwell there" (AP). Too much death has numbed the souls of the people, but the voice cries, "My life within you will heal your pain" (AP). Heaven is closer than we know, and there is nothing God cannot make new.

It is not esoteric prophecy that makes this book relevant but—in the midst of terrors and troubles—the extraordinary sense of God's nearness. The eternal surrounds us and lives within us, if only we will see it. Strangely enough, Revelation and the Christmas story share a common theme: the Word takes flesh and dwells among us, and a weary world is relit from within.

Recovering from illness, Thomas Merton traveled from his monastery to a nearby town for medical care. Coming from a life of silence and simplicity, he saw the streets filled with ordinary, everyday folks. He wondered if any of them knew what miracles they were, if any of them knew they were walking around shining like the sun, lit from within by the presence of God.

Can we become aware of the light within us? Can we learn to see it and treasure it in one another?

Eternal God, don't let my vision stop at the gray surface of things. Help me look deeper until I find you. Amen.

SATURDAY, DECEMBER 31 ~ *Read Matthew 25:31-46*

When Jesus blesses the actions of the righteous who have been feeding the hungry, clothing the naked, and welcoming the stranger, the righteous are taken aback. They have not seen themselves as doing or being anything out of the ordinary. They have never perceived a difference between themselves and those in prison, between themselves and those who are sick. Assuming that all present are brothers and sisters and in this life together, they do what is natural by caring for one another.

The sin of the unrighteous is not so much what they do not do as what they assume: that the hungry, the down-and-out, the ragged and lonely and lost are somehow qualitatively different, that theirs is a foreign reality, that there is no underlying family resemblance. They cannot imagine Jesus as one of these "least" ones because they do not see themselves there. Their sin, as ours can be, is a massive failure of self-awareness.

Dorothy Day, founding mother of St. Joseph's Houses of Hospitality and the Catholic Worker Movement, was famous for saying frankly that their homeless guests "are not grateful, and they smell." But she also embraced the rule that there would be no barriers, no difference between her level of living and that of the people she served. Love cannot be lived from a distance, only face-to-face. This story of a king who lives in identity with the "least of these who are members of my family" is less a judgment between those who do and those who do not do acts of charity as it is a challenge to our assumptions of who we are and with whom we belong. It becomes another version of the Incarnation story, of how love takes on flesh and becomes real. The message is this: The love that redeems the world begins with and proceeds out of a common identity. One family member connecting with another. No distance.

Jesus, as I hear you call my own name, let me also hear you call all those around me, "Brother!" "Sister!" Amen.

After the Birth

The Revised Common Lectionary* for 2011
Year A – Advent / Christmas Year B
(Disciplines Edition)

January 1–2
NEW YEAR'S DAY
Ecclesiastes 3:1-13
Psalm 8
Revelation 21:1-6a
Matthew 25:31-46

January 6
EPIPHANY
(may be used on January 2)
Isaiah 60:1-6
Psalm 72:1-7, 10-14
Ephesians 3:1-12
Matthew 2:1-12

January 3–9
BAPTISM OF THE LORD
Isaiah 42:1-9
Psalm 29
Acts 10:34-43
Matthew 3:13-17

January 10–16
Isaiah 49:1-7
Psalm 40:1-11
1 Corinthians 1:1-9
John 1:29-42

January 17–23
Isaiah 9:1-4
Psalm 27:1, 4-9
1 Corinthians 1:10-18
Matthew 4:12-23

January 24–30
Micah 6:1-8
Psalm 15
1 Corinthians 1:18-31
Matthew 5:1-12

January 31–February 6
Isaiah 58:1-12
Psalm 112:1-10
1 Corinthians 2:1-16
Matthew 5:13-20

February 7–13
Deuteronomy 30:15-20
Psalm 119:1-8
1 Corinthians 3:1-9
Matthew 5:38-48

February 14–20
Leviticus 19:1-2, 9-18
Psalm 119:33-40
1 Corinthians 3:10-11, 16-23
Matthew 5:38-48

February 21–27
Isaiah 49:8-16a
Psalm 131 (*or* Psalm 62:5-12)
1 Corinthians 4:1-5
Matthew 6:24-34

February 28–March 6
THE TRANSFIGURATION
Exodus 24:12-18
Psalm 99
2 Peter 1:16-21
Matthew 17:1-9

March 9
ASH WEDNESDAY
Joel 2:1-2, 12-17
Psalm 51:1-17
2 Corinthians 5:20*b*–6:10
Matthew 6:1-6, 16-21

March 7–13
FIRST SUNDAY IN LENT
Genesis 2:15-17; 3:1-7
Psalm 32
Romans 5:12-19
Matthew 4:1-11

March 14–20
SECOND SUNDAY IN LENT
Genesis 12:1-4*a*
Psalm 121
Romans 4:1-5, 13-17
John 3:1-17

March 21–27
THIRD SUNDAY IN LENT
Exodus 17:1-7
Psalm 95
Romans 5:1-11
John 4:5-42

March 28–April 3
FOURTH SUNDAY IN LENT
1 Samuel 16:1-13
Psalm 23
Ephesians 5:8-14
John 9:1-41

April 4–10
FIFTH SUNDAY IN LENT
Ezekiel 37:1-14
Psalm 130
Romans 8:6-11
John 11:1-45

April 11–17
PALM SUNDAY

Liturgy of the Palms
Matthew 21:1-11
Psalm 118:1-2, 19-29

Liturgy of the Passion
Isaiah 50:4-9*a*
Psalm 31:9-16
Philippians 2:5-11
Matthew 26:14–27:66
(*or* Matthew 27:11-54)

April 18–24
HOLY WEEK

Monday, April 18
Isaiah 42:1-9
Psalm 36:5-11
Hebrews 9:11-15
John 12:1-11

Tuesday, April 19
Isaiah 49:1-7
Psalm 71:1-14
1 Corinthians 1:18-31
John 12:20-36

Wednesday, April 20
Isaiah 50:4-9*a*
Psalm 70
Hebrews 12:1-3
John 13:21-32

Maundy Thursday, April 21
Exodus 12:1-14
Psalm 116:1-4, 12-19
1 Corinthians 11:23-26
John 13:1-17, 31b-35

Good Friday, April 22
Isaiah 52:13–53:12
Psalm 22
Hebrews 10:16-25
John 18:1–19:42

Easter Vigil, April 23
Exodus 14:10-31
Psalm 114
Isaiah 55:1-11
Romans 6:3-11
Matthew 28:1-10

EASTER DAY, APRIL 24
Acts 10:34-43
Psalm 118:1-2, 14-24
Colossians 3:1-4
John 20:1-18
   (*or* Matthew 28:1-10)

April 25–May 1
Acts 2:14a, 22-32
Psalm 16
1 Peter 1:3-9
John 20:19-31

May 2–8
Acts 2:14a, 36-41
Psalm 116:1-4, 12-19
1 Peter 1:17-23
Luke 24:13-35

May 9–15
Acts 2:42-47
Psalm 23
1 Peter 2:19-25
John 10:1-10

May 16–22
Acts 7:55-60
Psalm 31:1-5, 15-16
1 Peter 2:2-10
John 14:1-14

May 23–29
Acts 17:22-31
Psalm 66:8-20
1 Peter 3:13-22
John 14:15-21

Ascension Day—June 2
(*may be used June 5*)
   Acts 1:1-11
   Psalm 47 (*or* Psalm 93)
   Ephesians 1:15-23
   Luke 24:44-53

May 30–June 5
Acts 1:6-14
Psalm 68:1-10, 32-35
1 Peter 4:12-14; 5:6-11
John 17:1-11

June 6–12
PENTECOST
Psalm 104:24-34, 35b
Acts 2:1-21
1 Corinthians 12:3b-13
John 7:37–39

June 13–19
TRINITY SUNDAY
Genesis 1:1–2:4a
Psalm 8
2 Corinthians 13:11-13
Matthew 28:16-20

June 20–26
Genesis 22:1-14
Psalm 13
Romans 6:12-23
Matthew 10:40-42

June 27–July 3
Genesis 24:34-38, 42-49, 58-67
Psalm 45:10-17 (*or* Psalm 72)
Romans 7:15-25*a*
Matthew 11:16-19, 25-30

July 4–10
Genesis 25:19-34
Psalm 119:105-112 (*or* Psalm 25)
Romans 8:1-11
Matthew 13:1-9, 18-23

July 11–17
Genesis 28:10-19a
Psalm 139:1-12, 23-24
Romans 8:12-25
Matthew 13:24-30, 36-43

July 18–24
Genesis 29:15-28
Psalm 105:1-11, 45*b*
Romans 8:26-39
Matthew 13:31-33, 44-52

July 25–31
Genesis 32:22-31
Psalm 17:1-7, 15
Romans 9:1-5
Matthew 14:13-21

August 1–7
Genesis 37:1-4, 12-28
Psalm 105:1-6, 16-22, 45*b*
Romans 10:5-15
Matthew 14:22-33

August 8–14
Genesis 45:1-15
Psalm 133
Romans 11:1-2*a*, 29-32
Matthew 15:10-28

August 15–21
Exodus 1:8–2:10
Psalm 124
Romans 12:1-8
Matthew 16:13-20

August 22–28
Exodus 3:1-15
Psalm 105:1-6, 23-26, 45*c*
Romans 12:9-21
Matthew 16:21-28

August 29–September 4
Exodus 12:1-14
Psalm 149 (*or* Psalm 148)
Romans 13:8-14
Matthew 18:15-20

September 5–11
Exodus 14:19-31
Exodus 15:1b-11, 20-21
Romans 14:1-12
Matthew 18:21-35

September 1–18
Exodus 16:2-15
Psalm 105:1-6, 37-45
  (*or* Psalm 78)
Philippians 1:21-30
Matthew 20:1-16

September 19–25
Exodus 17:1-7
Psalm 78:1-4, 12-16
Philippians 2:1-13
Matthew 21:23-32

September 26–October 2
Exodus 20:1-4, 7-9, 12-20
Psalm 19
Philippians 3:4b-14
Matthew 21:33-46

October 3–9
Exodus 32:1-14
Psalm 106:1-6, 19-23
Philippians 4:1-9
Matthew 22:1-14

October 10–16
Exodus 33:12-23
Psalm 99
1 Thessalonians 1:1-10
Matthew 22:15-22

> **THANKSGIVING DAY
> (Canada)—October 10**
> Deuteronomy 8:7-18
> Psalm 65
> 2 Corinthians 9:6-15
> Luke 17:11-19

October 17–23
Deuteronomy 34:1-12
Psalm 90:1-6, 13-17
1 Thessalonians 2:1-8
Matthew 22:34-46

October 24–30
Joshua 3:7-17
Psalm 107:1-7, 33-37
1 Thessalonians 2:9-13
Matthew 23:1-12

**All Saints Day—
November 1**
(*may be used November 6*)
Revelation 7:9-17
Psalm 34:1-10, 22
1 John 3:1-3
Matthew 5:1-12

October 31–November 6
Joshua 24:1-3a, 14-25
Psalm 78:1-7
1 Thessalonians 4:13-18
Matthew 25:1-13

November 7–13
Judges 4:1-7
Psalm 123 (*or* Psalm 76)
1 Thessalonians 5:1-11
Matthew 25:14-30

November 14–20
REIGN OF CHRIST SUNDAY
Ezekiel 34:11-16, 20-24
Psalm 100
Ephesians 1:15-23
Matthew 25:31-46

> **THANKSGIVING DAY
> (USA)—October 10**
> Deuteronomy 8:7-18
> Psalm 65
> 2 Corinthians 9:6-15
> Luke 17:11-19

November 21–27
FIRST SUNDAY OF ADVENT
Isaiah 64:1-9
Psalm 80:1-7, 17-19
1 Corinthians 1:3-9
Mark 13:24-37

November 28–December 4
SECOND SUNDAY OF ADVENT
Isaiah 40:1-11
Psalm 85:1-2, 8-13
2 Peter 3:8-15*a*
Mark 1:1-8

December 5–11
THIRD SUNDAY OF ADVENT
Isaiah 61:1-4, 8-11
Psalm 126
1 Thessalonians 5:16-24
John 1:6-8, 19-28

December 12–18
FOURTH SUNDAY OF ADVENT
2 Samuel 7:1-11, 16
Luke 1:47-55
Romans 16:25-27
Luke 1:26-38

December 19–25
Isaiah 52:7-10
Psalm 98
Hebrews 1:1-12
John 1:1-14

December 24
CHRISTMAS EVE
Isaiah 9:2-7
Psalm 96
Titus 2:11-14
Luke 2:1-20

December 25
CHRISTMAS DAY
Isaiah 52:7-10
Psalm 98
Hebrews 1:1-12
John 1:1-14

December 26–31
FIRST SUNDAY AFTER
CHRISTMAS/OPTIONAL TEXTS
Isaiah 61:10–62:3
Psalm 148
Galatians 4:4-7
Luke 2:22-40

December 31
WATCH NIGHT/NEW YEAR
Ecclesiastes 3:1-13
Psalm 8
Revelation 21:1-6*a*
Matthew 25:31-46